THE LONG WAR AHEAD

AND

THE SHORT WAR UPON US

DEDICATION

October 9, 2007

To Albert and Roberta Wohlstetter, whose peerless careers were devoted to giving the Free World strategic choices other than surrender, suicide and genocide; to William Friedman, who in North Africa's desert, Italy's hills, at Omaha Beach from the first hour, and by the Yalu River in the dead of winter, risked his life to keep the Free World free; and to Bob Kupperman, whose warnings, if heeded, might have prevented 9/11's horrors, and whose advice can still guide us to safety.

With special appreciation to Bruce Chapman, who encouraged me to write this book.

THE LONG WAR AHEAD AND THE SHORT WAR UPON US

IMPERFECT CIVILIZATION, PERFECT BARBARISM AND WMD TERROR

JOHN C. WOHLSETTER

Description

The Long War Ahead and the Short War Upon Us analyzes the multiple wars against terrorist groups that ensued after September 11, 2001, and their roots. Topics of particular focus are the rise of Islamic communities in the West, and conflicts with non-Islamic communities, the debate in the West over civil liberties versus security, the role of the executive, legislative and judicial branches in applying national security law, the status of related battlefield conflicts around the globe, especially in the Mideast and Asia, personnel and material resource challenges in defending the homeland and fighting overseas, protecting critical infrastructures, especially communications, energy and ports, neutralization of WMD threats from hostile nations and sub-national groups, and lessons learned for policymakers since September 11.

John C. Wohlstetter is a Senior Fellow at Discovery Institute and author of the blog *Letter From the Capitol*. His professional background includes Wall Street, corporate and communications law, and national security telecommunications.

Library Cataloging Data

The Long War Ahead and the Short War Upon Us: Imperfect Civilization, Perfect Barbarism and WMD Terror
John C. Wohlstetter (1947–)
240 pages, 6 x 9 x 0.55 inches & 0.7 lb, 229 x 152 x 14 mm. & 0.32 kg
Library of Congress Control Number: 2007939852
ISBN: 978-0979014116 (paperback)
BISAC Subject Headings: HIS027170 HISTORY/MILITARY/IRAQ WAR; HIS026000 HISTORY / MIDDLE EAST / GENERAL

Publisher Information

Discovery Institute Press, Discovery Institute

Internet: http://www.Discovery.org/

208 Columbia St., Seattle, WA 98104.

Published in the United States of America on acid-free paper.

First Edition, Second Printing. February 2008.

CONTENTS

Acknowledgements

The origin of this book is somewhat serendipitous. In September 2006 I posted on my blog, *Letter From the Capitol*, a review of the five years since September 11, 2001. Upon reading my entries, Discovery Institute President Bruce Chapman, whose think tank sponsors my blog (the content is mine), suggested that I turn the postings into a book. The postings amounted to an extremely rough first draft, with many conclusions revised in light of information since acquired, and of events in a highly fluid war environment.

Bruce took three cuts at editing my work, and brought in Discovery's David Klinghoffer and Mike Wussow to edit further. Their contributions to the final product immensely improved the result. I am also indebted to Patrick Bell and Kenneth Pennock at Discovery for their contributions. Frank Dillow, a great friend who guided me to Discovery after I left the telecommunications industry, shared his wisdom on many subjects pertinent to my subject. Also at Discovery, Matt Scholz gave me a techie's perspective on Internet issues, and Yuri Mamchur a native's view of Russia.

I might never have written the book but for Josh Gilder, who urged me to continue my blog when I considered ending *LFTC* in late 2005. Josh has also provided much helpful commentary these past few years, including on nuclear energy. Josh's cousin George has greatly influenced my knowledge of communications matters, including those pertinent to this volume. Paul Hart and Paul Baran both helped me on technical and communication queries. Frank Gaffney, whose Center for Security Policy has been a valuable policymaker's resource on defense for 20 years, graciously invited me to make my first public presentation of my ideas, in December 2006. Tom Lipscomb and Bob Tyrell have enlightened me not only on the subject matter, but on writing and publishing a book. Al Regnery and Fred Siegel also counseled me on these considerations.

I owe an extraordinary debt to Herb London, who read my first, extremely rough print draft, and whose commentary over the past few years has greatly expanded my horizons. Above all, Herb brought me into the fascinating world of the Hudson Institute, where countless discussions and events over the past seven years have broadened my understanding of many things. Irwin Stelzer and Murray Weidenbaum provided much-needed guidance on defense spending, deficits and their consequences. Laurie Mylroie, Max Singer and Meyrav Wurmser have often sharpened my understanding of matters pertinent to the Mideast. Mia Lovink brought experience from life in Lebanon and dealing with unlovely Syria. Ed Whelan, another former telecom colleague and a legal mind supreme, enhanced my analysis of federal judiciary and legal issues. Mike Brewer has been a strong supporter of my effort, and raised many points that improved the product. Claudia Rosett, who virtually single-handedly exposed the oil-for-food scandal at the United Nations, has given me the benefit of her wide knowledge of many issues, in addition to unfunny follies at the UN.

Jack Oslund, who long ago taught me much about satellite communications, actually plowed through two versions, for which patience he deserves a medal. His comments were, as ever, incisive. Jim Graf, another veteran of my telecom years, brought his well-honed lawyerly skills to dissect my first draft and ask penetrating questions that first-rate lawyers can frame. Matters military are often mysterious to civilian types, and without much input over the years from Alan Salisbury, Stu Johnson and Steve Meader (all former telecom colleagues as well), I would be wondering which end of an F-22 points forward. Alan also kindly obtained comments on my first draft from Thomas Morgan of West Point, and has forwarded me many running accounts sent him from war zones afar, thus making me privy to eyewitness perspectives rarely presented in the news media, as has Stu Johnson. Chris DeMuth has over the years educated me on many policy matters, and treated me as part of the American Enterprise Institute's extended family.

Onorine Friedman offered her usual perceptive comments, and gave me much encouragement, as did dear friends Cheryl McMurry, Bart Kogan, Donna Reid, and George and Sarah Vassiliou. Other wonderful friends who helped me on various aspects were Neil Livingstone, Barbara Vazsonyi, Taffy Gould, Carl Oppenheim, C. Peter (Buzz) Beler, Tina Winston, Ron Rubin, Marion Maskin, Jim Koch, Neil Goldstein, Dennis Klein, Jeffrey Theodore, and Ed Barker.

Ed Weidenfeld and David Ginsburg each for nearly thirty years offered me the wise counsel of Washington insiders on countless issues, not only on specific points but also general wisdom on political and worldly matters. They both exemplify the refutation of the proposition, widely held outside the Beltway, that no D.C. denizen knows anything useful. A special tribute I give to Rosann Kaplin, neighbor and friend, for spirited, astute commentary on all subjects, and great encouragement to persevere. First-cousin Joan Wohlstetter added her intimate knowledge of Oriental cultures. My late father, Charles, shared his deep wisdom about the world and its often fickle ways. My late mother, Rose, and my brothers, Philip and Rand, always had a kind word for my efforts. My special gratitude goes to those to whom I dedicated the book. The stellar careers of Albert and Roberta Wohlstetter, William Friedman and Robert Kupperman, as much as their ever patient counsel, were of inestimable value to my own education.

A final gloss was provided by careful copy editor Anne Himmelfarb, who applied all those pesky grammar rules that smooth the reader's path. The talents of The Pinkston Group's Christian Pinkston, David Fouse, Amanda Race, and Sean McCabe introduced this book by a first-time author to a far wider audience than had I flown solo. I offer a sincere apology to anyone who I may have neglected to thank. I take full responsibility for the book's content. All errors of commission and of omission are mine alone.

PROLOGUE

NOVEMBER 4, 2010

You may not be interested in war, but war is interested in you.

LEON TROTSKY

The missile lifted off the launch pad and accelerated rapidly to several times the speed of sound, swiftly disappearing from human sight. The mother ship—disguised as a tanker—had come to a floating stop 300 miles off the Atlantic coastline of the American northeast, well inside international waters. The missile arced until it attained an altitude of 300 miles over Kansas. The instantaneous blinding flash that people looking skyward saw that Thursday mid-morning, exposed their eyes for milliseconds to the light of the sun. No one instantly died, vaporized by the mini-sun, no one ignited in flames from the blast's thermal pulse, no buildings collapsed due to the blast's immense over-pressure shock wave. But the lights went out and computers crashed by the millions, from Boston to Phoenix, from New York and Washington, D.C., to Los Angeles and San Francisco, from Miami to Seattle. Seventy percent of America's electric grid was fried by the powerful pulse of electromagnetic energy that suddenly surged through the American electric power grid. With a 360 degree radius of 1,470 miles from the detonation point, the pulse disabled America from coast to coast.

It would be many months—well into 2011, given the interdependency among electric, communications and other vital infrastructures—before power could be fully restored. In 2011's winter cold and summer heat, tens of thousands of elderly died. Trillions of dollars in economic damage sent America's powerful economic engine into reverse, headed for its worst and most protracted economic crisis since the Great Depression (1929–1941). The stock market crash of November 4, 2010, continued into 2011, knocking 50 percent off the value of America's trillions of dollars of pension funds, heavily invested in the market. Water and sanitation facilities were silenced. Food refrigeration was suddenly unavailable, necessitating resurrection of primitive freezing methods and investing much more daily time in shopping for food, much of which couldn't be kept safely more than a few days. Electric gas ranges, microwaves, dishwashers and washing machines ceased to work. Hospitals and doctors' offices were unable to run diagnostic machines; sophisticated surgery aids in operating rooms were unusable. Deprived of the ability to send emails or make phone calls, most of more than 300 million Americans resorted to writing letters, inundating the Post Office with mail volume well above its peak load capacity. But letters often took weeks to arrive, because automatic mail sorting machines no longer worked. America, in effect, had in an instant been returned to what life was in many ways in 1875, but without nineteenth-century technologies such as wood stoves and hand-run pumps.

The President's message to the American people was delivered over the broadcast networks, before their backup power sources had run out. Newspapers were delivered the next day, but then satellite transmission of newspaper text was silenced by damage to communications hubs whose back-up power generators expired within 24 hours. Most trucks were off the road by nightfall. The President promised decisive action as soon as the perpetrator(s) could be identified.

But that part was easy, as the perpetrator made no effort to hide. Iran's Supreme Leader appeared on Tehran television at 9 p.m. Tehran time on November 4; 1 p.m. Eastern Standard Time. His message was carried live to much of the world. The jubilant Iranian cleric began by reminding America of another dark day: the seizure of American Embassy hostages in Tehran, and their ensuing 444 days of captivity. The Supreme Leader continued:

America, two years ago you went to the polls to choose your new President. Now on the anniversary of your inglorious defeat 31 years ago, be advised that you have entered a new era. The Great Satan,

America, has dominated the world for decades. But now America's rule has come to an end. Before you retaliate for our action today, think—very, very carefully—of the consequences. Iran has enough nuclear warheads to destroy not only the Little Satan, Israel, but also the capitals of the oil-producing governments of the Mideast, and major cities in Europe too. If America lands even one warhead on Iranian soil, these countries will pay the price in the blood of millions.

Sound fanciful? The missile scenario involving electromagnetic pulse (EMP) is described in a 2004 report to Congress by a blue-ribbon panel, which warns it could happen well before 2020; Iran's known nuclear progress has accelerated since then. Iran has reportedly tested its Shahab-3 missile in EMP attack mode. The Shahab-3 has an 800-mile range, but the Shahab-4 has a 2,400-mile range, sufficient to reach the mid-point of the continental United States from offshore. Shorter range missiles could disable electronics on the entire East Coast.

The potential effects of EMP have been widely publicized since the late 1970s. They are no secret to anyone with knowledge sufficient to build a bomb. They are, however, probably a secret to many Americans, who do not have time to peruse reports to Congress, let alone those which receive little attention from the mass media.

While the CIA's latest estimate for an Iranian bomb is that the program, though suspended, will attain capability between 2010 and 2015, Israeli intelligence (though hardly perfect, its reputation is better than that of the CIA) believes Iran might go nuclear by 2009. British intelligence also disagrees with the CIA. U.S. intelligence failed to anticipate first atomic explosions by Russia (1949), China (1964), India (1974), South Africa (believed to be 1979), Pakistan (1998), and North Korea (announced 2002, explosion 2006). In 1962, 25 days before Soviet missiles were detected by aerial reconnaissance, U.S. intelligence declared missile-basing in Cuba "incompatible with Soviet practice to date and with Soviet policy as we know it." At the end of the Gulf War, analysts learned that Saddam was much closer—about one year away—from a bomb, than they had estimated. Yet in 2003 every major intelligence establishment believed that Saddam still possessed WMD. So, when will Iran go nuclear? No one knows. It could be much later, or it could be much earlier, than current estimates. The Iranians might obtain a missile and warhead from a WMD proliferator. Barring a miracle, a decision to destroy Iran's nuclear facilities will have to be taken with imperfect information. Knowledge certain can come only if Iran detonates a device.

Would we retaliate if Iran carried out an EMP strike? It is far from certain that we would. We would be under intense pressure from countries within range of Iran's missiles. Would an American leader retaliate, knowing that millions in allied countries might die as a result of our action?

Many American leaders and many of their constituents cannot stomach our plunging in water, for all of a couple of minutes, three senior al-Qaeda leaders, including the mastermind of the 9/11 atrocities that killed nearly 3,000—this during an interrogation designed to yield vital information about future attacks. Is such an America truly prepared to launch a massive retaliatory strike that would mean mega-scale mass murder of innocent Iranians, for what their leaders did without popular consent. And even if so, shouldn't we seek better choices?

It is in search of better choices, not just regarding Iran, but as to a broad range of theaters at home and abroad that are part of the worldwide war in which we are engaged, that this book has been written.

INTRODUCTION

A LONG WAR OF VALUES; A

SHORT WAR OF PREVENTION

Let us have the courage to admit that the fear of war is often the tyrant's opportunity, that the absence of war, that is, of open conflict between legally organized political units, is not enough to exclude violence between individuals and groups. Perhaps we shall look back with nostalgia to the days of "conventional" wars when, faced with the horrors of guerilla warfare and the atomic holocaust, the peoples of the world submit to a detestable order provided it dispels the agonies of individual insecurity and collective suicide.

RAYMOND ARON, *ON WAR*, 1956

Although we think of "the war" we really fight two wars in one: a long war that will likely last generations, and a short war the outcome of which may pre-figure the outcome of the long one. Our struggle is not just against Islamic terror groups, although they are most in focus at this writing. The book's basic thesis is that while much has gone right since the 9/11 attacks, America has faltered, and failed to invest enough material and human resources to ensure victory. Thus, urgent corrective action, in the form of a major shift in strategy towards more assertive policies, is needed.

My primary purpose is to offer readers a coherent intellectual framework to weigh issues pertaining to a conflict that is many-faceted and may run several generations, one in which our very survival as a civilization and society is at stake. Choosing policies begins with asking the right questions. That cannot be done if issues are obscured by a jumbled mass of categories and labels.

Sixty years of life in the United States have taught me that the American public usually gets it right if the relevant facts are presented and the issues are clearly framed. The adversarial debate that is essential to liberal democratic republics is thus sharpened by providing a clearer picture of the many wars that comprise what is called the "war on terror" or a war on radical Islam, or is given other, more esoteric labels, the most common of which are "Islamofascism" and "Islamism," both used in this book. Our war, in the event, includes adversaries like North Korea, hardly Islamic, and potential Unabomber-type apocalyptic terrorists, whose motivation for terrorism can be almost any deeply held grievance against society—from politics to religion to various forms of personal psychosis—and whose weapons of preference will likely be biological pathogens, perhaps novel and of unprecedented virulence.

For practical purposes, General John Abizaid, former chief of Central Command (which includes the Mideast), has offered the best label for the multi-generational struggle: "The Long War." It emphasizes the near-certitude that we will be fighting this war against radical factions within—and without—the Islamic world for a very long time. If the label is imprecise for want of naming a designated adversary, so was "Cold War" for the struggle against the Soviet Union and its "satellite" nations, from 1945 to 1991. As "cold" conveyed the essence of the earlier conflict—a war in which the main adversaries did not directly shoot at one another—so "long" conveys the most important fact about this war, its multi-generational prospect. The Long War is a *civilizational* war of *values*.

However, the Long War is neither a "clash of civilizations" nor a clash of cultures. Our terrorist adversaries are neither civilized nor cultured. We thus fight a war of imperfect civilization against perfect barbarism. We are fighting a bizarre death cult in which acolytes are indoctrinated in mosques and *madrassas* (Islamic religious schools). What separates a civilization from the uncivilized is a common predicate: Civilizations, in some form or another, celebrate human life's possibilities and achievements; Islam's great empires left us treasures, many of which we can see even today. Our enemies do not aspire to produce anything like what Islamic civilizations produced. They seek only to destroy. Not even Attila sent children and pregnant women to do his killing, nor did he hide behind them and use them as a shield.

We are not at war with the entire 1.3 billion people living in Islamic communities or with Islam itself. Such a conflict must be averted. True, Islam has not undergone a Reformation as did Western religions, and its relationship with modernity is an uneasy one. Yet Islamic communities live in peace in the U.S. and in India; they form the core of democratic societies in Turkey and Indonesia. The latter are fragile, but real examples that suggest that Islam is not inconsistent with forms of representative government. There is a serious problem of unassimilated Islamic minority communities in Europe, for which discrimination, rather than freedom of worship *per se*, has been a motive force. In France alone there are now an estimated six million Muslims, about ten percent of the country's total population.[1]

Western nations have become used to wars that last a few years. But the West has seen longer—much longer—wars, such as the Hundred Years War between England and France (actually it ran 116 years: 1337–1453). The Thirty Years War (1618–1648) devastated Europe. That war between Catholics and Protestants across continental Europe settled a fundamental principle as to wars within the West: No longer would major wars be fought over religious differences. Thus modern Western societies are temperamentally inclined to see religious conflict as unthinkable.

Our main adversaries, votaries of militant strains of Islam, are premodern. Thus, one assumption behind the invasion of Iraq parallels apparent assumptions made by European countries in admitting large numbers of Muslim immigrants: the assumption that, given a chance to adopt a modern, liberal western lifestyle, all members of Islamic communities would eagerly do so. This assumption has proven wrong in Eu-

---

1. Other continental European countries have smaller, but still significant, Muslim communities. Their places of origin vary greatly—mainly North African in Spain, France and Italy; mainly Southeast Asian in the Netherlands; mainly Turkish in Germany; mainly Indo-Pakistani and East African in Great Britain.

rope and looks shaky in Iraq, where one would have thought that after Saddam's "republic of fear" freedom would be eagerly embraced. Even in Afghanistan, where flowers greeted our liberating troops and where (as in Iraq) voters risked their lives to vote, they voted largely along sectarian lines. Historically, democracies have grown in cultural soil fertilized over centuries. The belief that in the modern world of open global communications this process of liberal acculturation can be greatly accelerated everywhere has proven a leap of faith over a vast, widening chasm.

In ways hard for us in the West to grasp, let alone relate to, in much of the Islamic world tribal "honor" cultures persist—fueled by what the eighteenth-century philosopher G. W. F. Hegel called "the struggle for recognition." Vice President Cheney said after the failure to find WMD that it was incomprehensible to him (as it was to others—myself included) that Saddam would not 'fess up, pass the official UN inspection, and rapidly resume his programs after the embargo and sanctions were lifted. We did not count on tradition-bound notions of honor that persist in Arab society. Author James Bowman has written of honor: "Morality is nuanced and subtle; there are shades of right and wrong, innocence and guilt. Honor is stark and unforgiving; either you fight or you run; either you are a hero or a coward." Westerners did not see this coming, because since the cataclysm of World War I (1914–1918), launched in the name of national honor, it has become unacceptable in the West to enter a war solely to preserve national honor.[2]

That tribal cultures flourish in the modern world, and that tribes will fight vastly destructive wars rather than concede what they regard as a matter of warrior pride, or some other source of honor, is anathema to most Westerners. Such a choice seems irrational, given unprecedented opportunities otherwise to pursue freedom and prosperity. Yet it is a choice many people still tragically make.

---

2. England was not enmeshed in the tangle of pre-war alliances that dragged the continental European powers into the First World War to the same extent as France. It largely entered to honor a treaty made in 1839, guaranteeing Belgium's territorial integrity. Germany invaded Belgium to begin the war; England honored a treaty made in vastly different circumstances and paid a vastly higher price than any imagined when the treaty was signed.

Author-soldier Ralph Peters asks: "Do we have the strength of will, as a military and as a nation, to defeat an enemy who has nothing to lose? [We] will often face men who have acquired a taste for killing." Peters sees powerful forces that will create increasing numbers of failed states unable to effectively participate in world economic prosperity, and that thus will be incubators and exporters of violence: tribal societies that deny freedom of expression, repress women, devalue education and the value of work, reject responsibility for their own failures, and follow restrictive religious norms.

Post-honor wars have taken many forms. The Second World War (1939–1945) came about in part because societies numbed by the vast carnage of World War I were unable to rally to prevent the early stages of aggression by Nazi Germany, fascist Italy and militarist Japan. The Cold War between the West and the Soviet Union was resolved without direct military conflict. There were several proxy wars, most notably Korea (1950–1953), Vietnam (1962–1973) and Afghanistan (1979–1989). The liberation of Eastern Europe in 1989, the ensuing collapse of the Soviet Union in 1991 (into Russia and 14 independent republics), and the 1991 defeat of Saddam Hussein in the Gulf War ushered in a "party decade"—a booming stock market and economy, and no major wars— that ended abruptly on September 11, 2001. Terrorist strikes in the 1990s against American assets overseas were disturbing, but were widely perceived as events at a distant remove from everyday life in America.

Americans found themselves scrambling after the atrocities of 9/11, trying to figure out who attacked us, why, and how to respond. Is it a war against terror generically? Is it a war against a stateless network, al-Qaeda? Are major terror-sponsoring nations like Iraq and Iran involved with al-Qaeda? To what extent are broader Islamic communities engaged? Are we hated for what we do? Or for what Israel does? Or simply because of who we are?

The Long War is one of *values*; the Short War is one of *prevention*. In the Long War our goal is victory: the global triumph of civilization over barbarism, with the threat of mega-death catastrophe reduced to an extremely remote prospect (it is never absolute zero). In the Short War our goal is defensive in essence: averting the kind of catastrophe whose vast harm can undermine the stable political, economic and social order upon which modern societies depend. To prevail will require nerve, either to destroy Iran's nuclear potential or to endure a new round of deterrence against fanatical adversaries. It would, however, be a grievous error to assume, as many apparently do, that we are destined to prevail.

Indeed, as dangers grow we dither. Fear of new attacks has receded as we go longer and longer without suffering another 9/11 attack on our homeland. Put simply: *America is not approaching this war as if it were a struggle for its national and civilizational survival. We are nowhere near a true war footing. We fight a war on the cheap, arguing about deficits and competing domestic priorities. The urgency that attends a true national war effort is not in evidence.*

Since 9/11

The years since 9/11 have seen much good news: not a single strike of consequence on American soil; al-Qaeda severely damaged, with its top leaders hiding in caves; Stalinist tyrant Saddam Hussein gone; Syrian troops leaving Lebanon; high voter turnout in Afghanistan, Iran, Lebanon and the Palestinian territory; better (if shaky) relations with Pakistan, to date the world's sole Islamic nuclear nation, whose arsenal would be the grand prize claimed by a radical Islamic takeover; a blossoming strategic partnership with India and an impressive strengthening of strategic cooperation with Japan and Australia; a host of partnership ventures with European and Asian governments, like the 70-nation Proliferation Security Initiative, that significantly augment counter-terror capabilities; and the abandonment by Libya, a major terror sponsor in the 1970s and 1980s, of its WMD programs.

Yet the bad news matches the good: the Afghan government controls little more than the major cities; the Iraqi experiment is precarious; Lebanon's Cedar Revolution has been compromised by Hezbollah and its masters; the Palestinian elections produced an avowedly terrorist government, Hamas, intent on destroying Israel, not even *faking* a desire for peace (as did its predecessor, Fatah); Iran pursues nuclear capability as we withhold support for popular resistance to the regime in order to preserve an atmosphere for negotiations; Pakistan is unable or unwilling to close in on al-Qaeda's chieftains; European countries have discovered that their restive Islamic populaces include sizable potential Fifth Columns—most notably in the UK, but also in France, Germany, Spain, Italy, the Netherlands and Denmark; Islamic terrorists all around the globe are energized by the U.S. faltering in Iraq and Israel faltering in Lebanon; North Korea staged a 2006 Roman candle rocket show, then tested a nuclear device while six-power talks stalled and other Asian nations pondered whether to go nuclear in self-defense. The United Nations, once again, has demonstrated that it is impotent at best and indifferent at worst. *Over all this is the shadow of Iran's nuclear quest.* If Iran's progress is fast enough it is conceivable that a decision whether to destroy Iran's facilities might need to be made before the next president takes office, or else face a nuclear-armed Iran.

Many terrorist groups are apocalyptic in orientation. Apocalyptic actors differ greatly from the terrorist groups who came to global prominence beginning in the revolutionary year of 1968. Groups like the Irish Republican Army (IRA) and the Basque ETA were "programmatic" in aim: the IRA sought to force Britain to end home rule for Ireland's primarily Protestant northern counties (a 1998 accord largely ended the violence); the ETA seeks to win the secession of Spain's Basque-speaking provinces (in the northeast).

Programmatic groups have an incentive to limit their violence, to use enough to force target governments to change policy in the direction the terrorists desire, but not so much as to galvanize the authorities to engage in an all-out war that eventually would surely result in defeat for the terrorists. Because victory can come at a high price in blood and treasure, governments often prefer to make concessions in hope of placating such groups, or at least take enough action to limit the violence to the occasional—and thus, tolerable—strike that while a nasty annoyance poses no real threat to the survival of the government.

Apocalyptic terrorism poses a vastly greater threat. Its practitioners seek total destruction. Such terrorists have no need to limit violence in pursuit of a political program or agenda of any kind. They don't want anything from a target state, because at the end of the conflict they hope the state will have been extinguished. Theirs is an elemental, winner-take-all struggle.

Against the backdrop of American efforts to quell apocalyptic terrorism, there are the challenges posed by all the wars subsumed under the "Long War" umbrella label—most of them not active shooting wars: one over the role of mosque and state in the Islamic world; one in the West over the legalist versus war-fighting views of how to respond to 9/11; one over whether unelected judges or elected representatives should make potential outcome-determining decisions in a war of survival; one over whether democracy can survive the poisonous climate of the Mideast; shooting wars on dispersed battlefields.

Also facing us are certain special challenges to protect the homeland, ones where acting sooner will be much cheaper than waiting until later, the latter a common but defective approach of democratic populations.

At present we have seen momentum shift in all these wars: within Islam for want of enough help from moderates; within the West because those with a 9/10 view that favors the institutional set-up antedating 9/11 are at odds with the 9/12 set, who believe current institutions and arrangements are unequal to the task; terrorists using the democratic process to gain legitimacy; and in the courts, where several key rulings by the Supreme Court have pushed aside decisions made by the elected branches. We are stumbling in Afghanistan and hanging in the balance in Iraq. And our key Mideast ally, Israel, by failing to destroy the Iran- and Syria-backed terrorist group Hezbollah in Lebanon, has lost its aura of invincibility in the Mideast.

Members of both parties regard the federal deficit as an economic barrier that denies them the ability to appropriate adequate resources to fight the war. We move too slowly in addressing threats to our infrastructure. We fail to act decisively to reduce our deepening dependence upon Mideast oil. We fail to take sufficient measures to fully, credibly inform the public about how to avoid mass panic in event of certain terrorist strikes.

We can fund the war without regard to a deficit over-rated in its economic significance. *In a war of civilizational survival the one thing we cannot afford is to lose the war.* We can deploy advanced forms of missile defense. We can harden our electronic infrastructure, which includes the electric power grid and the vast computer and telecommunications infrastructure, against the potentially grave threat of a high-altitude nuclear explosion. We need to create new, strictly bounded, emergency Presidential authority to govern effectively in event of a WMD catastrophe.

The hour is early in the Long War, but it is late in the Short War. Leaders and the public can turn matters around, with resolute effort. We can confront the Islamic world as to its objectionable practices— mistreatment of women, desecration of other religions' sacred sites, discrimination against other religions, suppression of free speech. We can better protect our homeland if we relegate law enforcement to its proper, vital place, working in the context of a larger war effort, by re-balancing civil liberties to allow us to focus on preventing catastrophic strikes— allowing high-tech database searches and aggressive interrogation of high-level detainees; preserving essential wartime secrecy and holding broadcasters responsible when they knowingly air enemy propaganda as if it were genuine news clips. We can relegate international institutions to their proper role, one narrower than we have allowed to date. In Afghanistan, we can invest more financial resources to wean recalcitrant tribes away from the Taliban. In Iraq, we must achieve an outcome that prevents the country from becoming a haven for terrorism or radical Islam. We must contain the ambitions of Iran to dominate the Mideast with prestige acquired from an American retreat prompted by Iranian support for the insurgency. We must pressure the Arabs—especially the Saudis—to end petrodollar financing of extremist ideology. It is realism and common sense, not hypocrisy, to insist on such things. In peripheral, but important theaters, we can leverage local allies to fight terrorists in Somalia to prevent their creating a new haven, and help allies like the Philippines fight terror.

Above all, we can—we must—win the Short War, by stopping Iran's nuclear program. Our hour of decision could be very near. Either we act or we don't. The latter course is as much a choice—made by default—as is the former. If we bet that traditional deterrence will work against Iran's leaders and thus guess wrong, we face a future with choices potentially as stark as the unholy trinity of surrender, suicide or genocide. As militant Islamic groups represent the primary threat today and over the near term, the book's main focus will be on terrorism from various militant Islamic groups and on the states that sponsor them.

Organization of the Book

This book is divided into eight chapters:

1. The Road to 9/11: Five Misperceptions Led Us Astray

2. The "Reformation Values" War: Islam or the West Reforms

3. The Law Values War: Lawfare or Warfare

4. The "Law-Giver Values" War: Mandarins or "We the People"

5. The "Vote Values War" : Export Votes or Import Violence

6. Resource Challenges: Cheap Now, Costly Later

7. The Short War: WMD and "Betting the Company"

8. Lessons Learned Since September 11, 2001

A Note on Sources

A desire to present the reader with ease of narrative flow limits footnotes to those that provide either historical context or collateral discussion. A document posted online at Discovery Institute's website will provide references for quotations and selected data. Other requests for references can be provided by e-mail to the address designated at the author's sub-page. Discovery's main page is located at www.discovery.org. The author's sub-page is found under the Fellows link on the main page.

For referenced online materials, putting lengthy Internet World Wide Web addresses in cold print forces readers to re-type a Web address—often a few dozen characters long—manually, a process that anyone who has tried (as I have) knows is error-prone and time-consuming. Thus for online references the reader need merely type in a simple Google search phrase (case name, statute title, etc.) in any widely-used Internet search engine.

A perennial problem with books covering topics that entail using foreign language terms is how to spell them. I have chosen to use commonly recognized spellings, and to avoid the use of diacritical marks except inside quotations.

Finally, for narrative flow I often use "the war" without specifying "long" or "short"; the context makes clear whether I refer to one, the other or both.

CHAPTER 1
THE ROAD TO 9/11
FIVE MISPERCEPTIONS
LED US ASTRAY

The traditional "nuisance" terrorism will continue. But fanaticism inspired by all kinds of religious-sectarian-nationalist convictions is now taking on a millenarian and apocalyptic tone. We are confronting the emergence of new kinds of terrorist violence, some based on ecological and quasi-religious concerns, others basically criminal in character, and still others mixtures of these and other influences. We are also witnessing the rise of small sectarian groups that lack clear political and social agendas other than destroying civilization, and in some cases humankind.

WALTER LAQUER, *THE NEW TERRORISM* (1999)

The terror threat of a generation past was socially disruptive; the threat we face now may prove lethal to our way of life. Most of the bill that we in the West will foot—in lives and treasure—has, in all likelihood, yet to be paid.

1968–2001: The Road to 9/11

Modern Islamic terrorism began in 1968, with the first high-visibility event being the September 6, 1970, hijacking of four jetliners in the Mideast by Palestinian terrorists. Israeli security thwarted an attempted hijacking of a fifth plane. Almost exactly 31 years later, a new phase of radical Islam's assault on the West began, targeted first and foremost at the United States and Israel.

From 1968 on, five misperceptions shared by eight American administrations led the West to 9/11:

+ We failed to understand Palestinian terrorism's regional revolutionary purpose, which is to destroy, not to compromise with, Israel.

+ We failed to limit the vast petrodollar bounty flowing to Mideast countries, despite knowing about the diversion of oil revenues to finance terrorism against the West.

+ We failed to take seriously the overtly revolutionary character of the Iranian regime that seized power in 1979, and also failed to grasp the equally revolutionary—albeit, not advertised—character of the dominant religious faction in Saudi Arabia.

+ We were unduly preoccupied with maintaining the Mideast's *status quo*—a "stability" that proved elusive and, ultimately, illusory.

+ Finally, with rare exceptions, we treated terrorism as primarily a law enforcement issue, rather than as a national security issue.[3]

Without understanding these errors clearly, the likelihood of continued miscalculation is great. We experienced the adverse consequences of such failure on 9/11. The task of painful re-appraisal was begun by the heroes of United Flight 93, who didn't wait to see if their government would change its policies. In making major policy changes the administration was following the choice, and honoring the sacrifice, of those who

---

3. There were numerous peace initiatives floated between 1973 (after the end of the Yom Kippur War) and 9/11. Most notable were the disengagement agreements separating the Israeli forces from Syria (1974) and Egypt (1975); the Camp David Accords (1978) establishing peace between Egypt and Israel (whose economic provisions have never been implemented by Egypt); the 1982 agreement allowing Yasser Arafat's Palestine Liberation Organization (PLO) forces to leave Lebanon for exile in Tunisia; the Madrid Conference (1991) that led to the Oslo Accords (1993), which restored the PLO to the Palestinian territories—an accord serially and flagrantly violated by the Palestinians, and arguably (as to certain Jewish settlements) violated by Israel; the 1994 peace treaty between Israel and Jordan which, as with Camp David, established a "cold war" peace—no shooting war, but, at the popular (street) level, continued animosity and consequent rejection of the Jewish state's right to exist; West Bank and Gaza agreements in 1994 and 1995; the Hebron Protocol, ceding Hebron (1997); the Wye Agreement, ceding West Bank territory (1998).

mutinied on Flight 93, who, in declaring their own war on al-Qaeda, saved the U.S. Capitol building.

Palestinian Terrorism's Purpose

Since 1967, the world, including every American administration from Lyndon Johnson to George W. Bush, has treated the conflict between Israel and the Palestinians as a territorial dispute over boundaries. This perception lies at the root of Mideast policy, except in the Mideast itself, where Arab and Muslim states ardently desire a Mideast free of Jews entirely. To them the issue is *existential*—the survival of Israel itself. Osama bin Laden's 1996 declaration of war against the U.S. cited Israel's *presence*, not its boundaries.

Critics of the Bush Arab-Israeli policy claim that the dispute is central to resolution of wider problems in the Mideast.[4] This is not true if the issue is merely one of defining a boundary line, as militant Islamic groups desire to destroy the Jewish state, not draw a new boundary line. It is partly true, however, if the conflict is *existential*, as is the struggle now called the Global War on Terror. Rejection of Israel and of Western influence in the Mideast reflect similar attitudes, despite many countries in the region turning to America for help as a matter of necessity.

The Palestine Liberation Organization was founded in 1964—more than two years before the 1967 War, at a time when the West Bank was controlled by Jordan. Thus the land to be "liberated" then was that of *Israel*, from Jewish control. The first PLO raid into Israel was launched January 1, 1965, aimed at the National Water Carrier.

United Nations Security Council Resolution 242, adopted after the 1967 war, does *not* require surrender of all the territory Israel occupied in the conflict. The settlements established by Israel are not clearly illegal, as the 1949 armistice between Israel and Jordan established cease-fire lines "agreed upon by the Parties without prejudice to future territo-

---

4. Mideast expert Barry Rubin notes that a peace accord between Israel and the Palestinians would enrage militant Islamists, who would target, as traitors, any Arab leader who supported the accord.

rial settlements or boundary lines or to claims of either Party relating thereto."[5]

Yet Israel, at the August 2000 Camp David Conference, offered the PLO 98 percent of the West Bank, two percent of Israeli territory as compensation for retaining two percent of the West Bank for security reasons, plus all of Gaza and shared sovereignty over Jerusalem, an offer rejected by Yasser Arafat. Arafat's rejection was not due to the two percent sliver of the West Bank that Israel was to retain. Rather it was due to the refusal of Israel to allow a "right of return" for Palestinians and their descendants, from a dispersion caused by the war five Arab nations started in 1948 to overturn the UN's 1947 Palestine Partition Resolution.[6]

Much misperception comes from the false historical narrative that since 1967 has been accepted, even by many who regard themselves as supporters of Israel. It holds that after World War I, in the postwar political settlements of 1919–1923, the Arabs were cheated by the treacherous diplomacy of Britain and France, who made a secret pact during the war to divide British and French territorial interests in the Mideast. The post-World War II creation of Israel, it is said, was the product of the Holocaust, and thus represents the imposition of European politics on the Mideast, taking away from the Palestinians territory that had been theirs, in author Joan Peters' phrase, "from time immemorial."

The historical reality is different. To begin with, outside Turkey and the Balkans, Arabs got 99 percent of the Ottoman Empire's lands (land ceded by England after World War I, plus land ceded by France during and after World War II), and 100 percent of the oil. Further, contrary to popular belief, the Arabs were aware 18 months before World War I

---

5. The armistice agreements of 1949 between Israel and Egypt, Jordan and Syria, did not establish legal frontier boundaries, because these three Arab states would not recognize Israel. Only the 1949 armistice agreement between Lebanon (then majority Christian) and Israel established final frontiers.

6. Popular belief has Israel expelling the Palestinians, whereas in fact there was no such general policy. But it was the policy of the *Arabs* that their brethren west of the Jordan should vacate, and then return after the expected Arab destruction of the nascent Jewish state.

ended that the French and British had competing claims; they were not betrayed at Versailles.[7] Five months before the end of World War I, the Arabs entered into an agreement by which lands they actually liberated would be theirs.[8] They failed to liberate any lands, and thus Britain was not obligated to transfer sovereignty unconditionally.

The Jews adopted Jerusalem, the City of King David, as their capital more than 16 centuries before the Prophet Muhammad founded Islam. The idea of a Palestinian national identity was first widely promulgated only after World War I. Most of the population of the Palestinian areas reflects emigration there from other Arab lands in the late nineteenth and early twentieth century.[9] There was no historic Islamic Caliphate over the entire Mideast, and thus the post-World War I settlements did not deprive the Arabs of territories that were theirs by historical right. Israelis entered the Holy Land in the nineteenth and twentieth centuries and got the land by purchasing it from absentee landowners, not by military conquest as with all Islamic occupations of the area. Thus Israel has, and thus the Jewish people have, a legitimate historical claim to land in the area. Jewish presence in the Holy Land was given qualified international recognition after the First World War, as well as a claim arising from the vital contribution Jews made during the First World War, enabling the British to have live ammunition in 1917 and 1918.[10]

---

7. In May 1917 Sherif Hussein met the British and French officials, Sir Mark Sykes and George Picot, who negotiated the map of the postwar Mideast. Hussein even threatened to switch sides, to the Turks, if the British failed to meet his territorial demands (for land outside what later became Saudi Arabia). The British paid Sherif Hussein over five million pounds over four years of war—some $225 million in 2005 dollars—to keep his allegiance.

8. On June 16, 1917, Britain issued a Declaration to the Seven Arabs, granting future Arab suzerainty to lands that had either been theirs before the Great War, or which they liberated during it; Britain would hold sway over lands it liberated, and people living in Turkish lands at the war's end would win their independence.

9. One noted visitor to the Holy Land, Mark Twain, observed how deserted the area was.

10. In 1916, as the British ran out of acetone, essential for the continued production of live munitions, a world-class chemist named Chaim Weizmann invented a way to synthesize acetone; the British thus were able to continue producing live ammunition. Weizmann was the Father of the State of Israel and its first President. His contribution was vastly more significant than the nuisance raids conducted by Arab irregulars under British adventurer T. E. Lawrence.

The 1922 Palestine Mandate ceded 77 percent of the land—what lay east of the Jordan River—to the Arabs and left the 23 percent that lay west of the Jordan to be shared between Arab and Jew. The 77 percent became what today is Jordan. Later, France ceded Lebanon (1943) and Syria (1946) to the locals (many not Arab). In 1947 the UN partitioned the part of Palestine that lay west of the Jordan, with Israel getting 56.5 percent.[11] The Partition Plan established a *Corpus Separatum* for Jerusalem whose ultimate fealty would be decided by referendum after ten years, which the numerically-superior Jews accepted and the Arabs rejected.[12]

Despite this history, which establishes the legitimacy of Israel's claims, Israel offered to surrender in 2000 (as noted above) 98 percent of the lands it held on the West Bank, plus all of Gaza. It got war for its troubles, featuring a wave of suicide bombings. Why? Because it would not accept an influx of Palestinian "refugees" sufficient to make Jews a minority in their own nation, which would lead inevitably to the abolition of the Jewish state. Moreover, the Palestinians planned the war in advance, after Israel vacated southern Lebanon (May 2000) and before the Camp David negotiations took place (July 2000).

It is not as if we do not know what real peaceful intent looks like in the Mideast. When in 1977 Egyptian President Anwar Sadat, the predecessor of Egypt's current president, Hosni Mubarak, went to Jerusalem and unequivocally accepted Israel's right to exist, a peace accord was signed within ten months. When in 1993 King Hussein, father of the present Jordanian monarch, King Abdullah, decided to make peace with Israel, an accord was signed in 1994. And we also know what happened to Sadat: Three years after Camp David was signed, Sadat was assassi-

---

11. Thus Arabs got 87 percent of the territory delimited by the Palestine Mandate (77 percent in 1922 and an added 10 percent in 1947), while Israel got but 13 percent (all in 1947)—territory it must share with the Arabs. Less than one percent of the original land was not assigned (allows for rounding error in figures).

12. In 1947 there were 99,320 Jews and 65,000 Arabs (40,000 Muslims and 25,000 Christian Arabs). Thus, some 60 percent of Jerusalem residents in 1947 were Jews.

nated by Islamic Jihad, an Egyptian terror group. One of its leaders then was Dr. Ayman al-Zawahiri, now al-Qaeda's number two.

So, to believe that a land settlement is a matter of finding the right formula, one simply assumes that Palestinians are prepared to compromise. Even before Hamas, a terrorist party that explicitly rejects compromise, won a fair election, this assumption was unsupported; now it simply strains credulity.[13] It would take a Palestinian Sadat making the unmistakable gesture of recognizing Israel's right to exist to create the genuine prospect of peace. Yet keeping such a leader from Sadat's grisly fate would be well-nigh impossible in the current environment, given a Palestinian polity envenomed with hatred of Jews and of Israel. To date, no administration has come fully to grips with the revolutionary character of Palestinian terrorism.

Petrodollar Poison

In October 1973, during the Yom Kippur War between Israel, Egypt and Syria, Saudi Arabian King Feisal imposed a targeted oil embargo on the United States. The embargo was rapidly lifted, but the message was clear: press Israel to surrender all lands won in 1967 or face oil supply problems. Saudi Arabia, in 1973 the world's largest oil exporter, could ration world supply. Feisal's political blackmail resonated in Europe, which already in the 1960s had abandoned support for Israel; the United States was also pushed to tilt less towards Israel. In addition to political blackmail by Feisal there had been, since 1969, oil price hikes engineered by the Organization of Petroleum Exporting Countries (OPEC), a cartel organized in 1960 that controls about 75 percent of the world's known oil reserves and 40 percent of world output.

Extortion like that should never be rewarded. Yet since 1973 it has been, by seven administrations, to the tune of a few trillion dollars over

---

13. One prominent Palestinian "moderate"—much touted during the 1990s—was the late Feisal al-Husseini. A few months before his death he gave an interview to an Egyptian newspaper, in which he said that the Palestinians wanted West Jerusalem as well as East Jerusalem (the latter referring to the sections forcibly annexed by Jordan in 1948), and that the 1993 Oslo Accords were—Husseini's words—a "Trojan Horse."

the past generation. Worse, what did the Mideast states do with this staggering petrodollar surplus bonanza? Partly they invested it in buying weapons, supporting terrorism, erecting immense palaces, pursuing pleasure and profit in Western countries, and underwriting the spread of radical Islam's hatred of the West.

How much surplus revenue has been paid OPEC above a fair market price? As recently as 1998, oil was priced at $10 per barrel. A rule of thumb is that every dollar increase in the per-barrel price of oil yields $7 billion annually to oil producers. By one expert's estimate, increased demand for oil since 1998 may make for a market price of perhaps $30 as of 2005. Thus, with the per-barrel price at $80, $350 billion annually flows into the coffers of oil producers as excess profit, much of it going to regimes in the Mideast. At $100, the excess would be $490 billion, nearly a half-trillion dollars. Even if one assumes a $60 free-market price for oil, the yearly cartel windfall at $100 is $280 billion. Cartel oil prices are in effect a *terror tax* imposed on Western consumers, as billions for terror are made available by petrodollar surpluses.[14]

America's passivity in the face of economic extortion is partially explained by another historical fable: that we got involved in the Mideast because of oil and exploited the locals. In fact, America's involvement in Mideast affairs dates back to 1803, when President Thomas Jefferson sent his fledgling navy to pursue the pirates of the Barbary coast. Muslim Barbary pirates had sailed the high seas since the fifteenth century. In 1631 a raiding party landed at and sacked Baltimore (the city in Ireland, not America), taking 237 captives. The Bey of Tunis and the Bey of Algiers presented a vexing problem, having kidnapped civilians and military personnel and held them for ransom, with many sold into Arab slavery. The mess was not resolved until 1815, partly due to American military action and partly due to covert transfer of American funds.

---

14. An emerging danger is petrodollar-endowed "sovereign investment funds." Over the next decade several trillion dollars will accumulate in the coffers of oil-producing countries. Strategic manipulation of that financial magnitude can exert immense pressure on oil-consuming countries to appease oil producers.

As for oil, it was first discovered for commercial exploitation in 1859 by Colonel Edwin Drake, in Pennsylvania. The first Mideast oil strike was in 1908, in Persia (Iran today). It was not until after the First World War that oil was discovered in the Gulf States. The British first engaged the Gulf sheikdoms in the 1830s, to combat piracy and slavery. The first strategic consideration given oil was in 1914 by the British, when Winston Churchill, as First Lord of the Admiralty, ordered the Royal Navy to switch from coal to oil on the eve of World War I. In the half century from the completion of the post-World War I settlements in 1923 to the imposition of the Saudi oil embargo in 1973, oil prices were kept very close to actual cost, with revenue participation deals given the American and British oil interests. Whether those deals fairly reflected the relative contribution of the parties is a matter of dispute, but what is beyond serious dispute is that American and British involvement in the Mideast had honorable, not colonial imperialist, origins.

Until (if ever) America reduces its import of foreign oil, billions monthly will flow to sellers who will divert some of it to fund terror, an enterprise generally far less expensive than the fight against it.

Revolutionary Terror

Petrodollars financed the diffusion of the two most radical versions of Islam: the Sunni version, Saudi Wahhabism, and the Shia version, Iran's Twelver Shi'ism.[15] The Saudis funded thousands of *madrassas*

---

15. Islam (which means "submission"), like all the world's great religions, has seen a major schism, and also numerous splinter offshoots of the twin major branches. The majority of Islam's community (in Arabic, *umma*) of believers are so-called Sunni (from the Arabic *sunna*, meaning "path"). These venerate the descendants of the Prophet Muhammad (570–632 AD), and owe allegiance to his successors ("caliph" means "successor"). The Saudi royal clan made an alliance in the mid-eighteenth century with a mystic named Muhammad ibn-al Wahhab; the Wahhabi version of Sunni Islam is extremely austere and puritan, and metes out harsh treatment for any religious offense. The second major branch consists of the Shia, whose name derives from *Shiryat Ali* ("partisans of Ali"). Ali was the son-in-law of the Prophet, and the fourth successor to Muhammad. The Shia look to their *imam* ("priest") for authority, not to a caliph. Twelver Shia are a splinter sect that take their name from the twelfth imam, whom they call the Hidden Imam, who is said to have disappeared at age five, *circa* 873 AD. Twelvers—such as Iran's President Mahmoud Ahmadinejad—believe that the Hidden Imam will return. All Muslims regard the Koran (*Quran*, meaning "recitation")

globally, providing 90 percent of funds to spread Islam—their radical branch thus dominated worldwide Sunni communities, despite Saudi population being less than one percent of Islam's 1.3 billion votaries. They also funded mosques in Western countries where radical messages could be disseminated behind the freedom of speech traditionally protected in the West. Sunni radicalism envisions a global Caliphate; al-Qaeda chieftain Osama bin Laden embraces this Sunni vision. The version of Twelver Shia belief that Iran's leaders have accepted since the 1979 seizure of power by the late Ayatollah Khomeini, holds that there will be a fiery Judgment Day when all the world is converted to Islam. Except for Lebanon and Iraq, the Arab Mideast states are predominately Sunni. Iranians are mostly of Persian, not Arab, descent.[16]

While Wahhabi Sunni and Twelver Shia have warred for centuries, they work together as well. Court cases in the U.S. and Europe have documented cooperation between Sunni and Iranian Shia terrorists. The two sects pursue in parallel a goal (albeit in different versions) that is *revolutionary*: establishment of a universal global Islamic community.

---

as the literal word of God. Islam's founder was both a warrior and prophet, the only founder of a major faith to have been a warrior. Islamic law, the *Sharia*, thus governs all activities; there has been no historical separation of church and state in a formal Islamic state, as eventually happened in Christian countries, after the (sixteenth-century) Reformation.

16. The current religious and political divisions of the Middle East have their origins in decisions made by the British and French at the Versailles Peace Conference. It was there that the fate of peoples living in the collapsed Austro-Hungarian and Ottoman (Turkish) empires was decided. The French took dominion over Lebanon and Syria, areas of French influence for the previous century. The British ended their colonial rule in Egypt and apportioned the Palestine Mandate, created in 1920 by the League of Nations: two Sunni Arab clans were the winners. Two sons of the Sunni Sherif (a titular religious office) of Mecca were placed, respectively, on the thrones of newly-created Transjordan (known as Jordan since 1946) and Iraq, which was put together from three provinces of the defunct Ottoman Empire: Mosul (north), Baghdad (center) and Basra (south). The north is primarily Kurdish. Muslim but not Arab, the Kurds were denied a state after World War I. The center is mostly Sunni (but with many Shia in Baghdad) and the south mostly Shia. The Kingdom of Saudi Arabia was unified, with British blessing, under Abdul Aziz ibn-Saud, in 1930, thus turning the two holiest cities in Islam, Mecca and Medina, over to the extremist Wahhabi sect. The Hashemite line, lineal descendants of the Prophet, ruled Iraq and Jordan. Turkey, a loser in World War I, evolved, in fits and starts, into a limited democracy, which in recent years has accepted a more political role for Islam. Turkey's boundaries were determined by the Treaty of Sevres (1923).

Joining will not be optional. Governance will be according to ancient notions of Islamic law. Such visions reject alternative religious beliefs, alternative civilizations, alternative anything else.

The challenge from the Iranian Revolution was open from the start. It seemed an atavistic vision few would embrace—Khomeini openly proclaimed his disdain for freedom: "Yes, we are reactionaries, and you are enlightened intellectuals: you intellectuals do not want us to go back 1,400 years." Attacking every variety of freedom, the Ayatollah decried "freedom that will drag our nation to the bottom."

Much impetus for the Iranian Revolution came from discontent with the regime of Shah Mohammed Reza Pahlavi, whose rapid Westernization offended Islamic clerics, and whose police state repression sparked dissent. His installation by the CIA in 1951 engendered much resentment.[17] The Carter administration pressed for departure of the Shah, and France allowed the Ayatollah Khomeini sanctuary, during which time he agitated for the Shah's downfall, and then left France to take power in Tehran.

Iran expert Michael Ledeen identifies the four foundations of the Ayatollah Khomeini's regime: a fascist-style constant mobilization of the masses; the transferring of benefits from the discredited elites to the poor; all-out war against the West; and judicial terror to instill fear in the population.

The parallel challenge from Sunni extremism was spread surreptitiously by Saudis, even while Islamic fighters were sent to Afghanistan to launch a *jihad* (literally "struggle"—often also translated as "holy war") to help defeat the infidel Soviet Russian invaders. Partly due to domestic legislative and political restraints, America was only too happy to engage Islamic assistance against the Soviet Union. But as radical Islam was helping defeat the Soviets in Afghanistan, it was establishing a base

---

17. Mohammed Mossadegh's regime nationalized the Iranian oil fields, seriously threatening Western economic interests. Nationalization with compensation likely would have averted the CIA coup.

there and also in neighboring Pakistan. As a separate matter, Pakistan ultimately became the world's first Islamic nuclear power.

Every U.S. administration that has made efforts to open dialogue with revolutionary Iran has seen American hopes dashed. The 9/11 Commission revealed two facts that have largely escaped domestic notice: First, Iran hosted al-Qaeda's senior financial planner, Ramzi Binalshibh, who wanted to be the twentieth 9/11 hijacker, twice within the year immediately preceding 9/11, the second time just days before the attacks. Second, Imad Muganiyeh, operational chief of Hezbollah, was on board the flight on which 9/11 hijackers departed Saudi Arabia, just before 9/11.

After nearly thirty years of failure the message should be clear. Iran's radical rulers are not interested in a negotiated compromise that would require them to abandon their revolutionary goals, objectives that form the conceptual foundation of their proclaimed right to rule over Iran and extend their revolutionary writ elsewhere. Meanwhile, the aftermath of 9/11 exposed massive Saudi funding of radical Islam globally, including in the United States. Americans were shocked to learn that 15 of 19 hijackers were Saudi.

One reason for this is that many American policy makers and analysts did not see militant Islam as revolutionary, but rather as a response to Western policies in the Mideast that Muslims deeply resented. Thus, the CIA's chief specialist on Osama bin Laden scoffed at the notion that bin Laden aspires to destroy Israel or America or the West, and has compared bin Laden to Robin Hood, Errol Flynn and Robert E. Lee. He filled out his portrait of bin Laden thusly:

> [T]here is no reason... to believe bin Laden anything other than what he appears: a pious, charismatic, gentle, generous, talented, and personally courageous Muslim who is blessed with sound strategic and tactical judgment... a reluctant but indispensable bloody-mindedness, and extraordinary patience.

Another factor in Islamic extremism is the influence of Nazism. It is easy to underestimate how deeply the Nazi poison from Europe penetrated the Mideast. Most Arab countries sided with the Nazis during World War II. Even in countries like Egypt, which sided with the Allies, young revolutionaries were pro-Nazi—even Anwar Sadat. But the most influential pro-Nazi was Muhammad Said Amin al-Husseini, the Grand Mufti (religious chief) of Jerusalem, who spent part of the war in Germany. The Mufti returned (courtesy of France) after the war and helped foment the Palestinian assault against Israel in 1948. He continued to spread hate until his 1974 death. By then derivative Nazism had taken deep root in the Mideast. Whether motivated by Wahhabi extremism, secular extremism, or Shia extremism, Middle Eastern dictators have pursued anti-Jewish policies and totalitarian political controls.

Embracing "Stability"

It was a desire to preserve a stable balance in the post-Cold War Mideast that led the U.S. to decide to spare Saddam Hussein, a Baathist secular dictator, after the Gulf War, despite his having nearly succeeded in gaining control over the heartland of global oil supply. Even the Gulf War victory was made possible by an attack the world—including the U.S.—condemned in 1981: Israel's destruction of an Iraqi nuclear reactor. Saddam was, we learned in 1991, about a year away from producing a nuclear bomb when he invaded Kuwait. Patience was never Saddam's strong suit. Had he waited a year or two he could have invaded Kuwait and even Saudi Arabia with impunity, shielded from retaliation by a nuclear arsenal.

In January 1991 the Gulf War was launched, its purpose expressed in UN resolutions: to eject Saddam from Kuwait. Passage of the resolution was made possible by the end of the Cold War, as Mikhail Gorbachev declined to exercise Russia's veto prerogative in the Security Council, overruling his foreign minister. In February, Saddam took two actions that went beyond the misconduct for which the UN authorized war: he spilled pollutants into the Persian Gulf, and his troops torched 700 oil wells before they retreated from Kuwait in late February, inflicting massive economic and environmental damage. It was only through heroic actions after the war that the immense fires were put out before the end of 1991. Saddam's actions eminently entitled the coalition to move beyond its original mission of simply ejecting him from Kuwait, and to force regime change in Iraq.

After 100 hours of ground fighting, the United States halted troops days short of totally disarming Saddam's elite Republican Guard, partly in response to media coverage of retreating Iraqis on the so-called "highway of death." As a result, Saddam's elite troops lived to fight another day. They got their chance.

During the war, President Bush had urged Iraqis to rise up against Saddam. In March 1991 they did so, and rebels controlled 15 of Iraq's 18 provinces within a matter of days. Saddam hung on to power by his fingernails. And then Saddam was saved—by decisions taken by the U.S.

General Norman Schwarzkopf permitted Saddam to fly helicopters, supposedly for civilian supply purposes. But Saddam used them in conjunction with his armor and his surviving Republican Guard units to turn the tide against the insurgents, who fought with small arms only. This was a clear violation of the cease-fire terms. Despite Saddam's blatant violations, and despite the literal massacre of untold thousands of Iraqis who had risen in revolt upon being encouraged to do so by the American President, more than 500,000 American troops stood just a few miles away and did nothing. American power could have blown Saddam's choppers out of the sky in minutes, and finished off his armor and the remaining Republican Guard in days, with minimal casualties.

Instead, Saddam massacred his out-gunned opponents and recovered control of the country. The U.S. had plenty of troops to establish control. It would have faced a grateful population in 2003, instead of bitter Shia in the south who remembered how America stood aside while Saddam butchered them in 1991. There was no problem of hostile Arab media coverage, as there was neither al-Jazeera nor widespread diffusion of satellite television in Arab and Muslim lands. Al-Qaeda was in its infancy, not ready for combat.

Further, it can be argued that America could then have finished off Iran, as the country was exhausted after eight years of ruinous war with Iraq that ended in 1988. Syria and Lebanon, the latter the main base of Iran's Hezbollah terrorist group, also seemed ripe for the taking. Keeping Yasser Arafat in Tunis would have isolated Palestinian terrorism. In theory, the U.S. and its allies could, in short, have cleaned up the Mideast long ago, ending the wave of terror directed against the West, and at far lower cost than the task will exact today—even assuming we are successful. There was just cause for doing so, due to many acts of terror committed against America and its allies in the 1970s and the 1980s. But there was little or no political support for such preventative action, which runs counter to the temperament and mores of modern liberal societies.

One question is, what would have replaced the regimes we thus would have toppled? The result might have been military dictatorships. But the new leaders would have taken office with sobering knowledge of what had happened to their predecessors. We could have warned them that adventurism on their part or sponsoring of terror would entail similar consequences.

It might be argued that the UN resolutions didn't specifically authorize deposing Saddam in 1991. True, but who, besides the U.S., would ask the UN for permission to use force? France, which lectured us about the imperative of staying under the UN aegis in 2003, has sent troops into post-colonial Africa more than three dozen times since 1960, without ever asking the UN for permission. The lesson is that no country should give the UN a veto power over its military operations.

One other factor played a role in saving Saddam. In November 1990 British conservatives jettisoned their party leader, Prime Minister Margaret Thatcher (for reasons unrelated to Iraq). It is hard to imagine the Iron Lady standing by while we let Saddam recover. It was she who, in August 1990, had famously told George Bush Sr., when he hesitated about taking action in Kuwait, that "this is no time to go wobbly." Thatcher's successor, John Major, lacked his mentor's resolve.

America ignored the famous dictum of Machiavelli: "When you strike at the king, you must kill him." Other expansionist and terrorist regimes would then have been put on notice as to the consequences of waging war against Western interests. We made the mistake of letting a priceless opportunity pass. Coalition considerations trumped broader American foreign policy interest, a perpetual hazard in such common enterprises. Instead we established shelter for the Kurds in the north, left the Shia in the south to largely fend for themselves, established northern and southern "no-fly" zones, spent more than a decade chasing WMD in Iraq, and enraged a scion of a Saudi construction family.

The scion was Osama bin Laden, who, to end the West's continuing presence in the Muslim Holy Land, established an organization called al-Qaeda (in Arabic, "the base"). Bin Laden established his base first in the Sudan, then in Afghanistan, where he allied himself closely with the Taliban rulers who took power in the 1990s. Bin Laden's original fatwa (in Arabic, "decree") also mentioned Israel; his quarrel, however, was not over what the boundary should be between Israel and the Palestinians. He called for the total destruction of the Jewish state. In al-Qaeda training camps Israel ranked only a fourth priority, behind secular Arabs, Shia Muslims (al-Qaeda is Sunni) and America.

The August 1996 original fatwa from bin Laden assailed the "Zionist-Crusader alliance." It bears quotation at length, that we may grasp why the 9/11 attacks were launched, from the enemy's point of view. Coming after terror attacks inside Saudi Arabia that killed Americans, bin Laden's text mocked us (all grammatical and spelling errors left in the original text, some Arabic deleted):

> Few days ago the news agencies had reported that the Defence Secretary [in 1996, William Perry] of the Crusading Americans had said that "the explosion at Riyadh and Al-Khobar had taught him one lesson: that is not to withdraw when attacked by coward terrorists."
>
> We say to the Defence Secretary that his talk can induce a grieving mother to laughter! and shows the fears that had enshrined you all. Where was this false courage of yours when the explosion in Beirut took place on 1983 AD. You were turned into scattered pits

and pieces at that time; 241 mainly marines solders were killed. And where was this courage of yours when two explosions made you to leave Aden in lees than twenty four hours!

But your most disgraceful case was in Somalia; where—after vigorous propaganda about the power of the USA and its post cold war leadership of the new world order—you moved tens of thousands of international force, including twenty eight thousands American solders into Somalia. However, when tens of your solders were killed in minor battles and one American Pilot was dragged in the streets of Mogadishu you left the area carrying disappointment, humiliation, defeat and your dead with you. Clinton appeared in front of the whole world threatening and promising revenge, but these threats were merely a preparation for withdrawal. You have been disgraced by Allah and you withdrew; the extent of your impotence and weaknesses became very clear. It was a pleasure for the "heart" of every Muslim and a remedy to the "chests" of believing nations to see you defeated in the three Islamic cities of Beirut, Aden and Mogadishu.

Further on bin Laden wrote:

I say to Secretary of Defence: The sons of the land of the two Holy Places had come out to fight against the Russian in Afghanistan, the Serb in Bosnia-Herzegovina and today they are fighting in Chechenia and—by the Permission of Allah—they have been made victorious over your partner, the Russians. By the command of Allah, they are also fighting in Tajakistan.

I say: Since the sons of the land of the two Holy Places feel and strongly believe that fighting (Jihad) against the Kuffar [unbeliever] in every part of the world, is absolutely essential; then they would be even more enthusiastic, more powerful and larger in number upon fighting on their own land- the place of their births- defending the greatest of their sanctities, the noble Ka'ba (the Qiblah of all Muslims). They know that the Muslims of the world will assist and help them to victory. To liberate their sanctities is the greatest of issues concerning all Muslims; It is the duty of every Muslims in this world.

I say to you William (Defence Secretary) that: These youths love death as you loves life. They inherit dignity, pride, courage, generosity, truthfulness and sacrifice from father to father. They are most delivering and steadfast at war. They inherit these values from their ancestors (even from the time before Islam). These values were approved and completed by the arriving Islam as stated by the messenger of Allah (Allah's Blessings and Salutations may be on him): "I have been send to perfecting the good values." [18]

Bin Laden described the WTC towers as icons of freedom—"those awesome symbolic towers that speak of liberty, human rights and humanity." In this, as in so much, he was ignorant of reality: The Twin Towers were in fact monuments to multi-state corporatist enterprise— for more than two decades tenants were nearly all government entities. Nearby stands the true symbol of American buccaneer capitalism, the New York Stock Exchange, nearly two centuries older.

Terrorism as a Law Enforcement Problem

In a February 1998 fatwa bin Laden explicitly called upon Muslims to kill Americans and their allies:

> The ruling to kill the Americans and their allies—civilians and military—is an individual duty for every Muslim who can do it in any country in which it is possible to do it, in order to liberate the al-Aqsa Mosque and the holy mosque [Mecca] from their grip, and in order for their armies to move out of all the lands of Islam, defeated and unable to threaten any Muslim.[19]

American law enforcement first learned of al-Qaeda in November 1996, when a Sudanese defector took his story to the FBI. At the time, al-Qaeda had all of 93 members—after more than eight years since its April 1988 founding. By 9/11 al-Qaeda had cells in 33 American cities.

Terrorist acts, whether or not regarded as acts of war, are always violations of criminal codes. Societies founded on the rule of law thus are tempted to prosecute violations, by targeting specific defendants. This legalist strategy has two shortfalls: First, it demotes to the level of

---

18. The full text of bin Laden's 1996 statement rambles on interminably. His February 23, 1998 declaration summarizes his views more succinctly.

19. Bin Laden does not specify, but the al-Aqsa (Arabic for "the far") Mosque is the mosque on Temple Mount (Haram al Sharif—Noble Sanctuary—to the Arabs) in Jerusalem, built in the ninth century. It lies across from the Dome of the Rock, built in the seventh century, and in Islamic scripture the place from where Muhammad ascended to Heaven on his steed. Thus bin Laden intends that Jews surrender Temple Mount, their holiest site.

common criminality acts that are far more dangerous in their ability to destroy a society's sense of security and cohesion.

The second, greater, danger of treating acts of war as mere crimes is that successful prosecution, by satisfying members of society that punishment has been meted out, can blind a society to national security threats posed by state-sponsored terrorism.[20]

Placing terrorist acts in the category of acts of war does not, however, mean that local law enforcement resources are not intimately engaged in fighting terror and seeking to prevent acts of terrorism. With 800,000 state and local police, versus but 12,000 FBI agents worldwide, it is far more likely that terrorists inside the U.S. will be spotted first by local authorities than by their federal counterparts. Thus, since 9/11 the FBI has more than tripled its information sharing bureaus (Joint Information Task Forces), to over 100.

The cost of misperceiving terrorism as a criminal matter is the butcher's bill we are now paying to fight a much larger, far longer multi-faceted conflict—one global in scope—than would have been needed a generation ago, and thus we face substantially graver risk of suffering vast, even potentially catastrophic, harm.

---

20. There have, of course, been a number of individual officials in prior speeches who spoke out forcefully in favor of treating state-sponsored terrorism as a national security priority. Perhaps most notable among them was Reagan's second Secretary of State, George P. Shultz, who publicly warned that American inaction against terrorism risked making us "the Hamlet of nations." But concerns about terrorism were first subordinated to broader national security concerns during the Cold War, and then hidden behind domestic "peace dividend" euphoria and its consequent shift in policy priorities, after the collapse of the Soviet Union in 1991. Efforts during the Reagan years to link terrorism to the Cold War, by citing abundant evidence that the Soviets aided many terrorist groups, failed, partly due to vociferous opposition from politicians advocating closer diplomatic engagement with the Soviets, and partly due to widespread, corrosive skepticism in the mass media.

CHAPTER II

THE REFORMATION VALUES WAR

ISLAM OR THE WEST REFORMS

You say that it is your custom to burn widows. Very well. We also have a custom: when men burn a woman alive, we tie a rope around their necks and we hang them. Build your funeral pyre; beside it, my carpenters will build a gallows. You may follow your custom. And then we will follow ours.

BRITISH GENERAL SIR CHARLES NAPIER, ON
SUTTEE (HINDU WIDOW-BURNING), 1842

Part of radical Islam's challenge to the international order is being mounted within Western countries. Radical groups aim to create separate confessional communities, with Islamic law regnant within their community. Radicals are pressuring schools to change their curricula, veiling their women from their community and even forcibly veiling non-Muslim females in some European cities. They are challenging security policies, and seeking to use multicultural political correctness norms to rewrite the terms of tolerance in public debate.

Thus, a central front in radical Islam's challenge to the international order established by the West is to undermine the West from within. Nowhere is this challenge stronger than in efforts by Muslim groups to use "sensitivity" as a weapon in silencing critics. If deprived of a vocabulary of vigorous criticism, proponents of traditional Western values will lose ground in debate with radical adversaries. In essence, the radicals demand that the West genuflect to their customs, and compromise ours.

In looking at trends within Islamic attitudes towards the West in Western countries it is useful to track three key reform battlegrounds: Europe, where Islamic radicals have mounted their strongest challenge; the United States, where the radical strain is weaker but growing; and Australia, where the Western response to Islamic challenges has been most forceful.

Europe: Demographic Day of Judgment

On November 2, 2004, just two days before the American Presidential election, the danger posed by militant Islam was dramatically illustrated. Dutch film-maker Theo van Gogh, great-grand-nephew of the Impressionist painter, was brutally murdered on an Amsterdam street. The murderer was a militant Muslim enraged by van Gogh's documentary on mistreatment of women by Islamic men, *Submission* (a title chosen because "Islam" is Arabic for "submission," as in submission to the will of Allah).

Van Gogh was not simply killed. The Moroccan immigrant, a recipient of Dutch welfare largesse, shot his victim twenty times, stabbed him several times, slit his throat and pinned on the corpse a five-page note that, in addition to threatening several Dutch political leaders by name, warned:

"I know definitely that you, O America, will go down. I know definitely that you, O Europe, will go down. I know definitely that you, O Netherlands, will go down. And I know definitely that you, O Hirsi Ali, will go down."

The last referenced name belongs to Ayaan Hirsi Ali, a Somali-born, Dutch immigrant who had written the script for van Gogh's film project. Although elected to the Dutch Parliament, Hirsi Ali eventually fled to the United States for security reasons. She remains under threat of murder by Islamic radicals.

Then came the July 7, 2005, London suicide bombings. In October 2005 widespread rioting by Muslim youths took place in France after two Muslims fleeing the police electrocuted themselves on a power transformer. The combined import of these and other events is clear: A major conflict within Islam is taking place within the West itself. Unless the progressive radicalization of Muslim youth can be reversed, the nations of Europe face a future with large unassimilated Islamic communities deeply hostile to fundamental Western values of liberty and tolerance.

Militant Islam's European roots are over 50 years old. Islam's first major postwar inroad in Europe, in 1956, was tainted by association with Nazism. In that year the Islamic Center of Munich opened. Figures who played key roles included: a Latvian Nazi who oversaw Muslim war efforts against Russia; an Uzbek (Central Asian) imam who served in the Nazi SS and then served as imam of the Center for several decades; the Egyptian son-in-law of Hasan al-Banna, who in 1928 founded the Islamic radical group, the Muslim Brotherhood; a Syrian terrorist financier who built the local mosque. The Islamic Center of Munich spawned a whole network of radical mosques around Europe. Ironically, the CIA also played a role, by supporting Islamic operations against the former Soviet Union during the Cold War.

Worse, Adolf Hitler's political manifesto, *Mein Kampf*, in which he aired his racialist Nazi ideology, remains a perennial best-seller in the Mideast under the Arabic title *Jihadi* (the possessive form of the Arabic word *jihad*, thus "My Struggle," identical to the book's German title). Anti-Semitism is central to Islamist radical ideology.

Some Palestinians assert what amounts to a right to make their territory *Judenrein* (Nazi Germany's "Jew-free" policy). Not long ago, Egypt ran a major series on television, centering on "The Protocols of the Elders of Zion," an infamous forgery that emerged from Tsarist Russia around 1900, alleging a Jewish conspiracy to control the world.

What ultimately became the epicenter for the spread of militant Islam was, of all places, London, whose main Muslim quarter is dubbed "Londonistan." There are at least 1.6 million Muslims out of a total British population of 60 million. They are far more religious than the Anglican majority. Church attendance in most European countries is less than five percent. British Muslims who arrived in the 1960s and 1970s came from Asia. Those who arrived in the 1980s and 1990s came from North Africa and the Mideast. Terrorists minted from these groups have executed attacks in twelve countries outside Britain, including in the U.S.

The Asians who arrived in the 1970s worked as cheap labor in Britain's cotton mills. To this day, some 85 percent of Pakistani and Bangladeshi households in Britain have incomes below the national average. Intermarriage rates for British Muslims are around ten percent, compared to as high as two-thirds in America. British Muslim immigrants mostly hail from rural settings rather than big cities, and carry with them the traditional tribal codes of honor, in which Muslim women are totally subservient to Muslim males. Other Islamic immigrants came to Britain after training to fight the Soviets in Afghanistan. The failure of Muslims to successfully integrate in Britain sets them apart from other Asian immigrants—Hindu, Parsi, Sikh and Jain (mostly from India)—who are better off economically than even British whites and Jews, due to superior education.

Author Melanie Phillips cites several factors behind the progressive radicalization of British Muslims. One was the 1989 Salman Rushdie affair, when a British writer produced a novel that Muslims found deeply offensive, and found himself sentenced to death by the Iranian Ayatollah Ruhollah Khomeini (when Britain awarded a prize to Rushdie in 2006, radical Islamic groups again threatened violence). A second factor was Europe's tardy response to the slaughter of Muslims in Bosnia. A third is the North London Central Mosque, in Finsbury Park, which did more to promote radicalism and terror than any other mosque in Britain. It is the mosque where the imam Abu Hamza, a disabled Afghan campaign jihadist, incited British Muslim youth, exhorting them to commit murder and mayhem against the infidel. The Finsbury Park mosque was funded by Saudis, who were persuaded to do so by none other than

Charles, Prince of Wales. The Prince, in fact, said in a 1993 speech that Islam respects women's rights as much as does the West.[21]

In 1999 a British newspaper reported that 2,000 terrorist trainees per year attended training camps located outside of Birmingham and London. In 2005 a former London police chief estimated that more than 3,000 British Muslims had trained in Osama bin Laden's terror camps. It was only in 2003, after the Finsbury radicals were tied to a plot to disseminate the lethal toxin ricin, that the authorities raided the mosque. But even then authorities continued to believe that they had a "gentleman's agreement" with radical Muslim leaders, what Phillips calls "the dirty little secret at the heart of Britain's "blind-eye' policy": Militants could conduct terror abroad so long as they did not do so on British soil. The compact held until the invasion of Iraq, when Muslim leaders decided it had been abrogated by British support for the war.

Another major factor in the rise of British Muslim radicals was the attitude of the police, who let fear of alienating moderate Muslims keep them from implementing strong measures. Thus, on 7/7, hours after the four suicide bombings, London's deputy police commissioner said to a television audience, "As far as I am concerned, Islam and terrorists are two words that do not go together." Meanwhile moderate Muslims were furious at the appeasement of radicals by the authorities. (Phillips states that authorities define anyone as moderate so long as they do not advocate violence; preaching hatred without actual incitement to violence qualifies under this definition.)

The broader British society adopted unprecedented measures of appeasement. One apartment complex went so far as to install toilets facing away from Mecca. Britain's prisons are also doing this, for half of their toilets, to accommodate Muslim inmates. The British flag—which depicts the Cross of St. George carried by the Crusaders—no longer

---

21. In November 2007 the Saudi government, apparently unmindful of the Prince's praise, affirmed a sentence of six months in prison, plus 200 lashes, for a Shia teenager, guilty of "illegal mingling" because she sat in a car with a man not related to her. That she had been gang-raped by seven (Sunni) males did not deter the authorities.

flies at British prisons, the Drivers and Licenses Agency and at London's Heathrow Airport. Other measures include provision of Sharia-compliant bank loans (the Quran forbids usury), and omitting criticism of Islam as a subject in university religious courses. Inland Revenue (Britain's IRS) is looking at granting tax status to polygamous marriages (Islam permits up to four wives); Muslims currently sidestep anti-polygamy secular law by getting married in mosques in ceremonies not legally recognized as civil marriages.

All this has been done despite scant evidence of widespread anti-Muslim feeling. One poll showed that 80 percent of Muslim respondents encountered no hostility even after the 7/7 bombings. But hostile minorities can pose plenty of problems. British authorities estimate that one percent of England's Muslims—16,000 people—are "actively engaged" in terrorist activity. According to British officials, al-Qaeda is actively recruiting Muslims attending British universities, seeking those with technical expertise.

A large number of young, UK-born Muslims in Great Britain hate the society that shelters them and gives them freedoms their co-religionists can but dream of in Muslim lands. Surveys show that hundreds of thousands of British Muslims, even Muslims born in Britain, put Islamic identity before country. A prime issue of cultural separation is the wearing of the veil. Veils have stirred controversy when worn by teachers, students, lawyers and even pedestrians. One 24-year-old Muslim female defended her decision to wear a *niqab* (only eye slits are open) as "not just a piece of clothing, it's an act of faith, of solidarity." She added: "9/11 was a wake-up call for young Muslims."

A December 2002 poll showed that 70 percent of British Muslims thought that America had declared war on Islam, nearly 60 percent did not believe that the 9/11 attack was al-Qaeda's handiwork, and 44 percent thought the 9/11 attacks justified. A poll taken after the London 7/7 bombings showed that 32 percent of Muslims believe "Western society is decadent and immoral and Muslims should seek to bring it to an end."

In 2006 a poll showed that in the UK only 7 percent of Muslims put country before religion, while 81 percent put their religious identity first. By way of comparison, a poll taken in Indonesia, the world's most populous Islamic country, showed that 39 percent put country first, and 36 percent put religion first. British efforts to reach out to young Muslims have not fared well. British Muslims are heavily influenced by Pakistan's radical Deoband sect. As of late 2007 more than 600 of Britain's 1,350 mosques are Deobandi. They run 17 of the country's 28 Islamic seminaries and thus train 80 percent of British Muslim clerics. The leading Deobandi cleric, Riyadh al Haq, openly advocates enmity towards all non-Muslims. Somewhat more encouraging are poll results showing that suicide bombing is "never justified" according to 83 percent of Muslims in Germany, 70 percent in the UK, 64 percent in France, and 60 percent in Spain.

After the June 2007 break-up of the Muslim "doctors' plot" and the attempted car bombing at Glasgow's Airport, London Mayor Ken ("Red Ken") Livingstone asserted, citing IRA and right-wing terror groups, that Muslims are less violent than non-Muslims and "have played a good and active and growing role in creating a multi-cultural society." Livingstone went on to note that just as Muslims were not all threats, neither were all white men. Missing from Livingstone's assessment is any indication that Muslim terrorists, unlike the IRA, seek WMD to inflict massive damage, and that thus the danger they pose is vastly greater.

The education front is active, too. In 2004 a Saudi-funded Muslim school in London was caught using textbooks that describe Jews as apes and monkeys, and Christians as pigs. In 2007 several British schools stopped teaching pupils about the Holocaust, lest it offend students who are Holocaust deniers. They also stopped teaching about the Crusades, so as to assuage Muslim sensitivities and avoid conflict with the subject as taught at local mosques. The history of the Arab-Israeli conflict has also been subjected to Muslim pressures. The British government is promoting a civics curriculum to be taught at mosques, in order to counter extremist tendencies among the young.

In October 2005 British Home Secretary Charles Clarke had this to say:

> [T]here can be no negotiation about the re-creation of the Caliphate; there can be no negotiation about the imposition of Shariah law; there can be no negotiation about the suppression of equality between the sexes; there can be no negotiation about the ending of free speech. These values are fundamental to our civilization and are simply not up for negotiation.

In his farewell address, former British Prime Minister Tony Blair urged his countrymen to confront militant Islamists: "We're not actually standing up to these people and saying: 'It's not just your methods that are wrong; your ideas are absurd.'"[22]

All over Europe, nations struggle to respond to a range of practices introduced by Muslim immigrants.

Especially appalling is the practice of female genital mutilation; to evade detection by authorities the act is often carried out on infants. While France requires mandatory medical exams to prevent it, the provision is rarely enforced, and the rule has not been adopted anywhere else in Europe. Swedish authorities have proposed a ban on the practice, with medical exam verification. Fortunately, the Grand Mufti in Saudi Arabia has recently pronounced against it.

But other practices are more insidious. One common custom is "dumping," sending children born in Europe to Quranic schools in Muslim countries of the parents' origin. A comparable result is achieved by sending Muslim children to private Muslim schools in Europe. Muslim school texts in Germany state that Muslims are threatened by Christians and Jews and that it is their duty to wage war against them. Family reunification laws enable the importation of relatives to Europe, who then are married to Muslim children, some born in Europe, without their consent. In Norway these are called "fetching marriages." Muslim women in Europe who socialize with non-Muslim boys risk honor-killing

---

22. In November 2007 British Prime Minister Gordon Brown proposed 53 new security measures, most notably, doubling from 28 to 56 days the length of preventive detention of terror suspects.

revenge from family members. And all this takes place despite Muslims being major recipients of government largesse in these countries. The five percent of residents in Denmark who are Muslim receive 40 percent of Danish welfare benefits.

Norway is so connected to Islamic immigration that there is an area in Pakistan called "Little Norway" (also known as "Little Scandinavia"). In 2005 a Norwegian Parliamentary candidate campaigned there. As for visa scrutiny, 94 percent of Muslim immigrants to Norway carry no identification. A 2001 report found that 65 percent of all rapes in Norway were committed by "non-Western" immigrants. Norway's response to such trends was to pass a law in April 2005 making unlawful "hateful" or "discriminatory" speech about race, color, and religion. *The accused is required to prove his innocence.*

Muslims in Europe are pressing for privileges truly extraordinary in scope and kind. At one Amsterdam school, Muslim students posted pictures of van Gogh's assassin on school walls. One teacher said that even a decade ago Moroccan students were predicting that Muslims would "take over the Netherlands." In Linz, Austria, Muslims have insisted that all teachers and students, regardless of faith, wear headscarves in class.

In France, some Muslim students have refused to engage in practices they have been told (by their Muslim elders) are un-Islamic: no singing, no pictorial drawing, no communal swimming and no music. More ominous by far are reports of French students and teachers being confronted by Muslim students demanding to know their religion, and of Muslim girls being shadowed by their brothers—even younger brothers—to see that they are observing traditional tenets of dress and behavior. Non-Muslim girls in France fear that if they go out at night in Western dress they will be called a "whore" and perhaps even be raped. In France, 70 percent of prisoners are Muslim.

France's tilt towards the Arabs has long between inextricably intertwined with anti-Semitism among its governing elites. It was a French consul who fomented the 1840 "blood libel" in the Damascus Affair.

(Damascus, capital of what today is Syria, was then under the control of the Ottoman empire; a "blood libel" denotes the false accusation that Jews use the blood of Christian children to make unleavened bread—matzoh.) The French spirited away from the British the pro-Nazi war criminal Haj Amin al-Husseini, the Grand Mufti of Jerusalem, after World War II. And it was the French who in 1978 gave the Ayatollah Khomeini asylum for several months prior to the fall of the Shah, allowing Khomeini to use the print and broadcast press to finish off the Shah's regime. While anti-Semitism helped fuel the Muslim youth riots of October and November 2005, the causes of Muslim alienation in France include economic and social separation, and incitement by radical imams. One notable French success story is the relatively peaceful co-existence of Muslims and others in the polyglot southern French port of Marseille, which has substantial Muslim and Jewish populations. But it has come at a high price: separation of the city into multi-confessional enclaves, with each religious community following its own laws.

Gestures by European political leaders have crossed the line of absurdity. In March 2004, Spanish voters responded to the al-Qaeda "3/11" train bombings by electing three days later, as the terrorists hoped, an anti-war and anti-American candidate. Millions of Spaniards turned out for demonstrations at first, when the bombings were thought to have been the work of Basque separatists; when Islamists were identified as the perpetrators, the demonstrations ended. Swedish authorities have hardly reacted at all to increasing Muslim immigrant violent crime, honor killings, and rising anti-Semitism. The Spanish demoted long deceased King Ferdinand III as patron saint of Seville's annual fiesta, because the King had led the fight to free Spain from Islamic domination (which in the south lasted nearly eight centuries). In another example of appeasing Islamic radicals, the mayor of Brussels rejected a permit request by groups seeking to publicly protest the Islamization of Europe on September 11, 2007, fearing violence.

The Dutch echoed Spain's post-9/11 abasement. Immediately after 9/11, Moroccan immigrants in one Dutch town gamboled through the streets in joy, and the Dutch Muslim TV station broadcast a passage from the Quran calling "unbelievers" "fuel for the fire." In a post-9/11 poll 21 percent of Holland's Moroccan immigrants expressed support for jihad against America. Yet while 60 percent of the Dutch public in one newspaper poll supported deportation of Muslim immigrants who approved of such acts, the Dutch Interior Minister was warning his countryman not to "disturb the peace and conduct a cold war against Islam." One Dutch bishop actually suggested that all religious references to a deity use Allah, even though Muslims had not proposed this. Perhaps the ultimate case of Dutch timorousness in the face of Islamic militancy is this: In 2005, Dutch parliamentarian Gert Wilders voluntarily moved into a *prison cell* for safety, because his own government would not protect him from death threats by Muslim militants. It is no wonder that an April 2005 poll showed one in three Dutchman wanting to emigrate; favored destinations are Australia, New Zealand and Canada. In 2006 the Dutch finally acted; their Parliament passed a law requiring would-be immigrants to pass a test showing Dutch language proficiency and understanding of Dutch society. Yet listen to a Dutch Justice Minister: "If a majority of Dutchman opt for [Islamic law] at some future date, this has to be respected."

Lest this seem far-fetched, a German judge in Frankfurt ruled in 2007 that a Moroccan husband had a right under Islamic law to administer corporal punishment to his wife; the judge was removed from the case, but that any Western jurist would apply confessional community law instead of long-settled public law suggests that the defense of the West is getting wobbly. One British Islamist, when asked about applying Islamic law in Britain, answered: "Who says you own Britain anyway?"

The November 2004 murder of Theo van Gogh (noted above) finally prompted the European Community to take steps to deal with the problem of militant Islam, by requiring immigrants to learn the local language and "European values." Several countries took steps to limit forced marriages by imposing age, residency and income requirements in various forms. In Denmark, where Muslim immigrants celebrated in the streets after 9/11, and called for "holy war" against Danish society, Danes elected a conservative prime minister, who strongly supported America. Denmark went so far as to ban residents who had attended Quranic schools elsewhere from importing brides into Denmark. A 2006 Swiss domestic security report found that radical Islamists based in Switzerland are exporting money and propaganda to the rest of Europe.

One segment of society determined not to conduct a cold war against militant Islam is European media. After Chechen terrorists butchered 331 civilians—many of them schoolchildren—at a Russian school in Beslan, at the start of the academic year in late 2004, European media reports ignored the Muslim religion of the terrorists, just as the BBC did after the July 2005 London bombings. In 2007 the BBC backed away from airing a plot involving Islamic terrorists on one of its top entertainment shows. Worse, when Britain's Channel Four network broadcast in prime time a show called "Undercover Mosque," depicting radical imams allegedly inciting their flocks to commit violence, the Crown Prosecution Service, far from pursuing the imams, threatened the network with a hate crimes prosecution, for allegedly using short, inflammatory excerpts out of context. This stands in stark contrast to the honest comments on Beslan by the general manager of the Arabic-language, Dubai-based TV station, *al-Arabiya*, who said that "not all Muslims are terrorists [but] most terrorists are Muslims" and asked if such barbarity "[tells] us anything about ourselves, our society and our culture."

Many Islamic news organizations dispense anti-Semitic propaganda; the sermons in the mosques and education in the schools are often no better, encouraging resentment and jihadist fatalism. The West leads with chin first, apologizing for past sins committed by the West against Islam. Few in the West seem to have the nerve to point out that the Crusades happened a thousand years ago or that Islamic rulers barring Christian pilgrims from the Holy Land prompted the Crusades.

Sadly typical of how Western leaders tread gingerly is the response to the Danish cartoon controversy that erupted in early 2006. They buckled under pressure from radical Muslim groups who protested cartoons published in a Danish newspaper as being disrespectful to Islam. The paper had published only 12 cartoons in September 2005. When the editor declined to apologize for publishing the cartoons, radical European Islamic clerics added three patently vicious caricatures to the original, less offensive, dozen. These they then took into the Arab world and re-published all 15, stoking public anger via orchestrated violent demonstrations in February 2006.

Western leaders condemned rioting around the globe by Islamic militants, but also chastised the paper for printing the cartoons. They could instead have defended the right of the press in free countries to criticize other religions. Robust criticism of Christianity is a commonplace in the Western press and especially in artistic circles; threats of Christian retaliatory violence are virtually non-existent. Western leaders could also have emphasized the successful ploy of radical imams in adding three especially offensive cartoons, and then passing them off as Danish creations.

Islamic radicals thus confected a cartoon controversy and the West sacrificed freedom of speech on the altar of Muslim sensitivity. Meanwhile, Nazi-style caricature of Jews is commonplace in Muslim lands. In Tehran the mullahs held a Holocaust cartoon exhibit and a Holocaust denial conference in a country that has the second largest Jewish community in the Mideast (after Israel). Palestinians trashed a major Christian church in 2001, abusing captives for 39 days, setting the Orthodox Christian and Franciscan sections on fire, and leaving behind forty explosive charges after they negotiated exile in Europe. Pope Benedict XVI's September 12, 2006, Regensburg speech set criteria for an interfaith dialogue with the Islamic world, one that contained a carefully circumscribed allusion to a fourteenth-century debate between Eastern Christianity and Islam. Riots were orchestrated around the planet, with at least one nun murdered. Neither apology nor clarification matters to the rioters. They seek to intimidate, and are succeeding.

Three months later, the Pope visited Turkey, and his trip was preceded by orchestrated demonstrations by radical Muslims. The head of Turkey's religious affairs office (a government position) proclaimed the "vast tolerance of Islam" and denied that Islam "was spread over the world by swords"—this in a country that disallows Christian activity as anti-Turkish and has locked the doors on the Eastern Orthodox Church seminary since 1971. Protesters at Haghia Sophia (originally an Eastern Orthodox Church, then turned into a mosque upon the arrival of the Ottoman Turks in 1453, and now a museum) shouted: "Pope, don't you make a mistake, don't wear out our patience." Fortunately, other Turks responded more favorably to the Pope's visit, as the Pope expressed regret for the effect of his earlier remarks, without retracting their substance.

Rome has synagogues and mosques, but where are the synagogues in Mecca and Medina (Islam's second holiest city)? In fact, non-Muslims are not allowed to set foot in either city. In Cairo? In Baghdad, whose Jewish community at the end of World War I was the leading minority community residing in the city?

A huge factor in the rise of Muslim influence in Europe—one exploited eagerly by radical Muslim factions—is the steep demographic decline of European populations. Italy has more people over 60 than under 20, an age-group inversion without precedent. Demographers peg the "total fertility rate" (TFR) necessary to sustain populations at 2.1 births per couple. Europe's TFR as a whole is but 1.38 (Japan's is 1.32). Such rates lie near a tipping point demographers call "lowest low": the rate (1.3) at which a self-perpetuating downward "death spiral" sets in, making recovery nearly impossible, barring radical change. At the top of the range is the U.S. at 2.11.

Noting that the decline in Europe's population in the next generation will be steeper than that caused by the fourteenth-century's Black Death, author Mark Steyn states: "We are living through a rare moment: the self-extinction of the civilization which, for good or ill, shaped the world we live in."

While today the Muslim share of population runs from two to ten percent in European countries, the Muslim share of children typically runs 16 to 20 percent. In Sweden a popular T-shirt among Muslim youth is "2030—then we take over." Graphically illustrative of how Islamicized Europe has become, Muhammad is now the most popular male child name in Amsterdam, Malmö (a southern port city in Sweden), and in the entire country of Belgium. European Muslim women produce 3.5 children on average, more than twice the 1.4 figure for non-Muslims. The impact is already felt in Europe's cities and in its urban schools. In Amsterdam, more than one-half are now non-native Dutch, and two of three students in school are non-Dutch.

These population numbers are but part of a larger trend that shows Muslims gaining worldwide *vis-à-vis* the West. Noting that in 1970 the developed world had a share of the world's population twice that of Muslims—30 percent versus 15 percent—but that in 2000 the two segments had equal 20 percent shares, Steyn concludes: "September 11, 2001 was not 'the day everything changed,' but the day that revealed how much everything had already changed." In the Middle East, an ominous portent for Israel in its conflict with the Palestinians is that in Gaza the median age is 15.8 years (in statistical terms, median age is not the average age, but the age level at which half of the population is younger and half is older).

The United States: Will Cultural Separation Defeat Economic Assimilation?

America, fortunately, does not face the same problems that Western European and Asian countries do with their Muslim populations. Yet trends in the United States contain troubling signs that the problems Europe faces are making landfall in the States. In the 1990s Osama bin Laden set up al-Qaeda cells in a host of cities, including New York City (in Brooklyn), Dallas, Tucson, Orlando (home of Disney World), and Herndon, Virginia (at the periphery of the interstate Beltway that delineates the heart of the extended Washington, D.C., government professional community). Muslims in New York City—at 600,000, more than seven percent of the city's population—report that since 9/11 they have felt "under suspicion." Recently a Muslim was convicted of planning to blow up the Herald Square subway station, located in Manhattan's West Side, near Macy's department store. His plot was detected due to police monitoring inside his mosque (there are 140 in NYC). Many Muslims resent such monitoring. Yet Muslims recognize that their treatment in the U.S. is far better than would be the case in their native lands.

Data on Muslims was released in 2007 in a major survey conducted by the Pew Charitable Trusts. Of America's 2.35 million Muslims, 1.5 million are at least 18 years old. Foreign-born are 65 percent of the total; of the 35 percent born here, one-fifth, or 7 percent of the total, are second-generation. Among immigrants, 37 percent of the total are Arabs, and 27 percent are from Asia, with Iran and Pakistan at 12 percent tied as the largest single countries represented. Muslims living here roughly match the non-Muslim population in education and income. In short, these are highly successful communities that are woven into the fabric of American life.

Even so, while most Muslims integrate, not all is well. Long Island Republican Congressman Peter King caught flack from Muslim activists for saying that 85 percent of mosques in the U.S. are funded by radicals, that Muslims inside the U.S. do not step forward with information about terrorist acts in the making (even if they do not participate in such acts), and that the U.S. should employ ethnic profiling (a bad idea, more on this later) of Muslims in airports. After six imams were removed from US Airways Flight 300 in late 2006, when their suspicious behavior alarmed passengers, including other Muslims, their lawyer immediately claimed ethnic discrimination. Three probes exonerated the carrier, but a lawsuit was filed nonetheless. In late 2007 the plaintiffs dropped the six "John Doe" passengers from the roster of defendants, while continuing their suit against the airline and the Minneapolis Airport Authority.[23]

Equally serious is a major controversy that erupted in August 2007 in New York City. A new high school that was to teach students Arabic became embattled when its Muslim-American principal was discovered to have distributed T-shirts with "Intifada NYC" on them. The principal protested that intifada merely means "shaking off" in Arabic, but clearly this was disingenuous, as the term is associated with the Arab-Israeli conflict. The principal was canned, but her temporary replacement, while Jewish, reportedly embraces academia's hard left politics. The ousted principal, who filed suit to regain her post, said: "Unfortunately, a small group of highly misguided individuals has launched a relentless attack on me because of my religion."

In a Detroit court there is a clash between law and culture, involving permissible head covering, of which four kinds are worn by Muslim females.[24] A Muslim plaintiff lost her small claims case (over who was to pay $2,750 in rental car damages caused by thieves) in 2006 when she refused to remove her veil in court, because the judge was male. The judge took the position that he needed to see the faces of those testifying to help him gauge witness credibility. But the plaintiff, calling this a violation of her civil and religious rights, filed suit.

This case, should it go the plaintiff's way and not be reversed on appeal, would establish a local precedent only in one part of Michigan. But if the rationale spreads to other jurisdictions it progressively will undermine a fundamental tenet of American law, that what the law terms "demeanor evidence" and considers essential to evaluating the credibility of witnesses must be surrendered to the demands of extremist Islam. One

---

23. The flying imams and their sponsor organization allege that threats of violence have been levied at them, and an acid bomb was allegedly tossed at one of the imams, at a mosque in Phoenix.

24. The four: the *hibab*, which covers only the hair; the *jilbab*, which leaves the face and hands exposed; the *niqab*, which covers the face and body save for a slit at the eyes; and the *burqa*, which entirely covers the face and body.

Florida judge ordered the driver's license of a Muslim woman revoked because she insisted on wearing a veil for her driver's ID photo.

In Minneapolis, Muslim cab drivers claimed a right, rooted in Islamic Sharia, to refuse to carry passengers who have liquor, and to refuse to carry blind passengers with seeing-eye dogs. Many such mini-battles will be fought, here and abroad. Thus, across the border in Canada, the issue of whether women can show up at the polls veiled has surfaced.

But as with any legitimate concern, it is possible to go overboard as to religious head wear: Another Florida judge denied court access to a Muslim woman because her wearing of a headscarf, which leaves the entire face visible, allegedly created a security risk and evinced disrespect for the court. The first concern can be addressed by a security search, and the second by appointing more sensible judges. Unlike veils, which interfere with assessment of vital demeanor evidence, a simple head-scarf imposes no undue burden, of any kind at all, on the courts. Similarly, Sikhs (an Indian religious sect, not Muslim) have protested their turbans being searched in public view by TSA personnel, but are willing to be searched in private. TSA has proposed to pat-down turbans without asking their removal.

A special challenge, to date not adequately met, is the infiltration of prison chaplains by Saudi-funded Wahhabi clerics who spread radical doctrines in the prisons. This includes stacking libraries with radical Islamic texts while freezing out moderate Sunni, Shia or Sufi texts. In 2003 New York Governor George Pataki fired the head of the State's chaplain system, but failed to fire other radicals.[25] At the federal level, an effort to purge libraries of radical texts was transmuted into an all-purpose purge that also tossed Christian and Judaic texts, including the writing of the great medieval Jewish theologian Moses Maimonides.

We must challenge Islamic leaders and their followers to condemn terror unconditionally; end efforts to make Islamic lands *Judenrein*; end

---

25. Shia inmates filed a federal lawsuit against the New York State Department of Corrections, claiming harassment by Sunni chaplains, and seeking the right to hold Shia services. The case, *Orafan v. Rashid*, goes to trial in 2008.

anti-Semitic tirades in Islamic lands; give aid—covert if necessary— to moderate voices in the Muslim world who are willing to speak out. Rare are the Islamic groups who condemn terrorism unconditionally (one notable exception is the American Muslim Congress). Many complain about profiling and Israel. Many wield the term "Islamophobia" to impede our describing the enemy accurately, and to promote profound group alienation. Contrast the fates of two authors: Salman Rushdie enrages Muslims by writing *The Satanic Verses,* and spends nearly twenty years in hiding to avoid a death sentence *fatwa;* Dan Brown enrages Christians with *The Da Vinci Code*'s inaccuracies about Christianity, and he rakes in a big fortune, *fatwa*-free.

A big problem is the West's adoption, over the past quarter-century, of "political correctness." P.C. denotes prohibitions on speech or conduct imposed on behalf of groups who deem certain speech or conduct offensive. Concerns over P.C. lead to self-censorship: At the behest of Muslims, gender-segregated swimming pools have been adopted in Seattle. A Catholic high school in California no longer goes by the name Crusaders; it's now the Lions. It often conflicts with America's traditional notion of free speech, which includes the legal right to say things someone might find offensive, tempered by a social custom of balancing legal freedom with reasonable constraints imposed by good manners. Mark Steyn aptly terms this a "societal Stockholm Syndrome" (identifying with one's captors).

A threat of lawsuits is used by advocacy groups to intimidate organizations from inviting certain speakers. The Council on American-Islamic Relations (CAIR), which instigated the "flying imams" suit, warned the Reagan Ranch that inviting Robert Spencer, a prominent critic of Islam, to speak risked provoking a slander or libel suit. Radical Muslim groups have attacked the Justice Department for naming them as unindicted co-conspirators in a Justice Department prosecution of Muslim charities for aiding terrorists.

On a positive note: CAIR's membership, 29,000 in 2000, is now but 1,700, *a 94 percent shrinkage.* As Presidential aspirant Fred Thompson noted, this suggests that moderate Muslims are opting out of a group they have come to see as radical.

The United States Supreme Court, in a landmark libel case, has called free speech rights "a profound national commitment to the principle that debate on public issues should be uninhibited, robust, and wide-open, and that it may well include vehement, caustic, and sometimes unpleasantly sharp attacks on government and public officials." Criticism of private groups is equally important.

There are certain boundaries, but they are minimal. Free speech has been held not to protect "fighting words"—"those that by their very utterance inflict injury or tend to incite an immediate breach of the peace." Yet in subsequent cases the Court has been reluctant to apply the doctrine, even in cases involving profanity and threats of violence. It stated in one famous case: "It is often true that one man's vulgarity is another's lyric."

Sensitivity of religious persons and groups has received little protection. In 1977 the courts held that Nazis could march in Skokie, Illinois, a town with thousands of Jewish Holocaust survivors; fortunately, the march was held elsewhere. In the early 1990s museums were permitted to display a painting showing a crucifix in a jar of urine; Christian sensitivities were ignored. There is no constitutional or moral reason why the sensitivities of Muslims should receive greater solicitude than the sensitivities of those who worship elsewhere—equal solicitude, certainly, but not greater. Above all, we must not allow militant Islamists to "define the territory of insult."

In September 2007 radical Islam's "insult" yardstick was deliberately tested by a Swedish cartoonist, who drew Muhammad's head on the body of a dog. The cartoon immediately drew a $100,000 reward for the cartoonist's assassination—$150,000 if "he were to be slaughtered like a lamb"—plus a $50,000 price on the head of the newspaper's editor-in-chief, all posted at an Islamist website. The initial response of authorities was silence, but the moderate Swedish Muslim Council answered: "We accept neither criminal acts nor attacks on individuals' rights to a safe and secure existence and to worthy and respectful treatment."

We must also take vigorous steps to prevent misuse of funds sent from the West to Islamic countries, which in effect funds hatred of the West. Examples are Iraqis naming a school built with American funds after Saddam Hussein, or Palestinians, who receive U.S. aid, naming a city block in Jenin (on the West Bank) after a suicide bomber who killed Americans in Fallujah, or a West Bank sports center named after the Palestinian terrorist group Black September, which killed American Ambassador Cleo Noel in Sudan and Israeli athletes at the Munich Olympic Games.

One practical impediment to vigorous engagement is the willingness of some radical Islamists to target for killing those who stand up to challenge them (as with terror expert Steven Emerson, targeted in 1994 for his PBS special "Jihad in America").[26] A remedy is the precedent established by the Supreme Court nearly fifty years ago, when it allowed the National Association for the Advancement of Colored People (NAACP) to keep its membership list confidential, lest its membership be exposed to the very real threat of violence from racist groups like the Ku Klux Klan. Those who wish to criticize Islamic groups—even question Islam itself—must be protected from violent retaliation, lest free debate be stifled. Organizations can be formed whose membership lists are kept confidential. Few will step forward if, as a result of doing so, they will make themselves or their families targets. Public support from legal, political and media groups can buttress this protection for free speech.

It happens that anonymous advocacy has a noble pedigree in American thought: In the time of the Framers, leading lights used pseudonyms chosen from Latin and Greek history to advance their views without pub-

---

26. Emerson has spent much time in hiding, to avoid death threats, since 1994, the year he produced his award-winning television special, which gave Americans their first serious close-up of radical Islamic activity in the United States.

lic identification. Thus Alexander Hamilton, James Madison and John Jay authored *The Federalist Papers* under the pseudonym "Publius."

In the 1990s the judge who presided over the terror trial of Omar Abdel Rahman ("the blind sheik" who inspired the first World Trade Center bombers and plotted to blow up several tunnels and the UN building) was targeted for assassination. Judge Michael Mukasey lived "24/7/365" for a decade guarded by U.S. marshals. (In 2007 Judge Mukasey became Attorney General.)

An added challenge when engaging Muslims—even moderate ones—in dialogue is that what constitutes "fact" in the Islamic world—especially as to America and Israel—is simply false; but try to tell that to *them*. The Arab world, in particular, suffers from an information deficit. Thus, a 2002 United Nations report noted that more books are translated into Spanish annually than have been translated into Arabic in the past *thousand years*. The factually challenged also live in America. Only *40 percent* of Muslim Americans residing in the U.S. believe that Arabs carried out the 9/11 attacks.

Failing to confront the problem now heightens the risk that the next generation of Arab and Muslim residents in America, as happened already in Europe, will be less integrated, and thus more susceptible to alienation and radicalism. We must engage and confront efforts in America to spread radical Islamist tenets in mosques, schools and prisons.

As we engage with Muslim moderates, we must isolate radical groups. The American Muslim Congress, the nation's oldest Shia group, condemned the JFK terror plot uncovered in June 2007 (to blow up fuel tanks at JFK airport and shut down a substantial part of the airline industry): "We categorically and vehemently condemn this evil plotting, which is criminal and abhorrent, threatening America as well as the security of all Muslims around the world."

Muslim moderates have emerged overseas, too. LibForAll, an Indonesian group, claims among its founders Indonesia's largest Muslim organization (*Gus Dur*), which has 40 million members—20 percent of

Indonesia's 200 million Muslims. It also features the country's top rock star, who has a major hit, *Warriors of Love*. In Bali, in 2007, the group held a conference on the Holocaust to counter a conference in Tehran that brought together Holocaust deniers.

Australia: Championing Western Values

When it comes to meeting the radical threat openly, things look better Down Under. In 2005 Australian leaders held dialogues with Muslim leaders after some attacks on non-Muslims. The Aussies bluntly told the activists that Western values prevail in Australia, that they are not negotiable and that anyone who does not accept them can leave.

Australian Prime Minister John Howard, a man of conviction and courage equal to any leader on the planet, went on talk-radio to answer Muslim protests about the Australian values push, which Islamic activists had said "infuriated" them:

> There is a small section of the Islamic population which is unwilling to integrate, and I have said, generally, all migrants have to integrate, and that means speaking English as quickly as possible, it means embracing Australian values and it also means making sure that no matter what the culture of the country they come from may have been, Australia requires women to be treated fairly and equally and in the same fashion as men.... And if any migrants that come into this country have a different view, they better get rid of that view very quickly.

Howard added, referring to Muslim attacks on Australian women, gang-rapes of targets called "white Aussie sluts:"

> There is within some sections of the Islamic community an attitude towards women which is out of line with mainstream Australian society. It needs to be dealt with by the broader community, including Islamic Australia. There is really not much point in pretending it doesn't exist.

In March 2007 another major conference between Muslims and non-Muslims was held in Australia. Cultural issues were discussed openly and vigorously. A poll taken after showed that the share of the Australian polity who regarded Muslim immigrants as a threat dropped from 35 to 21 percent, those who thought Muslim immigration bad for national security fell from 44 to 23 percent and those who felt that Muslim immigrants made Australia worse fell sharply, from 32 to 7 percent.[27]

Whither Reform?

In June 2007 England's then-Prime Minister Tony Blair addressed an inter-faith conference. Blair said of young Muslims with whom he has spoken that "the predominant complaint is about how they believe their true faith is constantly hijacked and subverted by small, unrepresentative groups who get disproportionately large amounts of publicity." Blair went on to cite efforts around the world to reform Islam, from programs in Indonesia and Pakistan to broaden the education of students at *madrassas*, to female suffrage in Kuwait and Bahrain, and reform underway in Morocco, Turkey, Afghanistan and Jordan.

English Orientalist Bernard Lewis told the *Wall Street Journal*, "In 1940 we knew who we were, we knew who the enemy was, we knew the dangers and the issues.... It is different today. We don't know who we are, we don't know the issues, and we still do not understand the nature of the enemy." Lewis has also said that Muslims "are about to take over Europe," and that the only question is "Will it be an Islamicized Europe or a Europeanized Islam?" In at least partial recognition of the problem, several European countries, most notably France, are adopting tough deportation rules for illegals, estimated at between 4.5 million and 8 million for the continent. Deportation is backed by biometric identification and sanctions against employers who hire illegals.

---

27. On November 24, 2007, Labor Party leader Kevin Rudd was elected Australian Prime Minister. Rudd has taken a strong stance on Muslim immigrants accepting Australian values.

Author Mark Steyn describes the spread of radical Islam as a fusion of terrorism, politics, religion and demography, which operates as a "franchise operation"—mosques incubating terrorists who then take up with cells. Meanwhile the Saudis bankroll Islamic lobby groups and the radicalization of prison chaplains, while an army of Arab-funded think tanks wages the PR war.

Author-professor Francis Fukuyama attributes much of the difficulty to "identity politics"—the concept of rights defined by group affiliation rather than individual status, "Modern identity politics," he writes, "springs from a hole in the political theory of liberal democracy. That hole is liberalism's silence about the place and significance of groups." Fukuyama concludes:

> The dilemma of immigration and identity ultimately converges with the larger problem of the valuelessness of postmodernity. The rise of relativism has made it harder for postmodern people to assert positive values and therefore the kinds of shared beliefs that they demand of migrants as a condition of citizenship....

If postmodern people (Europeans) fail in that task, Fukuyama warns that "they may be overwhelmed by people who are more sure about who they are."

While embracing Islam's moderates, we should say to the radicals—especially those living within Western societies—what British General Sir Charles Napier said to Hindus (quoted at the beginning of this chapter): If you practice violence in the name of your religion, you will be swiftly and harshly punished.

It is especially important that leaders defend Western values without apology. They have bodyguard entourages to protect them, and thus can speak openly at less risk than private citizens targeted by militant Islamists. Leaders should promote active public diplomacy as well. (More on this later.)

The Islamist project of transforming secularized Europe is well underway. Unless Europeans defend their traditions vigorously and on a broad front, they will fall before the energized, radicalized waves of

Muslim immigrants. America can see a brighter picture, but the same can happen here, if the chains of P.C. are not cast off once and for all. It may be too late to stop Eurabia, but we can, and must, stop the birth of "Amerabia."

Author Bruce Bawer, who has lived in Europe for decades, wrote of European calls for alternatives to resistance:

> What seemed lost in these calls for "nuance," moreover, was the fact that for Islamists, there *are* no nuances. In a war between people who had [sic] rock-solid beliefs and people who are capable of nuancing away even pure evil, who has the advantage?

Radical Islam's challenge to the West from outside is an overtly violent one. Its challenge within the West is more subtle: the establishment within Western countries of Islamic confessional communities based upon sectarian rather than established public law. Success in such endeavors would undermine the legal state that enables assimilation of communities into an integrated whole. One prominent academic frames the European contest as one for the ten percent of Muslim youth in Europe who waver between joining legitimate society and joining the one percent hard core militants, with the outcome very much uncertain, given a Europe not fully awakened to the homeland challenge posed by militant Islam.

In March 2007 moderate Muslims met in St. Petersburg, Florida, at a Secular Muslim Summit, and issued what has become known as the St. Petersburg Declaration. It affirms freedom of conscience, upholds separation of church and state, and condemns radical Islam and multi-cultural P.C. efforts to silence critics. And here is a recent proclamation that serves as a model for global religious tolerance:

Final Conference Communiqué

Religion, the art of peace, speaks to the peoples of the world of compassion, justice and mutual understanding. A blessing for all creation, religion is a constant reminder to humanity of the divine spark in every person. Yet today the world shudders as horrific acts are perpetrated in the name of religion. All too often, hatred and violence replace peace as religion is manipulated for political purposes.

Leaders of the world's religions have a special obligation to refute such claims, and to mobilize their communities to not only respect, but also defend the rights of others to live and worship differently. We, the undersigned, gathered here today in Bali, Indonesia, take a stand against wanton violence, and urge other religious leaders to follow our example in respect to our diversity and our commitment to end the violence.

Jimbaran, Bali, Indonesia

June 12, 2007

CHAPTER III

THE LAW VALUES WAR

LAWFARE OR WARFARE

1. The revolutionary is a doomed man. He has no interests of his own, no affairs, no feelings, no attachments, no property, not even a name. Everything within him is absorbed by one single all-excluding interest, one single thought, one single passion—revolution.
2. In the depths of his being, and not only in words but in deeds, he has broken all his links with the civil order and with the entire educated world, with all laws, with all the decencies, with the social conditions and the morality of this world. This world is for him a merciless enemy, and if he should continue to live in it, it would be for the sole purpose of all the better to destroy it.
SERGEI NECHAEV, *THE REVOLUTIONARY CATECHISM* (1871)

We find ourselves mugged in an alley, and the Marquis of Queensbury set wants a boxing ring. Our political discourse characterizes disagreement with administration policy as dissent on how to conduct the war, which implies broad agreement that the war is to be fought, but disagreement as to the means. But this underestimates the force of the objections to how America is conducting the war. There is, in truth, a "values" war within the U.S. as to how we should fight, based upon a deep split over fundamental societal values. Credit each side with patriotic motivation. Liberals (plus some libertarians on the right) who exalt civil liberties above catching terrorists think the country will lose its essence if it sullies its soul; conservatives who are willing to abridge civil liberties in order to pre-empt terrorist acts believe that the country should save its neck first, then worry about saving souls. Just how much dispensation should we give to adversaries who don't even engage in the pretense of compliance with basic norms of civilized humanity?

One side favors stressing liberty, the other stresses security. Values invoke the specter of irremediable moral taint, which renders a society unworthy of prevailing in a struggle or makes it appear the loser no matter how the shooting wars turn out. The most critical battlegrounds pitting law against war values are at the intersection of state prerogative and personal rights in war. State surveillance impinges upon personal privacy in the form of disclosure of information deemed private, or unlawful discrimination, or judgments based on a person's immutable genetic or demographic characteristics (profiling). State power to suppress information deemed harmful to wartime operations impinges upon rights of expression—most notably the freedom of speech accorded the press, which often entails disclosure of information the government wishes kept secret. State supervision also impinges, if less so, on such freedom.

Values

Begin with an enduring historical fiction: After 9/11 the country—and the world—was united, a unity that was later sundered by the administration's decision to launch a war against Iraq. Of the world, let us briefly note that there was jubilation in much of the Arab and Islamic world—Palestinians danced in the streets. (There were noble exceptions abroad, too: one million Iranians demonstrated in Tehran, ignoring the hostility of their own hated Islamofascist regime, expressing their support for America.)

We all remember the entire Congress posing together on the steps of the Capitol. But that show of unity and defiance was deceptive. In reality, for many, such unity extended only to a very narrow set of propositions: We would kill or capture the terrorists who mounted the 9/11 attacks, and target governments who supported them. This meant that we would carry the fight to al-Qaeda and the Taliban regime in Afghanistan, with which the terrorist group was allied. It meant more vigilance too, at home, but only if the balance between security and civil liberties was not fundamentally altered. It meant working within existing alliances and international organizations, including the United Nations. And it meant delimiting the President's war power.

As to the ambit of congressional authorization, on September 12 the White House sought authorization to use all necessary force to conduct military operations against those who carried out or supported the 9/11 attacks, and also to use force to "deter and pre-empt any future acts of terrorism or aggression against the United States." On September 14 Congress passed the Authorization for Use of Military Force (AUMF), authorizing "all necessary and appropriate force against those nations, organizations or persons [the president] determines planned, authorized, committed or aided the 9/11 attacks" only. Congress did not approve the broader charter President Bush sought to act against potential future terror threats. Much later, then-Senate Majority Leader Tom Daschle asserted that the AUMF excluded, as well, all operations against persons in the U.S., implying rejection of the administration's position that the battlefield against al-Qaeda is global in scope. But the AUMF's legislative history is silent on this point. In a nutshell, Congress narrowed its grant of authority to prosecute the war on terror days after the 9/11 attack. Already, *within 72 hours of the 9/11 attacks, as rescuers continued efforts to save people trapped in the rubble,* Congress collectively diverged from the President's view of his war powers. Thus, congressional "unity" was laser-targeted.

Senator John McCain seemed to catch the country's mood perfectly then, warning:

The terror our enemies have tried to sow in the hearts of Americans will now be the essence of their lives, however abbreviated their lives will be. And when they meet their Maker they will learn that they had their theology all wrong. Right, not hate, makes might. As they experience our power, so will they know the full measure of our righteousness. And as their last hour approaches they can ask an all-loving God for mercy. But don't ask us. We bring justice, not mercy.

Except that we did, in fact, show our enemies mercy, and continue to do so. Even Senator McCain, legendary warrior he, did so when in 2005 the subject of interrogation practices came up for Senate debate.

The best illustration of the divide that opened up immediately after 9/11 are the statements by Vermont Democrat Patrick Leahy, who has for more than two decades been deeply involved in legislation on national security and intelligence. He led the Senate majority in the debate on the USA Patriot Act, just weeks after 9/11, at a time when the fires were still burning at Ground Zero and the country was waiting for the next attack any day.

Senator Leahy spoke as floor leader when the Senate took up the original version of what later became the USA Patriot Act, on October 11, 2001—exactly one month after the atrocities of 9/11. Asserting that congressional intercession had induced the administration to remove unconstitutional proposals from the new law, he said:

> What I have done throughout this time is to remember the words of Benjamin Franklin... when he said: "A people who would trade their liberty for security deserve neither." We protected our security, but I am not going to give up the liberties that Americans have spent 220 years to obtain.

A fortnight later the Senate took up the House version of the proposed USA Patriot Act, passing it that day. Senator Leahy spoke again. Regarding sharing of intelligence on domestic investigations with law enforcement, he noted the pre-existing statutory laws enacted after a Senate Committee chaired by then-Senator Frank Church (a liberal Democrat from Idaho) had uncovered domestic spying abuses by the federal government. He warned:

> The gravest departure from that framework, and the one with the most potential for abuses, is the new and unprecedented statutory authority for sharing of "foreign intelligence" from criminal investigations with "any other Federal law enforcement, intelligence, protective, immigration, national defense, or national security official."

In fact, Benjamin Franklin is misquoted by civil liberties hawks like Senator Leahy. He actually said, "Those who would give up *essential* liberty, to purchase *a little temporary* safety deserve neither liberty nor safety." Even in the immediate aftermath of the 9/11 attacks plus the anthrax attack on Capitol Hill that targeted, among others, the offices of Senators Leahy and Senate Majority Leader Tom Daschle, the prime concern of liberals in Congress was to *restrain* the executive.

Three groups of elites have united in their own war inside the West—not against terror, Islamofascist or otherwise. Rather, they are making war against America's manner of making war against the terrorists. Our resisting elites—liberal and libertarian—are the mainstream media, most lawyers, and assorted intellectuals who are advocates of multilateral world government, or, short of that, of diminishing American power. Again, the resistance of the elites is not inconsistent with feelings of patriotism: Patriotism is a sentiment—noble, but not necessarily a synonym for sound judgment on any side of an argument. Today's civil libertarians can cite America's founders. James Madison wrote Thomas Jefferson, during the year when the Alien and Sedition Acts were passed: "Perhaps it is a universal truth that the loss of liberty at home is to be charged to provisions against danger, real or pretended, from abroad."

The "ace in the hole" held by elites is their mantra "our values," usually invoked to prevent us doing something that would prove effective in fighting the nation's adversaries. The campaign against American treatment of terrorist detainees began even as the first prisoners were brought to Guantanamo in January 2002. England's *Daily Mail* published a photo of a hooded captive in orange jumpsuit and shackles, captioned "torture." This in fact is standard treatment for dangerous prisoners—those at Guantanamo who would, given ten seconds in a room with the captioner, kill him (or her) with relish. Media reports of abuse directed at guards by detainees are rare, but stomach-turning.

What animates these elites? Primarily two things have led American elites to shrink from full engagement in wars long and short. As children of Watergate, with its widespread abuses of power by President Nixon and senior underlings, they fear their own government—especially so during a Republican administration—more than they fear the enemy. Politically and socially (mostly) liberal, such elites wish to win pretty. That ugly may be the only way to win, they simply reject. Liberal elites also embrace the seductive belief that all differences are in the end splittable, and thus negotiable. They thus are tempted to pursue a negotiated settlement with Iranian Islamofascism, just as they did with Soviet communism. Should a WMD strike occur that kills hundreds of thousands, let alone a few million Americans, elites finally might accept winning ugly.

A favored "values" trump card many war critics lead with is the "moral high ground." Thus Senator McCain: "We fight not just to preserve our lives and liberties but also American values, and we will never allow the terrorists to take those away. In this war that we must win—that we will win—we must never simply fight evil with evil." For example, critics say we lose this high ground by aggressively interrogating detainees. What exactly do critics mean by this phrase? Surely they do not really believe that making a prisoner stand hours on end, depriving him of sleep, or dunking him in water for a few minutes, is morally equivalent to atrocities committed by the terrorists, such as slitting the throats of unarmed flight attendants; crashing airplanes into buildings, thus dousing thousands with jet fuel burning at the temperatures of Hitler's ovens; or crushing victims under tons of rubble; or forcing people to jump from ninety stories up to avoid being roasted to death; or kidnapping innocent bystanders and beheading them, and recording their savagery to provide snuff video for the Internet. Others get this: In February 2007, as the "surge" of American troops was getting underway, al-Qaeda delivered to a Ramadi hospital an ice-chest containing the heads of several children from sheik families. The tactic, intended to intimidate, backfired badly, and the sheiks switched sides to fight alongside the Americans.

There is of course zero chance that Senator McCain believes Abu Ghraib or Guantanamo equate to such stomach-turning barbarism. Rather, those who play the "moral high ground" card do so to condemn practices of which they strongly disapprove, without regard to how our enemies behave. Many people think that dunking a terrorist mastermind in water for a few minutes is justified if thousands of innocent lives are thus saved. Those who condemn this practice apply Olympian moral standards never before met in wartime. And they express an absolutist preference that no harsh treatment of any kind be meted out to captives, for any reason whatsoever. To believe that is their privilege, but let no one be deluded into thinking that anything we are plausibly alleged to have adopted as standard practice comes close to the evils our adversaries regularly and gleefully commit. Rogue killings have apparently been committed, but those are few in number and not sanctioned by the authorities.

Yet terrorism can force us to choose between victory and peacetime values. Asked if we can "win an Eastern war with Western values," soldier-author Ralph Peters answered in the negative: "In warfare, the only moral stance is to win." His is another way of saying that "our values" cannot become a suicide pact. In a similar vein, Natan Sharansky, the great Soviet dissident, whose human rights credentials are gilt-edged, explains the dilemma facing free societies during wartime:

> By indiscriminately condemning a free society that upholds human rights but which is sometimes forced to encroach on certain freedoms to save lives, they do not advance the cause of human rights. Protecting the right to life, the most precious human right of all and the right that makes the exercise of all other rights possible, is the highest obligation of any government.

We let 200 Taliban attend a gangster funeral in the cross-hairs of a Predator—during 9/11's fifth anniversary week, no less—because of rules of engagement rigidly tied to our hyper-sensitivity as to targets thought to be of cultural significance. We are loathe to aggressively interrogate detainees, and thus deprive ourselves of potentially critical intelligence in fighting al-Qaeda and insurgents in Iraq. One senior intelligence official called Guantanamo "the single largest repository of terrorist, al-Qaeda, HUMINT on the planet." (HUMINT is CIA-speak for human intelligence.) We allow Guantanamo detainees to viciously assault the guards. Would this happen regularly if the first detainee to attack a guard had been bounced off the wall? To impose an idealized standard of "humane treatment" may someday cost us intelligence on a WMD strike that takes a huge toll in innocent lives. Will the families of those killed be consoled that we declined to subject detainees to stress in order to glean possible information that might have averted the attack? Is the "moral high ground" in its Olympian form worth preserving at all costs?

Perhaps the most extreme example of values-based skittishness is our reluctance to return terror suspects to their native lands, lest they be mistreated. They come to America to blow us up, and we are reluctant to send them home because there they might be mistreated. The concept of "that's your problem" is not one that sits well with our elites. Already an estimated 30 detainees set free have re-engaged in the war.

Yet Americans understandably want their government and people to behave better than terrorists. That much is fair enough and, fortunately, easily enough accomplished, and in fact by any fair appraisal we have indeed done so. What is not fair—egregiously unfair—is for a *differential* standard to be applied to our side versus our adversaries. We must demand that all be judged by the same yardstick. Applying Olympian standards to us while applying sewer standards to our adversaries gives them a partial moral free ride. Our falling below Olympian standards of conduct ought not to be equated to our adversaries lolling in the sewer. Doing so is enormously demoralizing to our war effort. We do not apply a lower standard to sociopathic killers than we do to the citizenry in general, and thus give killers a partial moral pass. We should not judge terrorists more gently than garden-variety sociopaths.

In sum, we legitimately expect our side to behave better. But we set ourselves a trap when we apply a pernicious double standard that spotlights our failure to meet the highest standards while our adversary lies in the gutter. We must apply a single standard and judge accordingly. It matters less whether the standard chosen is high, medium or low, so long as both sides are *equally* held to it. In the long run to do otherwise will undermine our will and thus our ability to fight Islamism, diminishing the prospect that civilization will prevail over barbarism.

Detention and Assassination: What Should We "Do Unto" Terrorists?

The "law values" tendency figures prominently in detention of terror suspects, as well as battlefield operations. The "law versus war" issue was framed sharply in 2006 when a prominent former Soviet dissident, Vladimir Bukovsky, and America's most famous Vietnam POW, John McCain, publicly cited their own horrific experiences under torture to argue against the administration's use of aggressive interrogation techniques (loosely labeled "torture" despite shaky legal grounds for doing so). Heroes who resisted torture with magnificent courage, they speak with a moral authority that makes disputation nearly impossible.

But there are differences between their situations and the present, both as to degree and purpose. Dissidents in the Soviet Union were being tortured to confess to political crimes and thus acknowledge the supremacy of totalitarian Soviet rule. McCain was tortured to extract an admission of false war crimes, plus to embarrass his father (John Sr.), then Commander-in-Chief of the Navy's Pacific Fleet. One can feel for their suffering and admire hugely their heroism in resistance. But interrogating al-Qaeda senior officials in an effort to learn more about the group's structure and plans so as to save thousands of innocent lives— as American officials did, with considerable success—hardly falls in the same moral category.

Nor should it fall in the same legal category. The matter was put crisply by Federal Appeals Court Judge Richard Posner:

The idea that torture is not only a cruel and ugly practice but just about the worst thing a government can do confuses torture as a routine practice of dictators, often intended to intimidate rather than to elicit information, and as a method long used to extract false confessions to political crimes and (necessarily false) confessions to non-existent crimes such as sorcery, with torture as the exceptional method of counterterrorist interrogation.

"Our values" require us, it is alleged, to extend Geneva Convention protection to al-Qaeda detainees, which would entitle us to learn name, rank, serial number, and date of birth. We can ask more, but the detainee may refuse. The monster airliner plot broken up in August 2006 was made possible by a tip gleaned from an al-Qaeda captive apprehended weeks earlier near the Pakistani-Afghani border. Under Geneva rules, unless the captive volunteered the information, captors could not have learned about it. Even offering inducements to captives to get them to talk violates the conventions. Any inducement whatsoever—a chocolate bar, an all-expenses paid trip to Las Vegas, Bill Gates's fortune—is unlawful under a literal reading of Geneva. Bribing captives to reveal a plot saves lives that could well be lost if instead we unilaterally follow Geneva.

One reason given for us to observe Geneva rules is that combatants' states or groups will then have an incentive to extend reciprocal courtesy to us. Thus John McCain: "[Mistreatment] of our prisoners endangers U.S. troops who might be captured by the enemy—if not in this war, then in the next." The flaw in this reasoning is that terror sponsors don't care how their minions are treated upon capture. McCain, of all people, should know this based upon his torture in North Vietnam, treatment not meted out by South Vietnam or America to prisoners. Indeed, sponsoring states or terrorist groups are *pleased* to reap propaganda benefits from alleging mistreatment of their own, as did North Korea and North Vietnam.

Another war values issue is the question of whether ever to permit assassination as a foreign policy tool for the U.S. Our laws (in the form of executive orders issued by Presidents Ford and Reagan) currently prohibit all assassinations.[28] History provides a sobering example of the cost of such a policy. In 1985 the Joint Chiefs rejected a strike at Hezbollah's Baalbek, Lebanon, headquarters that could have killed the group's entire high command—despite the organization having been responsible for the mass murder of 241 Marines in the October 1983 Beirut bombing, which drove American peacekeeping forces out of Lebanon. Incredibly, the Joint Chiefs didn't even trouble themselves to inform President Reagan of their decision, even though Reagan had famously promised "swift and effective retribution" for terrorist acts. During the Clinton administration lawyers argued that intentionally targeting Osama bin Laden violated the ban, and only were he killed during the course of an attempted capture would matters be fully legal.

By such logic, President Bush could invade Iraq but could not have had Saddam assassinated. Early in the Afghan 2001 campaign, a Predator drone had Taliban leader Mullah Omar in its sights. A request to take out the target was reportedly rejected due to legal advice at Central Command. Repeal of the existing rules would take the lawyers out of this one. Israel uses targeted assassinations. What makes the ban on assassinations so absurd is that taking out a leader is a lot cleaner an operation—with vastly fewer likely U.S. military direct, and civilian collateral, casualties—than invading a country. Who, given the mess Iraq has turned into, wouldn't rather that we had killed Saddam and his two sons instead?[29] Recognizing our reluctance to risk collateral casualties, in

---

28. Executive Order 11905 (Ford, 1976) prohibits government personnel from engaging in assassinations. Executive Order 12333 (Reagan, 1981) extended the prohibition to cover persons acting on behalf of the government.

29. The 1970s revulsion against assassination as a foreign policy tool stemmed from two developments: (1) the botched series of attempts on Fidel Castro's life, which included the clumsy stupidity of enlisting the Mafia's aid; and (2) a widespread belief, shared by JFK's successor, Lyndon Johnson, that Castro had JFK hit in retaliation.

the 2001 Afghan campaign al-Qaeda and Taliban fighters often brought along their families as human shields.

Administration lawyers have argued that assassinations are political, and wartime killings are military, and thus outside the assassination ban. But, the U.S. follows the Hague Regulations of 1907, banning "treachery," and bounties, and requiring acceptance of surrender.

It's easy to like such rules. But consider a cautionary tale. A British soldier on September 28, 1918, passed a German trench and spared the life of a wounded corporal lying helpless. For his heroic actions in that battle he won England's highest war decoration, the Victoria Cross. He didn't get it for sparing the corporal's life. The anonymous corporal lived to become Adolph Hitler. Misplaced gallantry can be costly (in World War II, some 50 million lives). Accepting the surrender of terrorist leaders could prove an expensive moral luxury, either in a botched trial or if terror operations are launched to try to induce our side to free them.

A "values" fixation also hampers Israel. Were Israel so inclined it could end forever the problem of rockets coming from Palestinian territory. How? Play by what *New York Times* columnist Thomas Friedman calls "Hama Rules," so called after the 1982 episode in which Syrian strongman Hafez al-Assad quelled a Muslim Brotherhood uprising in the town of Hama with tanks and bulldozers, killing 10,000 to 20,000 in two days.[30] Israel could easily use air power and armor to squash several Palestinian villages in a few minutes. Kill 20,000, and warn that future rocket attacks will cost another 20,000, and so on. Palestinian rocketry would soon cease. But Israel's own public would gag on this, as would America's.

The "international community," which ignored 800,000 Rwandans being hacked to death in 1994 in 90 days, would let out a collective primal scream if so many as 80 Palestinians were killed by Israelis. (The world mostly yawned when the late Jordanian King Hussein killed thousands of Palestinians in September 1970.) When Israel gives advance

---

30. The destruction of Hama, in March 1982, is told by Friedman in his superb *From Beirut to Jerusalem*, (1989), at pp. 76–105.

warning of strikes, as it did in Lebanon, just what do Israeli leaders think Hezbollah does? Move its minions into the area to be killed? Or bring hostages in to be killed, while Hezbollah fighters escape?

In judging how opposing sides conducted themselves during the summer 2006 war, three bedrock norms of the international law of war should be applied. A state must not only refrain from launching aggressive war against another state, it must prevent others from doing so. The attacked country may respond with force "proportionate" to achieve its lawful objective—a proportion that is measured not by the scale of force chosen by the attacker, but by the scale of force needed to eliminate the threat. The latter may be vastly greater than the first. Targeting civilians and using them as shields to protect personnel or other assets are both black-letter war crimes.

Hezbollah fights by committing war crimes, deliberately targeting civilians and using them as shields. True, Hezbollah, much like the Mafia in Sicily, provides social services too. But astute political sense does not make Hezbollah a social services organization. It is a terrorist group with political savvy, just as the Mafia is a crime syndicate with political savvy. Yet the world community blames Israel for striking terrorists secreted deliberately among innocents, as Israel has every legal right to do. This blaming of Israel is partly due to direct intimidation, such as kidnappings of journalists from news organizations that cover Mideast terrorist groups truthfully. Partly it is the latest round of Israel's being chastised for being too effective at protecting itself. But it also reflects a deeper antagonism toward vigorous prosecution of a war that cannot be won quickly and neatly.

In effect, lawyers and judges, human rights groups, media types, peace activists and other elites increasingly wage what has been called "lawfare": a concerted effort to impose criminal justice standards on how Western societies prosecute wars. As international lawyers David Rivkin and Lee Casey explain, lawfare would limit the scope of military response to a strict proportionality that can turn victory into defeat. Also, lawfare narrows the scope of key officials, by threatening them with legal liability if their decisions are judged illegal after the fact. Further, preventive detention of suspects is sharply curtailed by lawfare rules. Thus can lawfare trump warfare, to the detriment of civilized countries in fighting barbarian adversaries.

Surveillance: Redefining Public and Private Domains

Surveillance issues can be broken down into three broad categories: communications monitoring, profiling and new technology deployment. Begin with communications monitoring. Civil liberties groups have tossed around horror stories of government abuse and potential abuse as reasons to severely circumscribe wiretap powers, even in wartime. But at a 2004 hearing of the Senate Judiciary Committee on re-authorization of the three-year-old USA Patriot Act California Democrat Dianne Feinstein said, *"I have never had a single abuse of the Patriot Act reported to me. My staff e-mailed the ACLU and asked them for instances of actual abuse. They e-mailed back and said they had none."* Ignoring this record, civil libertarians argued the ever-present *possibility* of abuse.

Efforts by the administration to gather and share data on terror suspects met with ferocious opposition. The National Security Agency's Terrorist Surveillance Program (TSP), the SWIFT financial bank monitoring program, and data-mining efforts like the Pentagon's junked Total Information Awareness (TIA) were all opposed, even though machine reading of data already known to network companies violates no one's personal privacy in either law or common sense.

Former CIA Director R. James Woolsey has explained that the Foreign Intelligence Surveillance Act (FISA), a 1978 law enacted after Watergate and the CIA abuse hearings, when lawmakers were pre-occupied with guarding against abuses of executive power, doesn't suffice to chase down terrorists. Upon seizing a senior terrorist group leader's PC, one might find thousands of addresses and phone numbers on the PC hard drive. FISA requires getting a warrant separately for each single search. FISA establishes what is, in effect, a "Catch-22" as to tapping conversations (or e-mail): Obtaining a FISA warrant requires knowledge sufficient to convince a court to issue a warrant; but without the tap the necessary knowledge cannot be gained. The payoff rate for taps runs at best one tenth of one percent—1 hit in 1,000 taps. This hit rate is four times higher than that for airport firearm searches, which are done on everyone, without regard to probable cause or even suspicion.[31]

A *single* FISA warrant application requires joint preparation by the FBI and Justice Department, with the personal signature of the Attorney-General, and can run *one hundred pages.* In August 2007 the Director of National Intelligence advised Congress that intelligence analysts with specialized cultural and linguistic skills were being tied up by the time demands of completing FISA applications.

Another problem with FISA's coverage is that it applies only to "communications" sent by the sender to a recipient. It does not cover a message sender placing e-mail on his computer and allowing the recipient to access it remotely. With the information useful only so long as colleagues are unaware of the leader's arrest, time is of the extreme essence. No "one suspect, one warrant" court procedure can adequately address this issue under current law.

The TSP program is, in fact, a modest one. As of January 2006, shortly after the *New York Times* blew the program's cover, these details emerged. Since 9/11 the National Security Agency (NSA) has conducted a special surveillance program to monitor communications between al-Qaeda suspects overseas and persons in the United States. Some 7,000

---

31. There are broader Fourth Amendment search and seizure issues as well, but under the Supreme Court decision in *Smith v. Maryland* (1979) tracking numbers dialed is not a "search" within the Fourth Amendment, for want of what judges call the "reasonable expectation of privacy" as to numbers already known to the network provider. Remaining Fourth Amendment issues should be resolved simply by holding that unlawful combatants have no "reasonable expectation of privacy" when pursuing the destruction of our society.

terrorists overseas and 500 suspects within the United States have been thus monitored. Further "data mining"—harvesting vast quantities of calls and then pulling out targets based upon key words or phrases—is not being used. TSP employs "hot-pursuit" tracking based upon intelligence analysis. The President, in conjunction with the Attorney-General and key intelligence officials at NSA, has reviewed the program every 45 days. FISA warrants are sought for long-term surveillance; this program is short-fuse, aimed at preventing attacks. The FBI has used a data-mining technique called "link analysis" to identify calling patterns, including monitoring callers "once removed" from actual suspects. The technique, moreover, is one commonly used by commercial telecom firms to learn about their customers' calling patterns.

Each year total voice and data calls involving American users—adding together wire line telephony, wireless phones and Internet access, domestically and overseas—probably amount to 500 *billion* calls annually: that's two *trillion* calls during any four-year Presidential term. Each year Americans make 200 billion minutes of international calls. If each call averages five minutes, that is 40 billion calls—110 million calls per day. In a country of 300 million souls three million is one percent, and 500 domestic suspects is 1/6,000th of one percent. Further, for the 40,000 NSA employees to monitor all 1.4 billion domestic calls daily plus another 110 million international calls would require each employee to cover more than 1,500 calls per hour, 24/7. In fact, the Terrorist Screening Center recorded only 99,000 calls between December 2003 and May 2007, less than 100 calls per day—well under *one in a million* calls whose content is examined.

Surveillance of calls dialed is a long way from listening in on conversations. Flagging phone numbers by caller or recipient does not equate to hearing the conversation. Flagging a suspect e-mail address does not equate to reading a message. Addresses on the Internet are long strings of ones and zeroes, so that the human eye would see a meaningless jumble of encoded numbers. Only after decoding can a message intelligible to humans be revealed.

The TSP has produced positive results, including stopping efforts to smuggle a missile launcher into the U.S. and cut the cables on the Brooklyn Bridge. Yet due to judicial interference the administration had to cut a deal with Congress to save TSP (more on this in the next chapter).

A second surveillance issue is that of profiling. The American Civil Liberties Union argues, in essence, that profiling, even if neutral in intent, inevitably will at times be applied using ethnic or religious criteria.[32] That a sound policy is at times improperly applied is not an argument sufficient to reject it. Indeed, any policy will at times be misapplied, and thus the ACLU's standard amounts to prescribing paralysis. As it happens, TSA is—at last—taking advice from an ally and applying Israeli passenger screening techniques. Israel does not use ethnic profiling— the worst terror attack in Israeli history was 1972's Lod Airport Massacre, carried out by Japanese terrorists against Puerto Rican pilgrims, in which over 100 were shot.

Instead, Israel profiles suspects by *behavior* and *circumstance* (paid cash for ticket, one-way ticket, etc.), in the form of telltale signs terrorists can rarely hide. Instead of making flying an ordeal by searching thousands of low-risk passengers, airport security can focus on probables via behavioral profiling. The TSA is experimenting with trained security personnel who look for clues in "micro-facial expressions"—changes that can occur in less than 1/15th of a second. A properly calibrated profile would end up pulling out members from high-risk groups more often than low-risk. This may offend some members of the high-risk group, even though most will not be pulled out of line. Are Western societies ready for a market test as to whether security that makes flying safer for all—including Muslims—should be adopted? Searching low- and high-risk passengers equally raises the risk of a terror attack succeeding.[33] With limited resources, searches should be efficient. An overlay of

32. In November 2007 loud protests by civil libertarians forced the Los Angeles Police Department to shelve a plan to map Muslim communities in the city.
33. A RAND Corporation study of 508,540 cases in 2006 when NYPD cops stopped suspects on the street, showed that African-Americans were stopped at rates higher than

occasional random screening for low-risk passengers can be added, so as to inject an extra element of unpredictable behavior into the system.

A third area is new technology deployment. Surveillance cameras are widely used in major cities. In central London the average person is photographed an estimated 300 times per day. New York will have 100 cameras in Lower Manhattan by the end of 2007, with wider linkage planned. "Intelligent video" cameras that are programmed to detect suspicious behavior (such as someone in a parking lot peering into lots of car windows) are being tested. In the U.S., the administration has for the first time made available images and data gathered by spy satellites, so as to detect homeland security vulnerabilities (such as illegal points of entry, terrorist or smuggler staging areas). In the U.S. tests are underway for a scanner to detect material on or inside shoes. Another system being tested is an X-ray machine that enables simultaneous luggage scan from two angles, thus speeding security scans. The system is already installed at several major airports. But certain advanced baggage screening systems are not expected to come to market until 2024. Western publics accept the need for greater surveillance. One poll shows 71 percent of Americans favor and 25 percent oppose increased use of surveillance cameras. Another shows British acceptance, with 81 percent accepting monitoring communications and 80 percent electronic tagging.

Another innovation is "trusted traveler" programs, under which passengers can register in advance, provide certain data, and thus go through faster security lines at airports. Other countries are applying advanced technology to verify "trusted traveler" status. Indonesia's "Sapphire" program charges business travelers $200 annually so that they can bypass security screening at Jakarta Airport; verification is by iris-scanning technology. The venture is joint with the Dutch, and aims for 20,000 users (fewer than the 33,000 trusted travelers participating in a program at Holland's Schipol airport).

---

their share of the city's population, but lower than their share of the city's crimes. The New York Civil Liberties Union protested, claiming unlawful racial profiling.

One innovation that has to date encountered resistance is America's Real ID program, under which states are supposed to adopt biometric ID licensing and link their databases. Several states have passed resolutions of disapproval and others are considering following suit, despite a recommendation from the 9/11 Commission that the states adopt Real ID, and also despite poll data showing that 70 percent of Americans favor a national standard for drivers' licenses. Worse, visas are required for only 15 million out of 50 million annual visitors to the States. On the brighter side is that five states have passed Voter ID laws that have survived judicial review. Such laws, besides making elections more honest, will facilitate adoption of a national ID card in the future.

Judge Richard Posner argues that what Americans care most about as to privacy is not *what* information is revealed, but to *whom*. Americans voluntarily disclose private information not only to friends but to commercial providers. It is computer hackers, abusive government or private snoops, and other nasty fauna to whom Americans don't want their private data disclosed.

Media Wars: The Information Battlefield

Terrorists know well how to exploit Western media. In 2005, al-Qaeda's number two leader, Ayman al-Zawahiri, wrote a private letter to al-Qaeda commander Abu Musab al-Zarqawi (killed in 2006 by U.S. forces):

> However, despite all of this, I say to you: that we are in a battle, and that *more than half* of this battle is taking place in the battlefield of *the media*. And that we are in a media battle in a race for the hearts and minds of our Umma [Arabic for "community"]. And that however far our capabilities reach, they will never be equal to one thousandth of the capabilities of the kingdom of Satan that is waging war on us. (Emphasis added.)

Terrorists have their own television capacity, as well. One major, increasingly effective broadcast station, Al-Zawraa TV, uses Nilesat, a communications satellite largely owned by Egypt, a major ($2 billion annually) recipient of U.S. aid. Jamming is impractical, as satellite dishes are ubiquitous these days.

Short of jamming every terror media outlet, probably an impossible task, we can do little directly to prevent terrorists' lies from circulating. Yet there are two other factors in the global media equation: media outlets in the West, and public diplomacy practiced by Western governments.

Modern media contributed to the U.S. loss in Vietnam, by portraying the war as unwinnable and the famous 1968 Tet offensive as a North Vietnamese victory when in fact the North suffered a shattering military defeat. The My Lai massacre of 347 by American troops became a world symbol of American inhumanity, while the communist slaughter of 6,000 South Vietnamese at the 1968 battle for Hue (the French imperial capital) was largely ignored. In similar fashion, television broadcasts of Israel's 1982 bombing of PLO terrorists in Beirut so agitated President Reagan that he overrode objections from his Secretary of State, and called Israel's Prime Minister to demand that the bombing stop. It did, to Israel's (and America's) detriment. In 1985 it took more than one hour for Reagan's then-Secretary of State to persuade him not to make concessions to the hijackers of TWA Flight 847. However, TV did affect the Flight 847 crisis. Disclosure that Delta Force was being put into position for possible use induced the terrorists to move the captive plane from Algiers, an accessible and relatively neutral locale, to Beirut, a less accessible and more hostile locale for a possible rescue operation.

An especially egregious example of unnecessary and grave damage was the media frenzy following airing of the Abu Ghraib photos in 2004. No one defends gratuitous abuse of inmates. But there were already *three* government investigations underway when the photos surfaced, and several people facing charges. *All the photos did was raise one-thousand-fold the emotional temperature of the issue.* Were this done purely in the context of our domestic political debate, that would be defensible.

But surely terrorists were minted around the world due to the towering rage engendered by the photos—easily hundreds, quite possibly thousands of new recruits.[34]

In the first battle of Fallujah (spring 2004) media coverage of damage induced the Iraqi government to get the White House to call off a Marine offensive, despite the commander's estimate that only another 48 to 72 hours were needed for success. In the second battle of Fallujah (fall 2004) the shock value of four U.S. contractors hanging from a bridge spurred the White House into ordering an immediate offensive, despite the ground commander's assurance that quietly, within 30 days, his troops could find and kill those responsible. The result was major collateral damage, greater than that in the first battle. Yet due to less media pressure the Marines were permitted to finish the job this time.

Media coverage of the 2006 Lebanon-Israel War turned elite attitudes against Israel. Coverage during the conflict was shocking, with numerous cases where reporting either was stage-managed by Hezbollah itself, or censored by Hezbollah, or self-censored by reporters themselves so as to avoid reprisal by Hezbollah. After all, Hezbollah has photos of the passport page of any journalist working inside Lebanon in areas controlled by Hezbollah. To their credit, some reporters have openly acknowledged that terrorist intimidation was successfully employed to color news coverage.

The nadir was reached when Reuters had to pull photos after one was shown to have been altered to exaggerate the damage Israel did in Lebanon. The photos had been posted by an Arab freelancer. Hezbollah even set up staged photos for Reuters. Other abuses: The famous photo of the Qana building, where Israel was blamed for killing 60 civilians (later reduced to 28), turned out to have been *staged*, with bodies being moved in and out—and *with knowledge of journalists who published the photos anyway, and failed to inform viewers of the staging.* Another widely-

---

34. The December 2007 furor over the CIA's destruction of two videotapes may ignite another global firestorm, despite valid intelligence reasons—protecting sources, methods and data—for doing so.

circulated photo that purportedly showed two ambulances struck by Israeli missiles also was faked. The vehicles, which Hezbollah did not permit journalists to examine, showed no sign of missile impact. Photos of Hezbollah purportedly passing out $100 bills to victims of Israeli bombing likewise were faked—the bills did not have a telltale identifying strip on them. No wonder that Israel, despite at times giving three days warning of air strikes, lost the propaganda war in global mass media.

Human Rights Watch denied that Hezbollah uses civilians as shields. A Human Rights Watch report on the Israel-Hezbollah war, while finding no instances of Hezbollah deliberately hiding amongst civilians, did find numerous instances of Israel deliberately targeting civilians. This is as if in World War II a human rights group had accused the Allies of war crimes while exonerating the Nazis. Such coverage parallels the twenty years of Palestinian manipulation of network news, acquiesced to by Western news outlets, especially in Europe. After 9/11 security officers at the Palestinian Authority warned an AP reporter not to air pictures of Palestinians dancing jubilantly in the streets of Nablus; the reporter was told his life might be in danger were the footage aired.[35]

The media sophistication of Islamofascists is a sea-change from earlier times. Ex-CBS reporter Bernard Goldberg compared the 1979 Mike Wallace interview with the Ayatollah Khomeini to Wallace's 2006 interview with Iran's President Ahmadinejad. Khomeini exemplified seventh-century atavism; Iran's current President came off as up to date. He knows the Democratic Party's line about health-care for the uninsured and claims he enjoys "quality time" with his family. The World War II "Greatest Generation" of reporters understood that the press properly is not neutral in a time of grave danger, and did not give adversaries free, respectful air-time on radio. To be sure, at times news organizations do hold information at the request of the government.

---

35. Fortunately, some footage of Palestinian celebration briefly did make the airwaves after the 9/11 attacks. The footage was aired again by MSNBC on September 11, 2007.

Perhaps the most vexing problem is that reportorial bias is embedded within a permanent master narrative that trumps contrary information and places a fixed burden of proof on certain sides in given contests. *Newsweek* Bureau Chief Evan Thomas captured this tendency perfectly when he said, of the media's rush to judgment and resistance to contrary evidence for months in the Duke University lacrosse player false rape case, which pitted a black female stripper against three white male collegians: "The narrative was right but the facts were wrong." In other words, whenever white males are accused of wrongdoing by a black (male or female), because of the long history of racism that held back blacks in America, the black is right and the whites wrong.

Thus, reporters who follow the Thomas narrative idea—as many do—are not reporters presenting the facts as they unfold, but rather *storytellers* presenting the story that represents, per their biases, the permanent underlying "truth" that explains the events ostensibly being reported. One appalling example of this tendency is a British newspaper story on a September 2006 Afghanistan firefight in which British paratroopers killed 200 Taliban while suffering two wounded. The headline: "Two Paras Wounded in Clash With Resurgent Taliban."

Former British Prime Minister Tony Blair has eloquently framed the problem. He sees a fundamental shift in the relationship between politicians, media and the public, First, the news cycle has accelerated, so that whereas in 1997 (when Blair was first elected PM) the government could anticipate one news theme per day, by 2005—a mere eight years later—there would be a morning, afternoon and evening theme, to which the government must instantly respond: "Things harden within minutes. I mean, you can't let speculation stay out there for longer than an instant."

Blair expanded on his thesis, noting that the media "are facing a hugely more intense form of competition than anything they have ever experienced before." This competitive pressure has deleterious consequences:

The result, however, is a media that increasingly and to a dangerous degree is driven by "'impact." Impact is what matters. It is all that can distinguish, can rise above the clamor, can get noticed. Impact gives competitive edge. Of course the accuracy of a story counts. But is often secondary to impact.

Blair adds that "[t]he audience needs to be arrested, their emotions engaged." This, in turn, has six "acute consequences": scandal beats the ordinary; attacks are directed at motive, not judgment; fear of missing a story creates press wolf packs; reporting is commentary on the news, rather than the news itself; comment and reporting merge; and balanced reporting is rare.

It is one thing for reporters to bring a worldly skepticism to their task. It is not their job to make life easy for their government, or for allied governments, or for anyone else. But it equally is not their job to make life easier for enemies who seek to destroy the society that confers freedoms upon them. It is the juxtaposition of corrosive skepticism of their own governments, versus presumptive credibility accorded civilization's worst enemies, that reveals the poison in Western media today. (Yes, the Arab media are even worse, but they are hardly true news organizations, and have little, if any, tradition of fair reporting even as a professional ideal.)

Public Diplomacy: Winning Media Wars

The Government has one direct tool for influencing global attitudes: public diplomacy. Most famously, during the Cold War Radio Free Europe and Radio Liberty kept the flames of resistance alive inside the Iron Curtain. Programming included news about events inside the Soviet bloc and around the world, and American jazz, both broadcast and presented live via cultural exchange visits. Ronald Reagan's verbal eloquence, with an assist from Duke Ellington's musical elegance, helped win the Cold War.

In 1999, after a major re-organization, public diplomacy was centralized in a new federal agency, the Broadcasting Board of Governors

(BBG). BBG houses six entities that collectively reach a global audience of more than 155 million via radio, television and the Internet: Voice of America, Alhurra (Arabic for "the free one"), Radio Sawa, Radio Free Europe/Radio Liberty, Radio Free Asia, Radio & TV Marti.[36] BBG is severely restricted in communications with the American taxpaying public, due to fears that it might spread domestic propaganda.[37]

Radio Sawa, set up in 2002, targets the two-thirds of Mideast residents that are under 30 years of age. Alhurra, set up in 2004 as a satellite television station and funded at $70 million, has more public affairs programming. The two stations combined reach 35 million people in 22 countries, broadcasting 24 hours a day seven days per week. Each week the two stations reach an estimated 71 percent of Iraqi adults. A third all-news radio network, Radio Free Iraq, reaches more than one-fifth of Iraqi adults. VOA broadcasts into Iran, reaching some one in four Iranians at least once per week, with programming six hours per day. In Afghanistan, VOA reaches some half the population with 12 hours per day of programming. The State Department also has created a Digital Outreach Team of bloggers with foreign language skills who seek persuadable Muslims in online chat rooms; the bloggers always identify their U.S. government affiliation.

In December 2006 Alhurra aired most of a speech by none other than Sheik Hassan Nasrallah, chief of Hezbollah, ignoring that Nasrallah had invited all the world's Jews to come to the Mideast, so that it is easier to kill them. The station's former chief, an ex-CNN executive, approved this, and also had hired an executive from the virulently anti-American al-Jazeera. The infamous December 2006 Holocaust denial conference in Tehran was presented by Alhurra as if there was legitimate doubt of the Holocaust, in that deniers were not challenged. Despite such appalling deeds Karen Hughes, then Undersecretary of State for Public Diplomacy and Public Affairs, praised the management.

---

36. Though BBG is an independent agency, the Secretary of State serves on its Board.
37. The U.S. Information and Educational Exchange Act of 1948 (known as the Smith-Mundt Act, after its sponsors), bars domestic distribution of overseas broadcasts.

Other failures of public diplomacy abound. Our Ambassador to Egypt, one Riccardo Riccione, has openly praised Egyptian dictator Hosni Mubarak as being "loved in the U.S." and someone who could "win elections [in America] as a leader who is a giant on the world stage." The envoy also praised a film by an Egyptian artist best known for his hit single, "I Hate Israel." In 2001 the Voice of America's Pashto-language service interviewed none other than Taliban leader Mullah Omar, giving him a chance to comment on President Bush's September 20 address to the nation, in which the President demanded that the Taliban turn over al-Qaeda leaders or face the consequences. Asked to explain airing the interview, the news director defended the interviews of terrorists as "part of our balanced, objective and comprehensive reporting, providing our listeners with both sides of the story."

Lost on the news chief is the difference between a debate and a war. In a debate, two or more viewpoints are presented, with the underlying premise that no side has a monopoly on what is right and what is wrong. Thus, neither proponents nor opponents of capital punishment should claim that only their views have moral, legal, or other validity. But a war differs in that each side maintains that its side is indisputably right and the other side indisputably wrong. There is therefore *nothing to debate*. Thus did Franklin Delano Roosevelt speak to the nation after Japan's surprise attack on Pearl Harbor:

> The people of the United States have already formed their opinions and well understand the implications to the very life and safety of our nation.... No matter how long it may take us to overcome this premeditated invasion, the American people in their righteous might will win through to absolute victory.... With confidence in our armed forces—with the unbounding determination of our people—we will gain the inevitable triumph—so help us God.

Similar utterances can be found in the wartime speeches of British Prime Minister Winston Churchill, or in Ronald Reagan's Cold War speeches, and in President Bush's September 20 speech that Mullah Omar was allowed to discuss on the air. Conceding that there is another "side" to the question grants the adversary *legitimacy*, and thus undermines the justification for taking the fateful and perilous step of going to war. And it undermines, as well, the will of a nation to persevere in any protracted struggle.

Public diplomacy must thus reinforce a nation's will to fight, explain to allies why we fight, and put the foe on notice that victory is our only acceptable outcome. Author, scholar and former senior government official Carnes Lord explains the nature of public advocacy by a government, noting that just as commercial advertisers are not required to volunteer aspects of their product that may not be the best, so government, while avoiding lies, should present a positive portrait of our society:

> [I]t is important not to be misled by American or other defenders of psychological-political warfare into supposing that its various disciplines do or should communicate only "truth." In the commercial world, "truth in advertising" hardly requires companies to emphasize ways in which their products are inferior to the competition's. Effective propaganda certainly needs to avoid lies in the sense of counter factual statements, but it must also be selective in what it chooses to communicate.

The magnitude of the task confronting American public diplomacy after 9/11 is shown in December 2001 and January 2002 Gallup poll numbers drawn from Islamic communities around the globe. An astonishingly low 18 percent polled believed that Arabs had in fact carried out the 9/11 attacks, and only nine percent thought the U.S. invasion of *Afghanistan* to be morally justified. Lord cites two "complicating factors" in the Arab world: a mind-set oriented toward conspiratorial explanations, and the explosion in Arab-language mass media outlets over the past decade.

Public diplomacy challenges exist outside the Muslim world as well. A "documentary" aired on German *public* television on 9/11's sixth anniversary treated as a legitimate question who carried out the attacks, notwithstanding that al-Qaeda gleefully claimed responsibility. Conspiracy theorists were given free reign. An online vote after the show was aired tallied 25 percent of viewers blaming President Bush, another 25 percent blaming the U.S. government, 15 percent blaming America's gun lobbies, 27 percent fingering Osama bin Laden and 6 percent expressing no opinion. The audience numbers may reflect self-selection—viewers predisposed to crackpot theories—but what is shocking is that a public television station aired the program. Does the German government consider an open question who carried out the attacks? Presumably not, but treating it as open to serious debate is akin to treating the Holocaust as such. Holocaust denial is a crime in Germany, but 9/11 denial is perfectly legal. (Perhaps neither should be deemed criminal, for freedom of speech considerations, but neither should bear the government's implied imprimatur.)

Yet as Lord observes, the traditional distrust Americans harbor for government advocates has been amplified by a "cultural animus" among the "prestige media" towards any government effort to influence the war of ideas. Worse still, that elite distrust of vigorous public diplomacy has now spread to bureaucrats within the national security establishment. It was leaks from that bureaucracy to the prestige press that fatally undermined military assistance to pro-U.S. Iraqi media outlets. The idea was sunk because the U.S. influence was to be covert. Once it was publicly revealed, the Iraqi recipients would inevitably lose credibility. As well, they were at risk for their lives if "outed" as collaborating with the Americans.

In sum, America's airwaves and Internet public diplomacy should seek credibility but balance that against airing or posting inflammatory material that will produce terrorists by the carload, such as Abu Ghraib footage. A "light not heat" test should be applied to its material. Credibility means publicizing things that are going wrong, as well as those going right, our sins along with our virtues, and presenting diverse points of view. But it is simply perverse to present material that enrages impressionable youths around the world, in the name of enhancing our credibility. And it compounds such perversity to give air time to those who openly seek to destroy our civilization.

One form of non-verbal public diplomacy can be highly effective when done well: foreign aid. Americans export aid and import goodwill, with six out of seven dollars coming from the private sector: Of $192 billion in total aid sent abroad in 2005, $95 billion came from private sector donations (for-profit and not-for-profit combined), $69 billion from corporate lending and just $28 billion from official U.S. aid. Another widely-noted form of this is emergency aid, such as after the 2004 tsunami and the 2005 Pakistan earthquake. The U.S. military has unmatched ability to globally deliver humanitarian assistance with speed and volume.

There is one other growing factor—of huge potential impact—in public diplomacy: al-Qaeda's bloodthirsty campaign of terror, now often directed at Muslims. The two countries where support for Islamist terror dropped most steeply between 2002 and 2007 are Afghanistan and Iraq, where 90 percent of people disapprove of al-Qaeda and Osama bin Laden as well. Beheading children wins few converts anywhere. Large majorities in Egypt (88 percent), Morocco (66 percent) and Indonesia (65 percent) now condemn Islamic terror. The Egypt number is especially significant, as al-Qaeda's radical roots were planted in Egypt.

Re-Balancing Civil Liberties and Security

One of the legendary Supreme Court Justices, Louis D. Brandeis, succinctly explained the potential consequences of giving too much power to government:

> Experience should teach us to be most on our guard to protect liberty when the Government's purposes are beneficent. Men born to freedom are naturally alert to repel invasion of their liberty by evil-minded rulers. The greatest dangers to liberty lurk in insidious encroachment by men of zeal, well-meaning but without understanding.

Brandeis wrote his famous, oft-cited dissent in peacetime less than a decade after the infamous post-World War I "no-knock" raids against suspected Communist sympathizers, authorized by Attorney-General A. Mitchell Palmer. Between May Day 1919 and May Day 1920 four thousand suspects were arrested and detained without trial. Popular opinion turned against the raids. They were discontinued, and Palmer's Presidential ambitions were interred.

But destruction on 9/11's scale was not achievable in 1928, let alone the plausible prospect of WMD terrorism carried out by small terror cells. Such vastly greater potential lethality justifies tipping the liberty/security scale more toward security.

John Yoo, the Department of Justice official who found himself the chief point man for the Bush administration's legal strategy since 9/11, explained the difference between the threat posed by crime versus that posed by mass-casualty terrorism:

> Crime is an endemic, diffuse social problem that has persisted throughout human history. By contrast, war is a set of discrete and violent attacks undertaken by a nation or entity for political gain. Were the attacks organized and systematic enough to be considered "armed conflict"? The gravity and scale of September 11 surely crossed that threshold.

Thus, while naturally we should try to avoid mistaken detention of terror suspects, the mistake we should fear most is not compromising someone's comfort or "dignity," but that of failing to get the intelligence nugget that enables us to stop a WMD strike. Khalid Sheikh Muhammad, mastermind of the 9/11 atrocities, was apparently "waterboarded" (dunked two minutes in the water—a procedure used to test American Special Forces trainees) and broke in minutes, giving up a trove of information that probably saved thousands of lives. We are best advised to use aggressive interrogation sparingly, as Western publics cannot stomach widespread infliction of pain on hundreds, let alone thousands, of detainees. But it is imprudent never to use it as a tool.

Massachusetts Governor Mitt Romney has pointed out that while Americans value their civil liberties, the most important civil liberty is the right to be alive. In such a world, civil liberties must take a back-seat to terror prevention. Event probability must be juxtaposed with event severity, to produce an "expected value" for an event. A nuclear detonation would easily be a multi-trillion dollar event, so that even a minuscule prospect of a successful WMD mega-strike justifies immense investment of resources to prevent it. If this seems hard to justify before such a strike, afterwards it will seem self-evident.

Recalling Benjamin Franklin's maxim about not surrendering essential liberty for temporary safety, conversely, we should be willing to give up a little temporary liberty to obtain essential safety. As to the argument that the war will last decades and that compromise of civil liberties will hardly prove temporary, the threat to civil liberties from a successful WMD strike is greater.

Reflecting the new threat, the National Counter-Terrorism Center, formed in August 2004 as part of the homeland security reorganization after 9/11, now maintains a single integrated database with the names of all suspected terrorists, collected from 28 government networks and posted at a single classified web site. According to a senior intelligence official, radical Islamofascist groups in mosques and prisons are being monitored. But monitoring may not necessarily give rise to prosecution and punishment under current Constitutional law standards. Federal appeals Judge Richard Posner notes that Muslim clergy may encourage but not directly recruit terrorists, and that First Amendment law distinguishes between incitement and advocacy: "Incitement is a direct invitation to commit specific criminal acts in the immediate future and is punishable. Advocacy includes preaching the desirability of violent or otherwise criminal acts but without actually urging their commission forthwith, and is not punishable."

LAPD chief William Bratton and criminologist George Kelling advocates creating local intelligence units (NYPD already has one), as local police are more likely to be the first contact terror cell members cross, if only because most tips from locals will go to the local police rather than the feds. (Bratton also counsels against establishing a U.S. equivalent of England's domestic intelligence agency, MI5. He says that the FBI and local police can do MI5's work without creating a new bureaucracy.)

Judge Posner accepts local emphasis, as the U.S. has 17,000 police forces, which swamp the FBI's 56 regional offices. He adds that police forces, which discharge both investigative and preventive tasks, are better suited for counter-terror operations than is the FBI, which is a detective bureau only. Further, effective counter-intelligence, especially against domestic threats, requires intimate knowledge of, and seamless blending into, local Muslim communities. Monitoring of suspect activity can include watching activities for which probable cause cannot be established. Posner concludes that we are under-investing in countering the growing threat of homegrown terrorists who are not affiliated with foreign groups. Worse, security screening at the federal level rules out people from certain ethnic backgrounds, for fear of the risk of betrayal. Immigrants from Muslim and Arab lands are thus kept out of sensitive positions where their expertise would prove especially valuable. Judge Posner notes that few applicants sign up intending to betray; rather, they turn traitor later due to adverse circumstances.[38]

Another key civil liberties battleground is the media. That the media are the battlefield of choice for our enemy is simply intolerable. The First Amendment's free speech and press clause does not protect those who shout "Fire!" in a crowded theater. Neither should it protect those who recklessly aid and abet terrorists fighting a war of extermination against Western civilization. The press rarely aided the enemy in earlier wars. Yet political and legal realities sharply limit what can be done to limit national security harm inflicted by a free press in liberal societies.

There has never been a successful prosecution of a newspaper mass media outlet, or of reporters, under the Espionage Act of 1917. Passing an official secrets act that entitled the government to obtain prior restraint where disclosure poses substantial risk of grave damage to national security would encourage continuation of what everyone rec-

---

38. In November 2007 a Lebanese illegal was arrested. She had passed sensitive FBI and CIA data to Hezbollah. Both agencies hired her without discovering that she was an illegal immigrant. This argues for tighter screening of applicants from foreign lands, but not their total exclusion.

ognizes is the government's vast over-classification of materials. Where grave harm is threatened, an administration can always try its luck in federal court, in an *in camera* proceeding (closed chambers). Add to this the notorious penchant of legislators to write unwieldy laws (the proverbial camel as a horse designed by a committee) and the traditional American distaste for laws directly criminalizing speech, and inevitable judicial review of such laws, and it is better to cut out the middleman. It is better for the executive to seek judicial prior restraint if needed, and submit to judgment.

No war is an inquiry into the perfection or lack of it in the morally superior side. Yet media coverage of what is going wrong in a war—Iraq's 2006 slide towards civil war, for example—must be constitutionally protected. Voters need to have information if they are to assess whether their government is prosecuting the war properly and successfully. Disclosure of battlefield setbacks does energize the adversary, but is essential to spur corrective action.

How, then, do we distinguish between disclosure (Iraq insurgency) and secrecy (Abu Ghraib photos)? A balancing test is the best that can be applied by the courts—for the better part of the past century strongly sympathetic to press freedom, and thus highly unlikely to judge harshly at the expense of the media. That test should be, Does harm to national security outweigh the benefits of disclosure? Such a test may be highly subjective, but no more so than many balancing tests applied by jurists in other contexts. Legal judgments are as much a "slippery slope" as is life in general. However, the courts may not yet be up to this (see next section).

Former CIA Director R. James Woolsey proposes a reasonable multi-prong test as to when the media should hold a story: Ask if intelligence "sources and methods" might likely be betrayed, and don't assume that "everyone knows" about programs. Are the acts involved illegal or unconstitutional? Are there other arguable abuses of rules? Is it an area where people have some reasonable expectation of privacy? Is there oversight by Congress? Notably, during the 1979–1981 Iranian hostage crisis, the networks, to their credit, withheld their knowledge that several U.S. Embassy employees were being hidden at the Canadian embassy in Tehran. Yet even conscientious news reporters are ambivalent about the extent to which they should withhold similar information.[39]

Licensees are also subject to the FCC's authority, stated in the preamble to section 303, to regulate broadcasting "from time to time, as public convenience, interest or necessity requires." Thus, Presidential (and opposition party) access to airwaves can be mandated. The FCC's status as an "independent regulatory agency" gives it broad powers, greater than those given agencies lodged within the executive branch.[40]

The Federal Communications Commission has statutory authority to prevent transmission of "false or deceptive signals or communications." In September 2007 the FCC proposed a $4,000 fine against a cable company, Comcast, for not informing viewers that an ad imitating a newscast Comcast aired was paid for by the product vendor.

Thus the FCC can enforce "truth in sourcing": Any station that broadcasts photos without alerting viewers that the sources are hostile and unverified is fined or, with repeated instances, deprived of its broadcast license. Second, the agency can adopt a Presidential Media Access rule, under which radio licensees would be required to grant access upon request to the President to address the nation, with equal time granted the opposition party upon request. The federal Constitution may reasonably be interpreted to permit these measures, albeit in practice their survival would depend upon who sits on the Supreme Court when such measures are appealed by media organizations.

---

39. Thus former ABC News Correspondent John McWethy: "Probably the best way [in terms of a positive outcome] of dealing with a terrorist incident is to say nothing, but we live in a country in which freedom of speech is both a joy and a burden of our society, so when something like that happens, we report it. It's not just the way we do things in our business, it's the way we do things in our country; we have a very free press. But those of us who are engaged in this kind of journalism have to be careful."

40. An independent regulatory agency is not within the executive branch. It combines powers normally lodged in different branches of government. Besides the FCC, only the Federal Trade Commission qualifies for this exalted status.

How would such practices have worked to date, since 9/11? Presidential prime-time access would have enabled the President to directly present his case to the viewing audience, rather than have it filtered through a frequently hostile media. Should any President abuse the privilege, voters will let the White House know. Under the current practice, a small number of broadcast executives can act as *de facto* gatekeepers in deciding whether a President's speech is "political" and thus not to be carried over their networks. This is more power than the broadcast executives should have. To observe this is not to be pro-government, but rather to prefer the judgment of voters to that of corporate gatekeepers.

If monitoring media for truthful advertising sounds out of step with First Amendment freedoms, what is one to make of the Senate Minority leader, Harry Reid, having asked ABC in late 2006 to pull its 9/11 mini-series because, according to Democrats, it portrayed Clinton officials as being soft on terrorism in the 1990s, and because it contained purportedly inaccurate quotes? Television "docudramas" have raised controversy before, as when in 2003 CBS pulled a biased mini-series on the Reagans after vehement Republican protests. (It was aired on a cable channel.)

Thus, political leaders and their supporters today can sometimes get television networks to yank, or at least modify, programs to remedy asserted inaccuracies. So how is it that Hezbollah footage, or feeds from Hamas, are aired on television news without verification? Why not at least require truth in attribution and disclosure of lack of verifiability, while allowing the material to be aired?

A press not free enough to print criticism of the war effort cannot provide us with valuable corrective information that may be needed to win wars, as much necessary criticism comes from outside government. But a press can cost us wars, too, by demoralizing the public through relentless negativism, by airing footage supplied us by our enemy or gathered per our enemy's rules, or by revealing secrets that educate the enemy in how to fight us better. Proof of media negativism comes in a major Pew poll of global attitudes that shows that foreigners have a ten to twenty percentage point more favorable view of America if they have visited the U.S., or have friends or relatives in the U.S., than if they have no such connection—the latter getting their perception of America from global news and entertainment media. In wars of survival *every* freedom is at stake, including press freedom.

In a society premised upon the value of an essentially minimally-fettered press, such measures run against the grain. But it ought to be unacceptable even to the Western press corps that our deadliest adversaries in a war of survival regard our press as their prime asset in their crusade to destroy us.

The same holds true for Hollywood, which was subject to censorship in World War II, despite the manifest patriotic enthusiasm of the film colony then. Censorship was accepted then, partly due to recognition that inadvertent disclosure of certain facts or images could have a harmful impact on America's ability to fight effectively. And some Hollywood films today do express positive war values.

In the summer of 2007, however, Hollywood embarked on an unprecedented campaign to undermine public support for the war effort, by bringing antiwar films to the box office, aimed at the Iraq War, the CIA and other targets. One film, "Redacted," chronicles an isolated atrocity committed by American troops: the hideous rape, torture and murder of a 14-year-old Iraqi girl, and the killing of her entire family in March 2006.

The film relies on soldier film footage, blogs and other sources outside the mainstream media, which didn't air graphic images, and gave less prominence to the story than Brian De Palma, the filmmaker, thinks it deserves. De Palma explained his purpose thusly:

> This is an attempt to explain the reality of what is happening in Iraq to the American people. These pictures are what will stop the war. One only hopes that these images will get the public incensed enough to motivate their Congressmen to vote against this war.

The film director is of course entitled to his own opinion as to what "the reality" of the war is. Such atrocities have been rare, and thus hardly can be seriously said to be representative of the war. Five soldiers have been charged, with four already given sentences of between 5 and 110 years.

Besides the unrepresentative nature of the film, two other aspects are profoundly disturbing. First, it encourages viewers to base decisions on an emotional response to a highly inflammatory episode, hardly a reasoned way to decide whether or not to stay in Iraq. Worse still is that as with the images of Abu Ghraib, new terrorists will be created by the carloads among Islamic youth who do not realize how rare the event is. If these new terrorists kill innocent people, the director will (conveniently) never know.[41]

In sum, we should take these specific steps to re-balance civil liberties and security, and to advance American values in the world:

- Continue to aggressively interrogate key operatives.

- Mine databases broadly.

- Implement a national ID card, a long overdue end to a national hang-up.

- Repeal existing Executive branch prohibitions against assassination.

- Apply existing truth-in-advertising rules to broadcast licensees, to prevent airing of propaganda masquerading as news reporting.

- Require broadcast licensees to grant access to the President upon request, with equal access granted to the opposition.

- Seek prior judicial restraint against airing of inflammatory video images that clearly will motivate many youths worldwide to become terrorists, and who will thus place thousands of innocent lives at risk.

- Revive public diplomacy to shape global attitudes more favorably towards the United States.

---

41. Another film, by Robert Redford, "Rendition," attacks the CIA's practice of rendition, under which detainees are handed over to foreign authorities for interrogation. The practice is over 20 years old, and generally does not involve abduction and torture, as depicted in the film. The practice is dubious on practical grounds, as the CIA loses control of questioning.

Limits on State Power

To create political support for taking such steps we also need to adopt two sets of limits on state conduct: a self-imposed one on the boundaries of acceptable political discourse, and a corrective process that flags errors more reliably, so that innocent people can more rapidly clear their names.

As to the former, General David Petraeus was confirmed, unanimously, by the Senate. All senators should have lined up behind his plan and given it time to work. Yet senators were telling the world that the surge wasn't working, months before the full set of brigades were deployed. Silence until the General's interim report after eight months of effort would have reassured Iraqis that America intended to carry out the surge. Instead, while progress was made militarily, political leaders in Iraq worried that the U.S. might pull out even as the surge was working.

A prominent former Eastern Bloc intelligence chief, Ion Marie Pacepa, has recounted how important discrediting America was during the Cold War. In this the Soviets were aided often by the vitriolic dissenters on the Left in Europe and the U.S. It is one thing for a KGB stooge to slander America or its leaders, and quite another, vastly more credible abroad, if a slander (such as, "Bush lied, people died") is uttered by prominent Americans.

One restraint upon abuse of dissent has been enacted into law, one that well fits legitimate "time, place and manner" regulation of First Amendment speech. In 2006 Congress passed the Respect for Fallen Heroes Act, which prohibits demonstrations within 300 feet of a cemetery, for 60 minutes before through 60 minutes after funerals. Demonstrators shouting protests over the war in Iraq had been disrupting funerals of servicemen.

Better error correction procedures are essential to retain the trust of the citizenry. When Senator Kennedy turns up on a no-fly list and is stopped five times in one month, something is amiss—in this case, apparently, some terror suspects used T. Kennedy as an alias. Ditto for

Catherine Stevens, wife of Senator Ted, detained serially because her name crossed that of British pop singer Cat Stevens, a radical Muslim activist. Getting off the list, once on, is nearly impossible, as it matches names only, and thus those unlucky enough to share the same name as a terror suspect can find themselves on it indefinitely. A biometric ID card could enable rapid removal from such lists, by definitively establishing a person's unique identity.

Less prominent citizens have an even steeper uphill battle. One news report tells of a grandfather who needed two years to get off the TSA's watch list for special screening, and who in the end was not told that he had been cleared, but rather simply that his case had been "reviewed." Worse, a seven-year-old Muslim boy was stopped at three airports because he shares a name with a Pakistani terror suspect; the family missed its flight home to Pakistan. An effort to "scrub" suspect lists is underway at all major agencies, and a suspect complaint process that once took months now is supposed to take ten days. The government inevitably will make many mistakes, but unless corrections are more easily obtainable, support for vigorous security measures will surely wane. But Congress resists efforts to build databases with more data on the population, which would greatly facilitate clearing people who share names with suspects.

9/10 Versus 9/12

On 9/11 terrorists turned our technology against us; since 9/11 civil libertarians would turn us against our technology. The latter raised the specter of historical episodes to sow fear, yet nothing comparable to their Cassandra-like warnings has come to pass. President Lincoln jailed 12,000 civilian citizens and used military commissions to try civilians; the Bush administration has detained few civilians as al-Qaeda suspects, and will use military commissions to try non-citizens only. President Wilson authorized warrantless tapping of domestic phone calls in World War I, as did FDR in World War II; with rare exceptions the Bush administration tapped only international calls without judicial warrant, and now has accepted a compromise warrant procedure. Congress has consented to the administration's revised procedures, and repealed part of adverse Supreme Court rulings. As for detaining 115,000 Japanese from 1942 to 1945, not only has nothing like that been done, but the President himself urged Americans after 9/11 not to retaliate against Muslims, and policies prohibiting ethnic profiling are in effect. *No one has been detained solely for Arab or Muslim status.*

In pursuing conventional criminals we should be cautious and err on the side of being under-inclusive in casting the net, in order to avoid convicting the innocent. But against terrorists seeking WMD to kill tens or hundreds of thousands, if not millions, we cannot afford this luxury. If we are to reduce the risk of catastrophe to near-zero—it will never reach absolute zero—we must be prepared to err on the side of *over-*inclusion. This is what was done domestically in the immediate aftermath of the 9/11 attacks, after President Bush told then-Attorney General John Ashcroft, at the first post-attack Cabinet meeting: "Don't ever let this happen again." [42] Had the policy then adopted—of aggressively detaining immigrants suspected of visa violations—been employed earlier the 9/11 plot might have been stymied, as all nineteen hijackers had committed deportable violations in filling out their visas—all had lied on their applications, and five had overstayed their visas.

The fundamental "values" division begins with those who believe that 9/11 was a vicious attack, but one that can be dealt with by stepped-up efforts within the 9/10 "law values" framework: enhanced multilateral cooperation via the United Nations and European Union, enhanced law enforcement, preservation of the then-existing balance between civil liberties and security, and near-unlimited press freedom.

---

42. The unsung hero in the days following 9/11 was Ashcroft, who detained 750 Muslims for immigration violations. They were held, interrogated regarding terror matters, and then most were released. Ashcroft put possible risk of another terrorist act first, and liberty second, adopting what he called a "spit on the sidewalk" policy. All were suspected of immigration (or other) violations. Ashcroft details how several of the 9/11 hijackers escaped pickup despite staying illegally in the U.S. beyond their visas. Four of the hijackers were stopped by local or state police in the six-month period prior to 9/11.

Opposed to this is the 9/12 "war values" view that 9/11 opened a new phase of intensity in the war radical Islam has waged against the West for a generation. In this view, 9/11 "changed everything" and thus rendered obsolete traditional mechanisms for addressing the threat. Rebalancing civil liberties and escaping the chains of hidebound multilateral bodies are seen as essential to win the war.

Six years after 9/11 the country is thus deeply divided. Such a divide is not likely to be surmounted by argument, however persuasive. Rather, it will eventually be crossed after the occurrence of a transforming event—one that shocks either the 9/10 or 9/12 believers into reconsidering their position.

A series of mismanaged military ventures could demoralize the 9/12 set, and tilt America towards isolationism. Conversely, a massive terror strike that the public perceives as caused by laxity could galvanize public opinion in favor of more vigorous action. Many of the 9/10 crowd could be one WMD strike away from joining the 9/12 set.

CHAPTER IV

THE LAW-GIVER VALUES WAR

MANDARINS OR "WE THE PEOPLE"

Lawful, *adj*. Compatible with the will of a judge having jurisdiction.
AMBROSE BIERCE, *THE DEVIL'S DICTIONARY*

The Supreme Court: A Narrow 9/10 Majority

There have been four Supreme Court decisions addressing the rights of detainees held as unlawful combatants by the U.S., some held inside and others outside the country.[43] The High Court's rulings collectively prove anew what should be well understood by all: *Lawyers and judges can lose a war, but cannot win one; no country ever won a war by having the best legal system.* Decisions that could substantially affect our chances of winning the war are now held hostage to the intellectual and emotional sensibilities of five unelected judicial mandarins-for-life. Cases presented to the Justices offered alternative choices, including several plausible ways to interpret key provisions of laws passed by Congress, regulations

---

43. In 2004 the Supreme Court decided three detainee cases: *Rumsfeld v. Padilla*, 542 U.S. 426 (held: federal *habeas corpus* jurisdiction over prison commander located inside the U.S. is a sufficient predicate for jurisdiction to hear a *habeas corpus* appeal filed by a detainee held outside the U.S.); *Rasul v. Bush*, 542 U.S. 466 (held: federal jurisdiction to hear *habeas corpus* appeals applies to aliens held outside the U.S., where prison commander is located inside the U.S.); *Hamdi v. Rumsfeld*, 542 U.S. 507 (held: federal jurisdiction exists to hear *habeas corpus* petition of U.S. citizen held outside the U.S., and certain minimal procedural due process rights must be accorded detainees). In 2006 the Court decided *Hamdan v. Rumsfeld*. 126 S. Ct. 2749 (held: Detainee Treatment Act of 2005 does not preclude application of Common Article 3 of the Geneva Protocols to detention of unlawful combatants, and the military commission established by the administration does not meet standards required under the Uniform Code of Military Justice). The cases are superbly discussed in Ronald Rotunda, "Federalism and Separation of Powers: Holding Enemy Combatants in the Wake of *Hamdan*," *Engage*, Vol. 8, Issue 3 (undated).

established by Presidential executive authority, and international treaties ratified by the U.S. The Justices consistently have chosen interpretations that run contrary to the underlying purpose of the rule in question, and that expand the Court's judicial power, thus diminishing the power of the two other branches of government (legislative and executive).

Begin with what a Supreme Court decision actually signifies. A decision rendered on constitutional grounds is law of the land until either the Supreme Court overrules its own precedent or until the Constitution is amended to change the result. A decision interpreting a federal statute can be overruled by a subsequent law passed by Congress, as happened with the Military Commissions Act of 2005. Further, a litigant may win the case in federal district court, prevail on appeal before a three-judge appellate panel, but lose 5–4 in the Supreme Court. Despite winning 8 of 13 federal judges to his side, he loses. Indeed, if the entire appeals court of 15 judges re-hears a case on appeal (this is rare) a litigant could win all 16 lower judges' votes, but lose 5–4 in the Supreme Court. Then, despite 20 of 25 federal judges siding with him, he loses. Nothing makes the nine jurists sitting on the Supreme Court superior in constitutional interpretation to those sitting below—indeed, certain highly-regarded federal appeals judges have reputations equal to any of the nine Justices sitting on the Supreme Court.

Thus a litigant, or an administration, is not "lawless" because it loses in the final stage. In the words of Supreme Court Justice Robert H. Jackson: "We are not final because we are infallible, but we are infallible only because we are final." Chief Justice Charles Evans Hughes said: "We are under a Constitution, but the Constitution is what the judges say it is." Either you have the votes or you do not. And, as Justices come and go, the result may hinge on when a case reaches the court.

Turn now to the details of the 2006 detainee case, in which the Supreme Court considered an appeal on *habeas corpus* grounds.[44] The application for a writ was filed on behalf of Osama bin Laden's former

---

44. *Habeas corpus* is Latin for "produce the body." Jailers must bring prisoners to court upon issuance of the "Great Writ" by a court having jurisdiction—*i.e.*, power to hear the case.

bodyguard, an appeal that also challenged the military commission procedures adopted by the administration to try terrorist detainees. The Court issued a tripartite ruling in which it held that Congress did not clearly vest jurisdiction of detainees like Hamdan in a single court; that the administration's military commissions did not meet due process standards for such tribunals; and that one part of the Geneva Convention (Common Article 3) applies to detainee treatment.

In so deciding the Court ignored the plain intent of the 2005 Detainee Treatment Act in which Congress sought to vest exclusive jurisdiction of *habeas corpus* appeals in the U.S. Court of Appeals, D.C. Circuit, by an expedient parsing of legislative language and the record of the debates in Congress. It shoved aside decades of traditional deference to executive discretion, using a provision of the Uniform Code of Military Justice (UCMJ), a set of laws designed to try American service personnel, to find the Executive's procedures "impractical" and thus require the President to seek express congressional authorization for procedural deviations from the UCMJ. And it applied Common Article 3 of the Geneva Conventions, despite their hitherto unbroken historical application to civil wars only. As applied it could seriously degrade our ability to glean intelligence from detainees, a commodity for which we have immense need and few alternative sources to tap.

What the Court has accomplished, by expanding the ambit of non-reciprocal detainee treatment, to borrow an infamous expression of the Vietnam War, is to destroy the Geneva Convention's "village"—its bedrock of conditional legal protection only—in order to save it. The edifice of Geneva stands upon a foundation of reciprocal compliance.

From its 1949 inception there always has been the problem of dealing with state or non-state actors who refuse to comply with Geneva. From such we will never gain reciprocity. Imposing a unilateral mandate of Geneva compliance upon America removes the incentive for Geneva compliant adversaries to follow the rules, as their soldiers will get protection even absent Geneva rules.[45]

Common Article 3 (termed "common" because this provision, like with certain others, is found in all four of the 1949 Geneva Conventions), is worth a closer look. Language in 1(c)—" outrages," "dignity," "humiliating and degrading"—are a creative lawyer's dream. Terms like that pave the way for future judicial back-door importation of more non-reciprocal Geneva rules to treatment of detainees, with the requisite denial of ability to interrogate aggressively—or even, to interrogate at all, in any manner, without detainee consent. Such words are grist for any jurist to interpret as broadly or narrowly as personal taste dictates. But the legal definition of torture under U.S. law is a very narrow one—not the broad one applied by critics.[46]

What of one technique used to get Abu Zubaydeh, a top al-Qaeda leader, to name other key al-Qaeda leaders? The detainee, at Guantanamo, was exposed to music from the Red Hot Chili Peppers, played at high volume. Is this such "severe" pain as to fall under legal prohibition?

When the United States ratified the UN Convention Against Torture (CAT) it did so with many reservations. The U.S. has defined torture narrowly, following the adjective "severe" in the Convention. The term is "usually reserved for extreme, deliberate and unusually cruel practices... [such as] sustained systemic beating, applications of electric currents to sensitive parts of the body, and tying up or hanging in positions that cause extreme pain." However, once a practice is found to be torture under the CAT, the prohibition is absolute: "No exceptional circumstances whatsoever, whether a state of war or a threat of war, inter-

---

45. Americans who violate the Geneva Conventions face imprisonment or, if death results, the death penalty for violating them, per the War Crimes Act of 1996.

46. The legal definition Congress set for "torture," in ratifying the Convention, contains six elements: (1) intentional infliction of (2) "severe" (3) mental or physical (4) "pain and suffering" (5) on person(s) within custody or physical control (of the violator) and (6) done "under color of law." The last term means that to fall under this law's ambit an act of torture must have been committed by someone purporting to act with government sanction. The law is codified at Title 18 U.S. Code sec. 2340.

nal political instability or any other public emergency, may be invoked as a justification of torture." Court case law on this issue has been sparse.

Thus, our ability to glean valuable intelligence as to future attacks and possible changes in organizational structure of Islamofascist terrorist groups may rest, in event of additional adverse Court rulings, on the sensibilities of five Justices who showed more solicitude for Osama's bodyguard than for executive discretion in wartime. The Court displayed an unseemly eagerness to review trial procedures before an actual trial, which would have provided the factual context courts have traditionally deemed essential for effective judicial review. Reviewing a hypothetical case is impermissible in federal and most state courts, being what lawyers call an "advisory opinion." That the Court acted here in just such a case speaks volumes as to the probable mind-set of the majority Justices.

In the *Hamdan* case the Court succumbed to these judicial vices, not only as to what the law is, a temptation to which all judges, being human, are subject (albeit in varying degrees), but also as to *fact*, a relative rarity, even among activist judges. Five members of the nation's highest court assert that in going after al-Qaeda in their Afghanistan lair the U.S. was intervening in a conflict "not of an international character," giving as a reason that the conflict was not between nations, a glaring *non sequitur* (made no better by citing legal precedents that purport to justify similarly illogical findings). Justice Clarence Thomas, dissenting, aptly termed the majority's reasoning "too clever by half" and noted that the majority, in applying Common Article 3, ignored the fact that enforcing the Geneva conventions is a purely diplomatic matter.

Hijacked jetliners imploding Twin Towers in Manhattan—thousands crushed or incinerated; the Pentagon breached—incinerating more innocents; a plane headed for the Capitol, diverted by American heroism to crash in a field in Pennsylvania; terrorist bombs exploding around the globe—Bali, Madrid, Mumbai (Bombay), Beirut, all over Iraq—and what did five members of the nation's highest court do? Driven by their evident distaste for the administration's detainee policy, the majority adopted expedient constructions of law that make more likely that we at some future date(s) will endure atrocities vastly greater in scale than the death and destruction of 9/11.

Justice Scalia filed a withering dissent that showed how the majority selectively applied the legislative history behind the 2005 Detainee Treatment Act, and that showed how selective the Court majority was regarding the settled principle of judicial deference to the executive branch, especially in time of war. Justice Thomas's dissent noted that the same Justices who declined in *Hamdan* to defer to the executive did defer earlier, in upholding a ruling by the Army Corps of Engineers, no less, that a storm drain on private property is a tributary of a navigable public waterway, and thus subject to environmental regulation! So the Court majority deferred to the Army Corps of Engineers as to their prerogative to invade private property, limit its use and thus impair its monetary value. But that same Court majority could not find it in themselves to defer to other branches as to matters of gravest national security—matters as to which the Court is far less competent to assess and decide than either of the two other branches of government.

That the Court majority adopted three improbable constructions, each expanding their own judicial power at the expense of the legislative as well as the executive, brings to mind what James Bond's mortal adversary, Goldfinger, said: "Once is happenstance; twice is coincidence; three times is enemy action." The Justices are of course not literally our enemies, but their triple play suggests a deliberate choice to strongly boost the court's wartime role.

It is inconceivable that the Court majority would manipulate language about matters of readily ascertainable fact, simply to impose slightly different rules on military tribunals. Rather, the Justices have loaded their guns for future cases, in which one may expect more of Geneva to be applied to the detainees, if again what we do violates the sense of fair play held by five Justices.

Above all, there is a lesson for the administration in this: It was never a good idea to aim to put detainees on trial. It conflates punishment and prophylactic sequestration in the public mind. Common criminals, even mass murderers, are entitled to the full panoply of due process rights. They are wayward members of society, but with limited power to inflict harm. Lawful combatants are entitled to the full protection of the Geneva Conventions—provided they themselves comply. They are honorable adversaries. But unlawful combatants, as non-compliant actors, are entitled to absolutely nothing.

We may choose to extend certain dispensations as a matter of *discretion*. In some conflicts, including Korea and Vietnam, we have done so. In contrast, we have specifically declined to extend such protections to unlawful combatants.[47] In the Civil War we regarded irregulars as bandits, no different than pirates on the high seas and treated the same way, as war outlaws.

No one suggests that we detain or torture family members in pursuit of confessions. But practices such as forcing suspects to stand for four hours at a time hardly come under a serious definition of torture. In approving the practice, Defense Secretary Donald Rumsfeld, who worked in his office from a standing desk all day long even when past the age of 70, appended his own handwritten note: "I stand for 8–10 hours a day. Why is standing limited to 4 hours?"

The attitude of too many judges is perhaps best summed up by the tart comment of former Justice Sandra Day O'Connor: "A state of war is not a blank check for the president when it comes to the rights of the nation's citizens." The Supremes decline to give a "blank check" even as to non-resident alien detainees.

Below the Supremes: More 9/10 Judges

Nor can we expect better performance from lower courts than we have gotten from the Supreme Court. A quintessential example of ju-

---

47. President Carter signed the two 1977 Additional Protocols that extended Geneva protection to sub-national groups, but the Senate never ratified them. In 1987 President Reagan urged the Senate to ratify Protocol II, concerning humanitarian treatment of detainees, wounded, etc., with certain reservations. But he declined to submit to the Senate Protocol I, which would have entitled irregulars to be accorded full parity with nationals, and would have treated all irregular wars as "international" and thus under Geneva.

dicial obtuseness can be found in the November 2001 decision by the FISA Court which, ignoring passage weeks earlier of the USA Patriot Act, ruled that the "wall" between law enforcement and intelligence functions should *continue to stand*—this despite the Patriot Act debate in Congress, the anthrax attack and the atrocities of 9/11. The Court's ruling came at a time when four out of five Americans thought another attack within a year was at least somewhat likely, and when the CIA believed that 9/11 was part of a multi-stage series of attacks.

Nor is the culture at the Justice Department a comfort. Career types there advised then-Attorney-General John Ashcroft, "Let it go. We can work around it. Don't mess with the FISA Court." Ashcroft, to his credit, appealed, the first appeal to the Foreign Intelligence Surveillance Court of Review which, in late 2002, reversed the FISA Court ruling, thus allowing the "wall" to be taken down once and for all.

The FISA Review Court's opinion was extraordinary in two respects. Its ruling was the first appellate ruling ever issued since FISA was enacted into law in 1978. Equally extraordinary were its unanimous findings. The Court found that the original FISA law didn't create the famed "wall" between intelligence and law enforcement. Rather, the "wall" was initially created in a 1980 ruling of a federal appeals court. It was formally adopted in the 1995 guidelines issued by the Clinton administration. In turn, these practices were incorporated into FISA procedure by the FISA Court in November 2001, and affirmed by that Court in May 2002. It was this ruling that led Ashcroft to file a first-ever appeal with the FISA Review Court. That Court noted that the very purpose of the USA Patriot Act, passed less than one month before the lower FISA Court adopted the wall, was to take down the wall, because it contributed to the intelligence failures prior to 9/11. The FISA Review Court further noted agreement with all courts that considered the extent of Presidential authority re foreign intelligence taps: "[T]he President [does] have inherent authority to conduct warrantless searches to obtain foreign intelligence information."

But the procedures mandated by the Foreign Intelligence Surveillance Act of 1978, as amended by the Patriot Act in 2001, still require that within 72 hours a warrant be issued, on a case by case basis (extendable on emergency application). Many terror searches will require rapid movement, often without anything near to traditional probable cause. With searches allowing at most weeks, more likely days (at times, hours) to track down possible leads, FISA is an albatross. The law, in the event, was designed for a world when surveillance meant monitoring suspicious employees at the Soviet Embassy, none of whom were planning WMD terror acts or plotting to hijack airliners.

The American Civil Liberties Union stated in a complaint filed against the National Security Agency that FISA was designed to protect Americans from their own government, calling FISA a response to a 1972 Supreme Court case and a Senate Committee report on domestic intelligence activities conducted against Americans not suspected of any crime, and not national security risks. The ACLU quoted congressional report language: "Unless new and tighter controls are established by legislation, domestic intelligence activities threaten to undermine our democratic society and fundamentally alter its nature."

Critics point out that from the 1978 enactment of FISA through 2006, only 5 of 22,989 FISA warrant requests were denied by the FISA Court (four in 2003 and one in 2006). That reflects in part that FISA's rules are so specific that cautious bureaucrats submitted applications only if certain to win approval. And FISA has impeded foreign policy. One former senior Justice Department official has recounted how in 1985, during the TWA Flight 847 hostage crisis, she was advised by career lawyers that a tap on communications between the terrorists and supporters could not be sustained under the law, because the primary focus of the tap was catching those who had committed crimes, not obtaining foreign intelligence. Even when allowable, FISA warrant applications in non-emergency situations can take literally *months* to prepare, and even emergency requests cannot be done in mere hours. A joint congressional inquiry cited legal concerns as a key factor underlying the "wall" erected between law enforcement and intelligence gathering.

Continuing substantial modification is needed to bring FISA in line with the reality of twenty-first century WMD threats and the Internet jihadist. Some modification—prohibiting harboring of terrorists, and expanding conspiracy law—came with passage in October 2001 of the USA Patriot Act.[48] One worthwhile modification not yet on the table would be to allow tapping communications within the U.S. between persons who have communicated with overseas terror suspects. Thus if terror suspect A in Afghanistan calls B in Baltimore and C in Cleveland, calls between B and C should be included under warrantless intercepts, to obviate the need for cumbersome warrant preparation procedures; a subsequent report to the FISA Court could act as a check on unbridled executive discretion.[49]

Not satisfied with throwing one monkey wrench into foreign affairs, the FISA Court, in an unpublished ruling in January 2007, issued what may be its most astonishing ruling to date. The 1978 FISA statute required that before tapping lines of suspects located in the U.S. the government must obtain a search warrant. However, to tap suspects overseas did not require a warrant. In 1978, calls overseas exclusively traversed networks outside the U.S. Due to technology changes brought about by the Internet, calls between parties all located overseas frequently pass through network nodes inside the U.S. A FISA Court judge ruled that such calls only could be tapped per a warrant. (Some authorities dispute this report.)

---

48. The Act's title is a long acronym, creation of which is a talent that inside the Beltway abounds in Olympian measure. Thus: Uniting and Strengthening America by Providing Appropriate Tools Required to Intercept and Obstruct Terrorism.

49. From after 9/11 until late 2004 the NSA's TSP may well have included such domestic calls, but Deputy Attorney General James Comey and career Justice Department attorneys, objected to this, citing FISA's warrant requirement for domestic calls. White House Counsel Alberto Gonzales urged continuance based upon Presidential inherent power during wartime to monitor suspected enemy communications, but Attorney-General John Ashcroft sided with Justice. Such monitoring was terminated.

Judges handle cases where technology changes and statutes written long ago must be interpreted to fit an unforeseen situation. Good practice calls for applying the manifest intent, where clear, of legislators. Clearly the 1978 legislators intended that calls between foreign parties need not require a warrant to justify surveillance. That such calls traverse American soil in 2007 is a mere artifact of technology changes. As a result of the Court's ruling, call intercepts dropped by *two-thirds*.[50]

Fortunately, Congress and the President agreed on a six-month extension of NSA wiretap authority before adjourning for the August 2007 recess. The Protect America Act of 2007 permits tapping overseas calls without a warrant, even if the calls pass through networks in the U.S. It protects from privacy lawsuits telecommunications firms who cooperate with investigations, but the protection is prospective only. The FISA Court will be given an opportunity to approve procedures in advance, a vision of dubious constitutionality, as federal courts rule on specific cases and refrain from giving "advisory opinions" on matters not yet before them as a specific case. In October 2007 the President and Congress negotiated a six-year extension of the Act.

In September 2007 a plot to bomb multiple sites in Frankfurt, targeting thousands of American tourists, was broken up by German authorities. Critical to their success were intercepted Internet communications between Germany and Pakistan. The calls were made via Internet cafés in an effort to mask the identity of terror cell members. The communications interceptions were performed by American authorities, coordinating with their German counterparts.

Coincidentally, the news about the German plot emerged the same day that a federal judge declared part of the USA Patriot Act unconstitutional, specifically a provision requiring companies to turn over call records in response to "national security letters" from the government.

---

50. The 2005 TSP was slimmed down from the original version, so that relative to the original 2001–2004 TSP total call intercepts declined by more than two-thirds, after the FISA Court's January 2007 ruling. Thus the August 2007 restoration of warrantless NSA authority restores most, but not all, of the original program, returning it to the 2005–2006 level of coverage.

Such requests ask companies not to inform suspects that records have been turned over. The judge ruled that the companies' First Amendment rights were violated, and that the separation of powers was violated, in allowing executive branch officials to perform functions normally given the courts, and that thus court approval was required for issuance of such letters. The Justice Department will appeal. Given that between 2003 and 2005 the government issued 140,000 national security letters, a requirement of prior judicial approval is tantamount to killing the search technique.

Further, the President clearly retains some inherently constitutional authority to intercept foreign communications in the course of discharging his national security responsibilities. *Congress cannot by statute abridge such power, as the Constitution is the supreme law of the land.* That said, the Supreme Court, were the issue to come before it, could rule that certain Presidential acts are outside the scope of the President's inherent constitutional power. Given how the High Court has treated the administration's war cases, this is a risk that the administration may be wise not to take.

In June 2007 a military tribunal judge ruled that an al-Qaeda terrorist who killed one American soldier and wounded three others could not be tried before a military commission.[51] The reason was a wording discrepancy between the military's rules for Combat Status Review Tribunals and the Military Commission Act that Congress passed in 2006. The former refers to enemy combatants, while the latter refers to unlawful combatants. Yet as one former terror trial prosecutor has noted, anyone who fights for al-Qaeda is an unlawful combatant, because the terror group does not follow the laws of war. The judge's finding is, the ex-prosecutor states, akin to a finding that "a U.S. citizen who lived his entire life in Albany" is not a citizen of New York State. Fortunately, in September the decision was reversed by a military appeals court, citing applicability of the provisions of common-law courts martial.

---

51. On August 22, 2007, the Fourth Circuit granted a petition filed by the Administration for a re-hearing *en banc* (with all the circuit judges sitting, instead of the normal three).

The original ruling is no surprise, for that judge, one Peter E. Brownback III, made an earlier contribution to evolving military tribunal jurisprudence, one that should once and for all lay to rest fears that military justice is kangaroo justice. (Nothing could be further from the truth.) In August 2004 one detainee asked the Court if he could make a statement, and asked not to be interrupted. He began: "As God is my witness, and the United States did not put any pressure on me, I am an al-Qaeda member, and the relationship between me and September 11..." The judge cut him off and ruled the evidence inadmissible. This happened in August 2004, the month after the 9/11 Commission Report was delivered to the White House. (The panel reversed its ruling, but the defendant did not elaborate.)

A glaring example, in a federal appeals case, *Al-Marri v. Wright*, decided (2-1) in 2007, is a panel of judges holding that the government cannot detain indefinitely a "sleeper agent" of al-Qaeda. In granting the detainee's *habeas corpus* petition, the Court ruled that even if the detainee in question were a sleeper agent who had volunteered for a "martyr mission" inside the U.S. and had researched poisonous chemicals, still the government could not hold him indefinitely.[52] The Court majority found that because the defendant was a member of a private group he could not be at war with America—which will be news to terrorists who have openly declared war on us. Worse, the defendant has been fingered by 9/11 mastermind Khalid Sheikh Muhammad as having been sent to the U.S. to launch a follow-on attack.

Also in 2007 came the conviction of American citizen Jose Padilla on conspiracy to commit murder, and other felonies. Padilla was initially detained as an unlawful combatant and held pending trial before a military tribunal, but after Supreme Court rulings made such detention of Padilla problematical the government shifted Padilla to criminal court and tried him. Possessing only circumstantial (indirect) evidence, they

---

52. The Court did not, in fact, accept the government's allegations. But for purposes of deciding the issue it assumed that the government was correct.

managed to win because they offered an application form Padilla had filled out, as evidence of his intent.

While it is encouraging to see al-Qaeda developing bureaucracy and paper trails, the case is a poor model for future prosecutions. International law expert David Rivkin notes that trials entail complex rules as to "chain-of-custody" and preservation of physical evidence. In terms of strict criminal procedure, the former means that the AK-47 seized on the battlefield must be accounted for every step of the way to the courtroom, or else it is inadmissible as evidence against a defendant. Contamination of physical evidence renders it inadmissible. Both failings are highly likely on a battlefield. Indeed, Padilla was transferred to the criminal justice system from military detention as an unlawful combatant because when he was picked up he was not read his Miranda rights. Contrary to public perception, military trials give defendants considerable due process rights. Moreover, while there are procedures for handling classified information, the government at times faces "graymail": being forced to choose between dropping a prosecution or revealing sensitive evidence that may assist America's adversaries. This last concern is real, as Judge Michael Mukasey, who presided over the 1993 trial of the "blind sheik," Omar Abdel Rahman, explains. The government had to turn over a list of unindicted co-conspirators to the defense. The list included Osama bin Laden's name, and ten days later bin Laden found out he was on the list. In the 1996 trial of Ramzi Yousef, the mastermind of the first World Trade Center bombing, information that terrorist cell phones were being monitored came out in court. The terrorists immediately stopped using the phones.

During World War II we held 400,000 opposing soldiers, many of whom were lawful combatants (unlike terrorists), without conceding them rights under American law. No *habeas* petitions were filed. It seems preposterous that today we would give *unlawful* combatants more due process than hitherto we have given *lawful* combatants.

Illustrative of the hyper-legalist frame of mind is this nugget from lawyer Michael Ratner, who represents numerous Gitmo plaintiffs:

The litigation is brutal for [the United States]. It's huge. We have over one hundred lawyers now from big and small firms working to represent these detainees. Every time an attorney goes down there, it makes it much harder [for the U.S. military] to do what they're doing. You can't run an interrogation... with attorneys. What are they going to do now that we're getting court orders to get more lawyers down there?

Claims filed by detainees alleging "mistreatment" include Kuwaitis who have been denied high-speed Internet access to their lawyers, others seeking more exercise and recreation and a detainee alleging medical malpractice.

Meantime, foreign courts are not encouraging either. Dutch judges refused a prosecution request to deprive the Muslim assassin of Dutch film-maker Theo van Gogh of his right to vote and run for elective office. A London judge allowed a Muslim defendant the privilege of being tried before a jury free of Hindus and Jews, on grounds that their presence would have denied the defendant a fair trial. Do you think a white Christian defendant in an English court could get Muslims excluded from his jury on similar grounds?

Once again, turn to Supreme Court Justice Robert H. Jackson, who neatly summed up why the judiciary should leave foreign affairs to the executive.

The President, both as Commander-in-Chief and as the Nation's organ for foreign affairs, has available intelligence services whose reports neither are nor ought to be published to the world. It would be intolerable that courts, without the relevant information, should review and perhaps nullify actions of the executive taken on information properly held secret. Nor can courts sit in camera in order to be taken into executive confidences. But even if courts could require full disclosure, the very nature of executive decisions as to foreign policy is political, not judicial. Such decisions are wholly confided by our Constitution to the political departments of the government, executive and legislative. They are delicate, complex, and involve large elements of prophecy. They are and should be undertaken only by those directly responsible to the people whose welfare they advance or imperil. They are decisions of a kind for which the Judiciary has neither aptitude, facilities nor responsibility and have long been held to belong in the domain of political power not subject to judicial intrusion or inquiry.

Can anything be done to reduce the risk judges pose to our ability to vigorously and effectively prosecute a war of survival? The risk of releasing detainees can be substantial (whether done by judicial intervention or executive discretion). One detainee released from Guantanamo, Abdullah Meshud, returned to the field as a top-level Taliban commander driving the insurgency in Afghanistan and Pakistan. He was killed in 2007 in a raid conducted by Pakistani forces.

Taming the Courts and the Law

In October 2006 the President signed into law the Military Commissions Act (MCA), to address issues raised by the four Supreme Court rulings. The new law preserves some, but not all, of the aggressive interrogation techniques that to date have saved thousands of lives, and defines compliance with Geneva in specific statutory terms, rather than give judges open-ended discretion to fashion standards of humane treatment.[53] Senator Lindsey Graham (R-SC) explained:

> Without congressional authority we run a real risk a federal court will either take over or impede our efforts at Gitmo. We are winning in some courts and losing in others. I firmly believe that the Executive branch will fair [sic] better in court now that Congress has given guidance regarding the operations at Gitmo.

The administration had demonstrated tangible results that saved lives by using its war powers. Also, as Senator Lieberman noted in 2004, instances of documented interrogation abuse—ignoring deliberately false allegations made by terror detainees trained to lie, and spurious allegations by politicized human rights groups—were *less than one-tenth*

---

53. Waterboarding, though used rarely, and discontinued in 2006, has received the most publicity. Former terror-case prosecutor Andrew McCarthy has written that absent precise disclosure of how the technique is used, a definitive assessment cannot be made (a position taken by Judge Mukasey in his confirmation hearing). A 2004 Justice Department memo adopted a 2002 federal court formulation of "severe": "intense, lasting and heinous agony." How "lasting" waterboarding pain can be is unclear.

of one percent out of tens of thousands of interrogations. The CIA's interrogation program targeting top-level terror leaders has identified terror cells, thwarted attacks aimed at military and civilian targets, and uncovered an al-Qaeda anthrax cell within al-Qaeda's bio-weapons program.

Congress further addressed the Supreme Court's concerns about military commissions, by establishing by statute an exclusive review procedure for detainees, to determine if there is a legal basis to hold them. Under current rules each detainee has the right to appear before a Combat Status Review Tribunal, a right that in effect substitutes for *habeas corpus* appeals to the federal courts.

What Congress did recognize by implication is that we should not place rulings that can alter the course of wars in the hands of unelected mandarins for life. Our courts have too many judges who, like Oscar Wilde, can "resist anything but temptation." Thus Congress, in passing the MCA, delivered what former Justice Department counsel John Yoo termed "a stinging rebuke" to the Supreme Court, in several areas. The law strips the courts of *habeas corpus* jurisdiction over alien enemy combatants, a contraction of court jurisdiction not seen since FDR's 1930s New Deal, and the first time *habeas* authority has been limited since the Civil War. It confines the Geneva Convention authority of the Court to *congressionally-defined* war crimes, and directs the Court to ignore foreign or international judicial case law in reviewing the work of military commissions.

The (Judicial) Empire Strikes Back

On June 29, 2007, the Supreme Court reversed its April 2, 2007, *Boumediene v. Bush* ruling and agreed to hear an appeal from 375 detainees at Guantanamo. The Court will review whether Congress has the Constitutional authority to strip the courts of jurisdiction over *habeas corpus* appeals filed by non-resident aliens held abroad. The Supreme Court's action is highly unusual, and suggests that a majority on the Court rejects the idea that Congress can strip the federal courts of *habeas* jurisdiction. At least one human rights organization is planning to flood the courts with lawsuits over Guantanamo, with the objective of paralyzing interrogations there.

The *Boumediene* case, argued December 5, 2007, may well prove an historic landmark in judicial intervention into the national security arena. The fundamental question appellants will raise is whether the Congress may suspend *habeas corpus* for terror war detainees per the U.S. Constitution's Suspension Clause, which provides for suspension of the *habeas corpus* writ only "when in Cases of Rebellion or Invasion the public Safety may require it." This was done by Abraham Lincoln during the Civil War, in 1863.

Astonishingly, briefs supporting the petitioners have been filed by 383 members of the European Parliament, 53 bar associations of the British Commonwealth, and even by the ranking Republican on the Senate Judiciary Committee, Arlen Specter. Having voted for the MCA in 2006, the Senator now asks the Supreme Court to declare the law he voted for to be unconstitutional. The rarity of the Court's action and the intervention of major international groups plus a ranking Senator, and the decision turning on constitutional questions, makes the case—likely to be decided in early 2008—one of immense importance.

What makes this so worrisome is what former CIA Director George Tenet said of information gleaned from the administration's interrogation program:

> I know that this program has saved lives. I know we've disrupted plots... I know this program alone is worth more than the FBI, the Central intelligence Agency, and the National Security Agency put together, have been able to tell us.

Corroborating Tenet's assessment is a September 7, 2007, address by the CIA Director, General Michael V. Hayden, on the value of detainee information. He stated that *more than 70 percent* of the human intelligence that went into the Agency latest National Intelligence Estimate came from detainees.

Consider another example from scholar Benjamin Wittes: American forces capture the wife and children of a high-value al-Qaeda target and interrogate the wife at an air base. After she refuses to divulge her husband's whereabouts, the Americans tell her that she has ten minutes to talk, or else they will put her three sons on a plane immediately and send them to Saudi Arabia, where her husband is a wanted man, and thus the children likely will be killed. She talks. The terror leader is captured and brutally interrogated, to the point where the medical officer warns the commanding officer to stop the beatings "unless you want to take back a corpse." When human rights lawyers learn of this, they file suit in court, but the administration refuses to concede that the courts have any jurisdiction.

This actually is a true story, except that the year was 1946, the plane was a train, the forces were British, the country of extradition was Germany and the target was Rudolf Höss, the commandant of Auschwitz, a star witness at the Nuremburg war crimes tribunal.[54]

There is a more recent example: Ramzi Yousef and a colleague, who were plotting to blow up a dozen jetliners over the Pacific, were arrested by the Philippine security forces. An American confidential source told author Robert Kaplan, "[They] tortured the dog meat out of him. But it wasn't until they threatened to turn him over to the Israeli Mossad that he cracked."

If, as Justice O'Connor says, war doesn't give the President a blank check, neither should the Judiciary have one. The judges have insinuated themselves into questions affecting the conduct of a war, to a degree without prior historical wartime precedent. (Israel is bedeviled by judges as well, as Israel's Supreme Court has several times ordered relocation of segments of Israel's security barrier, after the Palestinians complained.)

An Emerging Danger: High-Profile Trials of Terrorists

There is a fantasy, widely held, that were Osama bin Laden or his top deputy, Ayman al-Zawahiri, captured they should be put on trial. It would, supporters of this idea believe, replicate the dramatic 1961 trial

---

54. The author, Benjamin Wittes, offered no parallel for the Saudi Arabia role.

of Nazi butcher Adolf Eichmann in Israel, when his deeds were revealed in their full genocidal horror.

But times have changed. First, Eichmann was a chillingly bloodless bureaucrat; the top al-Qaeda leaders have charismatic appeal to many in the Islamic world. Second, the audience of the 1962 trial was mostly in America, Europe and Israel—and most of what they watched was on brief news clips or movie newsreels; today there is a global satellite television audience, with many viewers of non-Western orientation. Third, the media were four-square behind Eichmann's conviction; today, media in the West, let alone Arab media like al-Jazeera, will tilt to defendants, and obsess over whether defendants are getting a fair trial. Fourth, Eichmann oversaw the killing of six million Jews; al-Qaeda's leaders would happily replicate the ghastly horror if they could, but to date their toll is far, far lower—well under one million. Finally, Eichmann was hanged; today most Western governments oppose the death penalty, even for mass murderers. With terror chiefs living in prison, if convicted—which is far from certain, given the capriciousness of many courts today—there would be endless efforts to free them by hostage-taking and terror.

Even a non-charismatic defendant can turn the tables in a trial, as did al-Qaeda terrorist Zacarias Moussaoui in the penalty phase of his terror trial, held after the defendant, ignoring advice from his lawyers, entered a guilty plea. The trial was a farce, with the defendant telling the courthouse upon receiving a life sentence and not death: "America you lost! I won." The jury, from the normally sane state of Virginia, had given the admitted terrorist life instead of death by finding as a mitigating circumstance that the defendant had grown up in a home with an abusive father and in a "hostile" country—France.

Terror trials have done even worse damage. In one trial arising out of the first World Trade Center bombing, and related terror plots, despite complex safeguards designed to prevent vital information from being leaked, Bin Laden learned one critical nugget: that the WTC towers had been designed to withstand an accidental crash by a Boeing 707 jetliner. Our adversaries figured out that larger jets, flying at the higher speeds that an intentional terror strike would entail, and angled to hit corners to maximize vertical floor penetration, might bring the buildings down.

The administration plans to try before a special tribunal 14 top al-Qaeda leaders. There is no assurance that further rulings by the Supreme Court might not result in exclusion of evidence they declare was obtained unconstitutionally, which could seriously complicate these prosecutions. Even a *single* acquittal of a senior detainee would be a monumental loss of valuable prestige for the U.S.

In addition, juries are skeptical of charges in complex cases alleging money laundering via Muslim charities that aid terrorist groups, and equally so in any case where free speech can plausibly be raised as a defense, as with academic Islamists. The result has been several acquittals or hung juries in high-profile cases. Overall, the administration since 9/11 has been successful in only 29 percent of terror case criminal prosecutions, compared to its 92 percent success rate in ordinary criminal cases.

Values and Civilizational Survival

According to critics, the Bush administration supposedly has pressed executive wartime power to unprecedented lengths. Yet in 1994, the Clinton administration issued a legal opinion holding that the President "could decline to enforce a statute that he views as unconstitutional." To the extent that the Supreme Court sets itself up as Lawgiver, our future will depend in significant measure on whether judges apply prudential limits to cases, or instead yield to doctrinaire concepts of civil liberties as existing in a permanent state, without regard to conditions of war or peace.

Law is *process-oriented*; national security is *result-oriented*. The 2004 episode when a military tribunal judge cut off a detainee who was about to explain his relationship to the 9/11 attacks encapsulates this profound cultural gap. A legalist mind-set focuses on whether litigants are treated fairly. At times, the law protects them from even self-harm by excluding evidence, even if relevant, if admitting the evidence violates a legal norm (illegally obtained, inflammatory etc.). A national-security mind-set cares not at all for procedural niceties, but only for information pertinent to national security concerns. Anything that anyone with knowledge connected to the 9/11 attacks wishes to say, the national security specialist wishes to hear. Lawyers and judges are trained to think above all of *the integrity of a given proceeding.*

Former Bush Justice Department official Jack Goldsmith, in a book that criticizes the administration for its expansive interpretation of executive power, nonetheless defends its commitment to principles of law:

> Many people think the Bush administration has been indifferent to wartime legal constraints. But *the opposite is true:* the administration has been *strangled by law,* and since September 11, 2001, this war has been *lawyered to death.* The administration has paid attention to law not necessarily because it wanted to, but rather because it had no choice. (Emphasis added.)

Goldsmith goes further, noting

> ... the daily clash inside the Bush administration between fear of another attack, which drives officials into doing whatever they can to prevent it, and the countervailing fear of violating the law, which checks their urge toward prevention.

Goldsmith adds that whereas senior officials act on the assumption that they will be pardoned in event of legal trouble arising out of performance of their government duties, junior members of the bureaucracy fear "retroactive discipline"—application of law *ex post facto* to find legal liability. The result is extreme caution exercised by junior officials. One prominent legal scholar has warned that even a President can be liable for violations of the Geneva Conventions.[55]

In a 1949 free-speech case Justice Jackson wrote a landmark dissent that contains his famous "suicide pact" warning to his judicial brethren:

---

55. The Bush administration withdrew the Clinton administration's acceptance of the 1998 Rome Statute establishing the International Criminal Court (the Senate did not ratify the treaty). The treaty became law in 2002, but the Bush administration has negotiated over 100 bilateral "Article 98 agreements" that exempt U.S. personnel from prosecution by the authorities of such countries.

The choice is not between order and liberty. It is between liberty with order and anarchy without either. There is danger that, if the court does not temper its doctrinaire logic with a little practical wisdom, it will convert the constitutional Bill of Rights into a suicide pact.

If our Constitution is not a suicide pact, neither are international law or our values.

Federal appeals Judge Richard Posner has written:

The Constitution is not different if it is the [P]resident who suspends *habeas corpus* instead of Congress; the [P]resident's suspension of it is unconstitutional, and so justification for it must be sought in a "law of necessity" understood not as a law but as the trumping of law by necessity, as in the case of rebellion or invasion. There can be such a thing as excess of legalism, as President Roosevelt recognized when he violated the Neutrality Act in 1940 by supplying munitions to Great Britain to keep it in the war.

If America's jurists fail to heed such admonitions, Congress must act to remind them. It took the carnage of 9/11 to galvanize the American public to support a major escalation of America's response—from crime-busters to bunker-busters. Having not been hit in six years, the American public feels less of a sense of urgency than right after 9/11, when everyone was certain we would be hit in months, if not weeks or even days.

Above all, decisions that can materially affect the outcome of a war of survival must be commended to, in a democratic republic, the *representative* branches of government. Mandarins answerable only to their own conscience should heed Alexander Hamilton's assurance in Federalist 78 on the limited role to be played in the American republic by the courts:

Whoever attentively considers the different departments of power must perceive, that... the judiciary, from the nature of its functions, will always be the least dangerous to the political rights of the Constitution; because it will be least in a capacity to annoy or injure them.... The judiciary... has no influence over either the sword or the purse; no direction either of the strength or of the wealth of the society; and can take no active resolution whatever. It may truly be said to have neither FORCE nor WILL, but merely judgment....

Hamilton, whose vision of federal power more closely matches today's federal establishment than any of his fellow Framers of the Constitution, said this of national security in Federalist 36:

> And as I know nothing to exempt this portion of the globe from the common calamities that have befallen other parts of it, I acknowledge my aversion to every project that is calculated to disarm the government of a single weapon, which in any possible contingency might be usefully employed for the general defense and security.

Writing in Federalist 41, James Madison, architect of the Bill of Rights, warned:

> The means of security can only be regulated by the means and the danger of attack. They will, in fact, be ever determined by these rules and by no others. It is in vain to oppose constitutional barriers to the impulse of self-preservation. It is worse than in vain; because it plants in the Constitution itself necessary usurpations of power, every precedent of which is a germ of unnecessary and multiplied repetitions.

Actions taken by activist courts have often crossed Hamilton's lines. If anything would seem to activate Hamilton's and Madison's principles, it would be WMD threats from terrorists whose fanaticism and possible anonymity put effective deterrence and retaliation in doubt. And if we accept the maxim that war is too important to be left to the generals, then war is surely too important to be left to the judges.

CHAPTER V

THE VOTE VALUES WAR

EXPORT VOTES OR

IMPORT VIOLENCE

The effort is difficult and the outcome uncertain but I think the effort must be made, because either we free them or they will destroy us.
BERNARD LEWIS, SEPTEMBER 11, 2006, AT A HUDSON
INSTITUTE CONFERENCE ON THE UNITED NATIONS.

In the wake of 9/11 there was a debate within the Bush administration between those fearful that promoting democracy would undermine regime stability, and those who believed that only a transformation of the Mideast from tyranny and terror to some form of representative government could drain the swamp where terrorists breed. Events since then have proven both views flawed. The stability sought by the former helped produce 9/11. But nascent democracies midwifed at the urging of the latter show little promise to date of realizing the hopes of their progenitors.

The late Jeane Kirkpatrick, former U.S. Ambassador to the UN, concisely summed up the problems of attempts to rescue failed states:

[N]o one knows much about how foreign forces can help civil societies or modern states emerge in very different cultures. No one knows how to harmonize hostile elites, end violent behavior, or induce respect for law and restraint in the use of power in another culture without a larger commitment of personnel, money, and time than any president or any administration is prepared to make.

One grave miscalculation, noted by John Agresto, a former university president who spent nearly a year advising the coalition on higher education in Iraq, is our failure to realize the strength of the appeal of religious fanaticism, especially among the young:

> [T]he pre-eminent reality of the day is a religious fanaticism, self-assured, unafraid of death, unafraid of killing, medieval in its outlook and yet armed with powerful modern weaponry, growing in its mass appeal and able to co-opt democratic forms and elections.

Agresto also encountered the conspiratorial way of thinking that makes many Arabs susceptible to entirely fantastical notions about America and the world. One Iraqi told him why Arabs could not have done 9/11: "Absolutely not. Couldn't be. Arabs can't fly planes like that." Of America he said that while blacks are no longer slaves, "[Y]ou could have Arabs for slaves, and I think you flew the planes into the buildings to blame it on the Arabs so you could come here to take Arabs to be slaves in their own houses." President Reagan's speech after the Challenger space shuttle disaster, which memorialized the astronauts for sacrificing their lives in pursuit of scientific knowledge, was, he explained, proof that Reagan blew up the orbiter to gain scientific knowledge.

President Bush first spoke of promoting democracy in the Mideast in 2002, but it was in his Second Inaugural Address that he laid out his vision most clearly:

> At this second gathering, our duties are defined not by the words I use, but by the history we have seen together. For a half century, America defended our own freedom by standing watch on distant borders. After the shipwreck of communism came years of relative quiet, years of repose, years of sabbatical—and then there came a day of fire.
>
> We have seen our vulnerability—and we have seen its deepest source. For as long as whole regions of the world simmer in resentment and tyranny—prone to ideologies that feed hatred and excuse murder—violence will gather, and multiply in destructive power, and cross the most defended borders, and raise a mortal threat. There is only one force of history that can break the reign of hatred and resent-

ment, and expose the pretensions of tyrants, and reward the hopes of the decent and tolerant, and that is the force of human freedom.

We are led, by events and common sense, to one conclusion: The survival of liberty in our land increasingly depends on the success of liberty in other lands. The best hope for peace in our world is the expansion of freedom in all the world.

The President made it clear that instant global democracy is not feasible:

The great objective of ending tyranny is the concentrated work of generations. The difficulty of the task is no excuse for avoiding it. America's influence is not unlimited, but fortunately for the oppressed, America's influence is considerable, and we will use it confidently in freedom's cause.

Norman Podhoretz sums up the Bush Doctrine's four "pillars": promoting democracy as a moral imperative; identifying the lack of democratic rule as a fundamental cause of terrorism; asserting America's right to act in pre-emptive self-defense; and supporting the establishment of a non-terrorist Palestinian state on the West Bank and Gaza.

Agresto states the counter-argument: It may well be that all people yearn to be free themselves, but it is less clear that they equally desire that *others* be free: "If the desire to be free is natural to mankind, so is the desire to oppress or control others. And a ' bad' democracy simply changes the locus of power from one person or group of persons to a popular majority."

President Bush compounded this problem by giving the UN a role in postwar Iraq, stating with regard to UN supervision over the making of a new Iraqi constitution that "they're good at that." The UN pushed proportional representation, thus apportioning power among interest groups, whereas, as Agresto notes, the American Founders created electoral districts and states where those aspiring for power had to represent diverse interests in order to be elected.

The battlefield "vote values" wars are scattered around the globe, ranging from the televised carnage in Iraq to unseen engagements in Somalia and the Philippines. These battles are being fought not for the traditional goals of territorial expansion, political subjugation, religious conversion or economic imperialism. Rather, the United States and its coalition partners (who differ from battlefield to battlefield) are engaging militant Islam's forces in pursuit of victory in the Long War, the triumph of moderate over radical strains of Islam, and the growth of societies where voting rather than violence determines who rules.

The Mideast: Vortex of Violence

Iraq. We had hoped for a World War II-style victory in Iraq, but the "surge" of American troops begun early in 2007 has produced results beyond what anyone, even its authors, thought possible in a few months.[56] Yet despite stunning initial success and the prospect of further success, the situation is extremely fluid, with gains reversible should troops be withdrawn before Iraqi units are fully able to take over the task of providing security for the population. Also, while the ultimate structure of the Iraqi polity is unclear, it is likely to feature strong federalism with a weak center.

Our own worst case is a possible ignominious Vietnam-style defeat. A middling outcome—vastly better than outright defeat—would be a face-saving Korea-style stalemate. Should the surge fully succeed in creating security that makes political reform possible, we might even do better. There are already many common elements between the two wars American-led coalitions have fought in Iraq and the coalition America led in Korea. The diplomatic maneuvering in 1950 resembles that for the Gulf War in 1990 and early 1991, after Saddam invaded and occupied Kuwait in August 1990. In 1950 we went in under the diplomatic aegis of a duly authorized UN "police action," which happened only because Moscow made a one-time mistake of boycotting the Security Council and thus was not present to cast what would have been a certain veto.

---

56. The "surge" plan was devised in late 2006 by American Enterprise Institute scholar Frederick W. Kagan and retired General Jack Keane, a former vice-chief of staff of the U.S. Army. It was implemented in late January 2007, and by June 2007 some 30,000 troops had been positioned inside Iraq, bringing total U.S. troop strength there to 165,000, for a planned surge of 12 to 18 months.

When Saddam invaded Kuwait, he took the world by surprise much as North Korean dictator Kim Il-Sung (father of the present leader) did in 1950. In 1991 the UN response was a coalition under the aegis of an enabling UN resolution, a rare occasion when no permanent member of the UN Security Council cast a veto.[57] The Gulf War was thus, if not formally so named, a "police action" akin to Korea. In 2003 France, having learned from Moscow's blunder, informed the world that even if the U.S. got the required three-fifths majority of the Security Council to authorize UN support for invading Iraq, France would cast its Security Council veto to block approval.

Three military parallels between Iraq 2003 and Korea are haunting. First, just as in 1950 MacArthur's Inchon masterstroke landing got U.S. forces up to the Yalu River at lightning speed, in 2003 General Tommy Franks's cavalry stormed into Baghdad in record time. Second, just as in 1950 China launched a massive counter-attack across the Yalu, which sent American forces reeling all the way back to the Pusan perimeter in the south, in 2003 insurgents launched a major counter-stroke in Iraq, aided by al-Qaeda and pro-Iranian militias backed by Iran. Third, just as the result was protracted stalemate in Korea after victory seemed within the coalition's grasp, in Iraq things hung in the balance once the insurgency gathered steam, with relative stability in most of the country and massive instability in four provinces. Even stalemate in Iraq could have serious consequences. We are still dealing with the consequences of failing to liberate North Korea fifty-plus years ago. Failure to get a better result in Iraq will leave us facing an Iran immensely emboldened by our failure to win and determined to become the region's hegemonic power. Were America's credibility shattered, it could well succeed.

The main factors creating the mess in Iraq were these:

---

57. The five permanent members of the United Nations Security Council are the United States, Great Britain, France, Russia and China; permanent members possess a veto power over Security Council actions. There are ten other council slots, filled on a rotating basis, with slots occupied for two-year terms. The chairmanship of the Council rotates on a monthly basis among the 15 members. The rotating non-permanent members are elected by vote of the UN General Assembly, comprised of all member states.

+ The WMD intelligence fiasco that shredded American international credibility for years to come.

+ The pushing aside of Iraqis in selecting an initial interim government after the fall of Baghdad, thus depriving Iraqis of governance—this despite a coalition of Iraqi exiles prepared to step in.

+ The failure to rapidly stabilize Iraq and pre-empt a large-scale insurgency, due to an astonishing confusion between liberty and anarchy.

+ The failure to confront Iran and Syria immediately upon their intervention, if necessary supplementing warnings with military strikes, when the U.S. was not yet bogged down in Iraq and thus could instill fear.

+ The worldwide display of the gratuitous prisoner abuses at Abu Ghraib.

+ Adopting a national party list system—strongly urged by the UN, no friend of democracy—instead of a winner-take-all local district system, thus giving more power to minority sectarian and pro-terror parties.

+ The defining of elections as ends in themselves, rather than defining *liberal* democracy as our goal—liberty under law.

A complicating operational shortcoming was that of 1,000 U.S. embassy employees in Iraq, there were only 33 Arabic speakers, of whom *six* were fluent in the language. The Defense Intelligence Agency had fewer than ten capable analysts who specialize in the Iraqi insurgency, and these were being rotated to new positions by bureaucratic routine and replaced periodically by novices. Put simply, we lacked enough skilled personnel who could rapidly deal with cultural issues.

The WMD credibility collapse came about in part because the State Department would not agree to base the public diplomatic case for war on anything other than Saddam's WMD. The Defense Department wanted as well to stress Saddam's support for terrorism and his massive human rights abuses. Administration spokesmen kept referring to *stockpiles* of WMD, when what mattered was *capability*. Saddam could have (and surely would have) rapidly re-started his programs after passing inspection. As a result of the WMD fiasco, no claim by U.S. intelligence that Iran is about to cross the nuclear threshold will be deemed credible by much of the world. It should be noted, however, that the failure *vis-à-vis* WMD was *bipartisan*—in the words of arms inspector David Kay in 2004, "We were all wrong." Worse, of 100 Senators, only *six* actually read the 90-page summary of the intelligence assessment, which contained numerous caveats to the overall conclusion.

As for Saddam's support for terror, the Salman Pak air hijacking training facility was well known, as was his support for families of Palestinian suicide bombers. That he met with al-Qaeda operatives was known as well. We did not know what transpired during such sessions, but does anyone think they were discussing the future of classical music? It also was known that Saddam had tried to assassinate former President George H. W. Bush. The administration should have stressed the terror support factor much more.

Great credit for the American foundering in Iraq must go to Iran, which has backed Shia factions and fomented hideous ethnic carnage. It underwrites terrorist operations inside Iraq, trains terrorists at camps in Iran, has provided sophisticated munitions to insurgents that they could not have made themselves, and even increased its operational tempo since talking with the U.S. in May 2007. By August 2007 Iranian-backed insurgents carried out roughly half the attacks against U.S. forces inside Iraq. Iran's potential to cause trouble in Iraq is illustrated perhaps best by the fact that 90 percent of Iraq's population lives within 100 miles of Iran's western border.

We made other mistakes of consequence. We did not shoot looters on sight upon taking Baghdad, when establishing instant order was essential, we confused liberty with anarchy—Iraqis literally vandalized their own country as if it were one giant stolen-car "chop shop" operation, where everything of monetary value was ripped off, stripped down and then either sold for profit or kept for personal use.

In another major mistake, we rejected a six-man Iraqi group, whose membership (two each of Sunni, Shia and Kurds) was established before the war, to place in an interim governing authority. We turned down a pre-war proposal to train 10,000 police to immediately help secure Iraq once the regime was toppled.

We sought unity of command in the form of a MacArthur-style regency—ignoring that Japan was a homogenous society that had been reduced practically to rubble, with no insurgency possible. Better by far was the proposal to name, in parallel with the Coalition Provisional Authority (CPA), a tribal council (akin to the Afghan *loya jirga*), as proposed by then-U.S. Ambassador to Afghanistan (later, envoy to Iraq and after at the UN) Zalmay Khalilzad. Instead the CPA alienated the tribes, who then joined the insurgency. The tribes only re-engaged with us more than three years later. The CPA was given absolute authority, and Ambassador L. Paul Bremer III was given MacArthur's proconsul powers.[58] The result, however unintended, was a Soviet-style central-planning disaster, imposed from inside Baghdad's Green Zone.

Further, we fired too many people and thus we sent thousands of people home without a job and with their guns—a bad combination; a better combination is giving people jobs (a future) and taking away their guns. A perfect illustration of this is that one company, American-Iraqi Solutions Group, as of summer 2007, got 90 percent of its workforce from Sadr City in Baghdad, home of militant Shia militias.

We failed to secure Iraq's energy supplies. Even as the surge showed signs of progress, Baghdad was with electric power but a few hours daily. Insurgent sabotage is rampant, and local gangs divert power so that it stays in the outlying regions, which Saddam deprived of power dur-

---

58. The decision, reportedly, was taken at a May 6, 2003, lunch, after Bremer made a "unity of command" plea to President Bush, who accepted it and announced his decision publicly without troubling to notify, let alone consult, his then National Security Adviser, Condoleezza Rice (later Secretary of State), or Secretary of State, Colin Powell.

ing his rule. Oil and natural gas production is far below targets. Iraq is at least three years and perhaps close to a decade away from being self-sufficient in energy, despite immense oil reserves (second largest on the planet). The sole bright spot is that Western firms think there is oil in Sunni areas, which if found could end the oil revenue disparity that Sunnis deeply resent.

We failed to kill charismatic pro-Iran thug-cleric Moqtada al-Sadr, instead letting him run for office without disarming his militia, thus making him a player in Iraq. We failed in general to disband Iraqi militias. In September 2007 Sadr, having once before pulled his faction out of the governing coalition, did so again. But this time his position was weaker than before the U.S. surge began. While his action may impede rapid political reform at the national level, it isolates Sadr and radical militias.

Finally, and perhaps most astonishingly, we defined holding an election as an end in itself, without regard to how victory was obtained. In the January 2005 Iraqi parliamentary elections Iran pumped $11 million per week to its favored candidates. The CIA proposed putting up $20 million to start, with more to follow if needed, to aid liberal parties. President Bush signed a covert action finding, and congressional leaders were briefed. The project began, only to be halted due to objections that covert influence would compromise the integrity of the election.

That the Iranians were tilting the table surely entitled us to tilt it back to at least level. But we should have tilted it in our favor if possible. Faced with totalitarian adversaries, we should promote liberal democracy, by illiberal means if necessary, as when the CIA funded pro-Western publications in Europe during the Cold War.

We were to repeat the same mistake in Lebanon and in the Palestinian territories. As Natan Sharansky recalled, "I told Bush before and after [the vote] that quick elections cannot replace the democratic process. Elections require a free society. Elections have to be the last step of the democratic process." Thus declining to promote democracy tomorrow everywhere is not hypocrisy; it is elementary common sense and self-preservation.

Sharansky differentiates between "free societies" and "fear societies." He defines a free society as one in which people can express opinions without fear of arrest, imprisonment or physical harm. If a person can walk into the town square and speak freely, the society is a free society. A fear society is composed of a small cadre of true believers, a small group of dissidents, and a large mass of "doublethinkers." Doublethinkers hide their true sentiments, lest they be punished. Thus, outsiders always underestimate the support for freedom on the part of subjects living in a fear society. (Ironically, President Bush expressed admiration for Sharansky's book on democracy, yet failed to follow Sharansky's advice on the proper sequencing of elections.)

The result of this series of major miscalculations was an Iraq that, at the close of 2006, was on the brink of total chaos, a civil "war of all against all," the end result of which would likely have been slaughter on a genocidal scale. Our goal until 2007 was political progress above all, with security rapidly devolved to the Iraqi forces. This gave us the parliamentary elections of 2004 and 2005, plus the Constitution adoption in 2005. But in 2006 al-Qaeda bombed the Golden Mosque at Samarra, sacred to the Shia, and the Shia militia went after the Sunnis. It was only when al-Qaeda overreached that the Sunnis turned to us, just prior to our adopting the surge plan. The terrorist group lost favor with Sunnis due to their brutal rule when they took over villages: forcing inter-tribal marriages, executing children for playing soccer with a U.S. ball, cutting off fingers of smokers, killing families in front of the youngest child, and letting the child live to tell others the grisly tale.

The surge represents a fundamental shift in strategy, from a failed policy of trying to kill insurgents to one of protecting the local population, village by village, district by district, enclave by enclave. The problem, and the solution with the best chance of prevailing, has been explained by David Kilcullen, Senior Counterinsurgency Adviser to the Multi-National Force in Iraq. A counter-insurgency clears not physical terrain but "human terrain." It focuses less on killing insurgents than in getting them to vacate each area for enough time so that stable political, economic and security structures can be built. Sustained success will prevent the insurgents from being able to return. Kilcullen notes that in insurgencies the enemy is fluid while the population is fixed, and thus a killing strategy fails if the enemy "goes to ground." But if we stabilize and secure the population, "we can asphyxiate [the enemy] by cutting him off from the people. And he can't just 'go quiet' to avoid that threat. He either has to stand and fight or risk permanent marginalization."

Kilcullen further explains that the challenge in Iraq (and, to some degree, also in Afghanistan) differs from the classic counterinsurgencies of the twentieth century, forcing the military to adjust on the fly. First, classic insurgencies aimed to overthrow a state and replace it with a new regime. But many of the terrorist groups in Iraq have no political agenda other than to destroy the nascent Iraqi democracy. Second, classic insurgencies were initiated by the insurgents, but today governments also initiate action. Third, whereas the classic insurgent was the agent of revolutionary change, today, as in Iraq, revolutionary change is represented by the government. Fourth, sanctuary in a classic insurgency was purely geographic, within a state and perhaps across the border of neighboring states. Today, the Internet and globalization of media have created what Kilcullen calls a "virtual sanctuary." Recruitment, communication, operational advice, financial assistance and sharing of intelligence are being accomplished via the Internet's jihadist websites. Fifth, instead of a static contest between one or more unified guerilla movements against a state, today we see myriad splinter groups with diverse objectives, by instant networking "creating a self-synchronizing swarm of independent, coordinating cells," and thus confronting the government with continually morphing adversaries. Finally, rather than seek to achieve a practical objective—to *do* something, the new insurgents often seek to *be* something—a *mujahid* ("God's warrior"). All this, the author writes, makes counterinsurgencies more unpredictable, and creates via media an environment where *perception* of who wins a battle trumps who actually wins. One iconic image can be exploited to change a result.[59] Above all, Kilcullen maintains that there is no such thing as a single counterinsurgency model; each one stands on its particular facts and evolves unpredictably.

For the foreseeable future we will have to put stability over democracy as an interim goal. The mismatch between resources and strategic goals meant that America's goals had to be recalibrated to fit a rapidly changing environment. Preventing Iraq from becoming a terror-incubating failed state is now the top priority. Critical to this is completing the expulsion of foreign fighters, who, according to the military, carry out 80 to 90 percent of all suicide bomb attacks inside Iraq. In the summer of 2007 U.S. forces turned increasing attention to fighting Iran-backed units, including Iran's elite forces, who, according to General David Petraeus, aim to establish Hezbollah-style units to continue operations against Iraq and Coalition forces.

Military analyst Anthony Cordesman warns that Iraq's grave problems should not be underestimated. Its government can provide for perhaps a population of 16 to 17 million, not the current 27.5 million number. Iraq's oil revenues were, in constant 2006 dollars, $55.3 billion in 1980 (when Saddam Hussein launched the ruinous Iraq-Iran War that September) and at most an estimated $22.9 billion in 2007. Oil revenues today, at 41 percent of 1980's figure, must support a population that has increased 63 percent since then. The U.S. has sent $2.7 billion in oil industry aid since 2003, but the industry remains worse off today.

If somehow the country descends after the surge into total civil war the U.S. should not abandon its truest friends in Iraq, the Kurds. According to a 2005 poll, 98 percent of Iraq's four million Kurds desire independent status. The major sticking point is Kirkuk, which lies in oil-

---

59. Kilcullen notes that both of these factors greatly influenced Vietnam. The January 1968 "Tet" offensive launched by the North was a battlefield disaster, but footage of Viet Cong sappers at the gates of the U.S. Embassy in Saigon fueled public perception that the North had won. A photo of a South Vietnamese police chief ostensibly executing a prisoner, and one of a naked child running down the road screaming after a U.S. napalm bomb burned her, further turned American elites irrevocably against the war.

fields just outside the official boundary lines of Iraqi Kurdistan, and has a substantial Turcoman population whose ethnic brethren in Turkey are opposed to the city's incorporation into an independent Kurdistan.

Columnist-author Thomas Friedman sees the Kurdish renaissance since 1991 as a model for all of Iraq, in that it creates a reasonably free, democratic state with no territorial designs on its neighbors (including Turkey): "Iraq's only hope is radical federalism.... with Baghdad serving as an A.T.M." The next opportunity for change at the top comes when in 2009 parliamentary elections are held; these may take place in a higher-trust climate than did the 2005 elections, largely boycotted by Sunnis. The felicitous result could well be politicians who are more moderate and thus more able to compromise. Ambassador Ryan Crocker testified to Congress that Iraqi politicians in Baghdad are becoming increasingly receptive to devolution of political power and a loose federal structure.

In Iraq, all options are high-risk, with a significant chance of failure. Worst of all would be the disastrous consequences of America suffering a Vietnam-like defeat that surely would result from our rapid, total withdrawal. Iran would reign pre-eminent in the region, and our Mideast "allies" would immediately recalibrate their policy to take note of the power shift. A Mideast nuclear arms race would go into high gear, with potentially ghastly consequences for the future of an already staggeringly violent region. In all, defeat in Iraq would be far worse than defeat in Vietnam. We lost in Vietnam to a power on the wane; in Iraq we would lose to a power—militant Islam—on the rise. Pakistan, a nuclear-armed Muslim country with many radical forces, would be in greater danger of falling to Islamist factions, because a U.S. defeat in Iraq would discredit America as a strong ally.

Retreat is what al-Qaeda, just like earlier Mideast adversaries, counts on. In 1975, Syrian President Hafez al-Assad (father of the current dictator) told Secretary of State Henry Kissinger: "You've betrayed Vietnam, someday you'll sell out Taiwan and we'll be around when you get tired of Israel." Thirty years later Al-Qaeda number two Ayman al-Zawahiri (who may be operational chief as well) wrote the following in his 2005 letter to al-Zarqawi, in which he cited "the aftermath of the collapse of American power in Vietnam and how they ran and left their agents" and added that "[the Americans] know better than others that there is no hope in victory. The Vietnam specter is closing every outlet."

In December 2004 Osama bin Laden said this about the importance of the battle for Iraq's future:

> I now address my speech to the whole of the Islamic nation: Listen and understand. The issue is big and the misfortune is momentous. The most important and serious issue today for the whole world is this Third World War, which the Crusader-Zionist coalition began against the Islamic nation. It is raging in the land of the two rivers. The world's millstone and pillar is in Baghdad, the capital of the caliphate. The whole world is watching this war and the two adversaries; the Islamic nation, on the one hand, and the United States and its allies on the other. It is either victory and glory or misery and humiliation. The nation today has a very rare opportunity to come out of the subservience and enslavement to the West and to smash the chains with which the Crusaders have fettered it.

But let the 9/11 Commission have the last word on the stakes in Iraq: Noting the twenty-first century trend toward "remote regions and failing states" the panel warned: "If, for example, Iraq becomes a failed state, it will go to the top of the list of places that are breeding grounds for attacks against Americans at home."

Lebanon. Israel failed to win decisively against Hezbollah.[60] This deprived it of its aura of martial invincibility, strengthened Iran and weak-

---

60. Hezbollah, which means "Party of God," was founded in 1982, after Israel defeated the Palestine Liberation Organization (PLO), the terrorist group co-founded by, and headed by, until his 2004 death, Yasser Arafat. Israel's victory in Lebanon led to Arafat and the PLO being expelled from that country, to exile in Tunisia, where they remained until inept American diplomacy after the Gulf War, compounded by even more inept Israeli diplomacy, resuscitated Arafat's group and delivered the Palestinians to his dictatorial, corrupt clutches. America, smitten by the idea that the Israel-Palestine problem was ripe for solution after the Gulf War, shoved Israel into the 1991 Madrid Conference with Yasser Arafat's PLO— *despite the fact that Arafat had backed Saddam during the Gulf War.* Israeli leaders Yitzhak Rabin and Shimon Peres then negotiated the disastrous Oslo Accords with the PLO, under which Israel surrendered land for lies, thus leading to the parlous situation when in late 2000 Arafat launched the suicide bomber campaign in an effort to bring Israel, once and for all, to its knees. It failed, in part because of Israel's Ariel Sharon, who came to power in 2001,

ened Israel and the United States. A case can be made—one that does not entirely convince, but should be presented here—that Hezbollah was defeated because it lost a few hundred top-flight fighters; its physical infrastructure was badly damaged; and that the Lebanese knew that Israel did in fact limit infrastructure damage, and that Hezbollah encouraged it. Lebanon's March 14 Movement (the pro-democracy movement started one month after the February 14, 2005, assassination of political leader Rafik Hariri) recovered momentum at the expense of Hezbollah. The UN force will serve as a buffer and prevent re-establishment of Hezbollah's positions on the Israeli border. Finally, Sheikh Nasrallah's own August 27 statement was hardly a victory cry. "We did not think, even one percent, that the capture [of two Israeli soldiers] would lead to a war at this time and of this magnitude," he said. "You ask me, if I had known on July 11... that the operation would lead to such a war, would I do it? I say no, absolutely not."

But the more credible assessment is that Israel's aura of invincibility and martial ferocity was shattered. What do Iran's mullahs make of a country that announces three days ahead that a certain village will be targeted, so that civilians can leave, knowing that the military utility of such a strike is surely attenuated by giving such advance notice?

Israel's abortive thrust against Hezbollah also helps Iran. It greatly enhanced the prestige of terror groups and their sponsors, Syria and Iran. It energized Islamofascists all around the globe. It also demoralized Arab countries that backed the U.S. and Israel in the hope that Iran could be contained. It dimmed hopes for a democratic Lebanon raised by the 2005 Cedar Revolution by strengthening Hezbollah's grip on the Lebanese government. It gave the UN—endemically hostile to Israel and world Jewry—a stronger hand in the Middle East. And it reduced

---

after the Palestinians spurned the absurdly generous offer Israel made in August 2000. In September 2000 the PLO used a visit by Sharon to Temple Mount—negotiated in advance with the Palestinians—to launch an all-out assault on Israel. Part of the motivation for the campaign was Barak's May 2000 decision to unilaterally withdraw from southern Lebanon, which convinced Arafat that Israel was on the run, and thus ripe for the taking.

the already slim chance that Iran can be induced by diplomatic pressure to curtail its quest for operational nuclear weapon capability.

Lebanon's hopes lie in the hands of the U.S., the UN and France, plus Arab states fearful of Iran. Israel's military credibility is severely damaged. Hezbollah proved that terrorists embedded in civilian populations can sufficiently constrain military operations of Western nations so as to deny the West outright military victory. Actually, four percent of Lebanese territory remains in Syrian hands, a creeping annexation made despite UN "supervision" of the area.[61] Worse, Iran is backing land purchases aimed at driving out non-Shia from the south of Lebanon, so as to create a contiguous rump state for Hezbollah.

We must find a way (if possible) to enforce Resolutions 1559 (Lebanon independence) and 1701 (disarm Hezbollah), despite the manifest lack of intention of the UN and many member states to allow that to happen. Pressure must be put on Syria to force it to allow constructive change in Lebanon.

Yet Israel's defeat led to one unintended, felicitous development: Sunni Arab states—all Arab countries save Syria, Lebanon and Oman (a Gulf Coast state)—have turned to the United States and Israel, as a joint bulwark against a rising radical Shia Iran. Many Sunni Arab leaders fear Iran more than they dislike America, for America may keep them in power.

The Palestinians. Despite the 2007 Mecca pact between Hamas and Fatah, the main contending factions, the conflict remains not resolvable anytime soon, if ever, because it is not a mere border dispute. It is *existential*, and despite ambiguous declarations from Fatah leaders about co-existing with Israel, there is no serious prospect that Hamas would accept this, even if (against all odds) Fatah somehow did so. Any attempt by Fatah to make peace with Israel would re-ignite civil war. Despite massive foreign aid—$7 billion in all—the Palestinian entity remains

---

61. The four percent sliver is the equivalent of Arizona in terms of the U.S. continental land mass. By contrast, the Shebaa Farms area that Syria claims (without merit) from Israel is 11 square miles.

a failed terrorist proto-state. Aid has even *increased* since explicitly terrorist Hamas won the 2006 elections, to $300 *per capita* in 2006, seven
times the per capita aid to sub-Saharan Africa. At close to $2,000 *per
capita* total aid over the years, aid to the Palestinians is several times the
per capita aid given Europe under the Marshall Plan. Would that the
Mideast investment had yielded comparable results.

The Arab League's Beirut Declaration of 2002 ends the state of war
and establishes normal relations with Israel (which implies recognition
of its existence), only if Israel surrenders all gains won in 1967 (including the Jewish Quarter of Jerusalem's Old City) and allows Palestinians
to return to Israel, thereby creating an Arab majority inside the Jewish
state. Even Israel's celebrated peace treaties with Egypt and Jordan do
not create anything close to true peace. In both Arab countries there
is massive public agitation against Jews and the idea of a Jewish state.
The two Arab states who have signed peace accords with Israel formally
have recognized Israel's status, but when they agitate their populations
to continue to hate the Jews and reject the idea of Israel, they wage, in
effect, a Cold War. It is one-sided. Israel declines to reciprocate. The Palestinian conflict remains hot. In the first two years since Israel vacated
Gaza in August 2005, the Palestinians fired 1,964 rockets into Israel.
"Land for rockets" is an odd way to make peace.

In summary, no one wins points in the Mideast for meaning well
and failing. We would become the famous "weak horse" that Osama
bin Laden saw when we retreated in the 1990s; and the radical Islamic
forces, not just in the Mideast but worldwide, would become a highly
energized "strong horse."

President Bush has at least separated his peace initiative from prior
attempts, by insisting that Palestinians actually "walk the walk": arrest
terrorists, dismantle their infrastructure, turn in illegal weapons, end
attacks against Israel, free hostages and end corruption. Perhaps more
significantly, President Bush emphasized the American commitment
to "the security of Israel as a Jewish state and homeland for the Jewish
people," a clear repudiation of a "right of return" that would enable Arab

refugees to flood Israel and set the stage for a demographic takeover of Israel. Asking Palestinians to choose between "a future of decency and hope" or one of "terror and death" the President quoted a 16-year-old Palestinian girl who told a reporter in Gaza City: "The gunmen want to destroy the culture of our fathers and grandfathers. We will not allow them to do it. I'm saying it's enough killing. Enough." Yet her voice may be one in a vast wilderness. A 2007 poll showed some nine out of ten Palestinians between ages 18 and 25 rejecting a right to exist for Israel. The airing of Walt Disney cartoon characters being murdered by Israelis has further poisoned the minds of Palestinian children. The effect of Palestinian dictatorial rule stands in stark contrast to that of Israeli administration of the territories. In 1996 a poll showed 78 percent of Palestinians giving Israel a favorable rating. Under Israeli rule Palestinian life expectancy rose from 47 to 70.

Any chance—an extreme long-shot at best—of a final peace settlement must deal with the harsh facts of geography. Israel's 6.3 million people (20 percent are Israeli Arabs) live on 8,000 square miles, with its "waist" (between Jerusalem and Tel Aviv) only nine miles wide. Israel's main airport is but three miles from Palestinian rocket launchers. The total Palestinian population is about 3.7 million, of which 1.4 million live in Gaza's roughly 160 square miles and 2.3 million live on the West Bank's 2,500 square miles. Adding the Israeli Arab population to the numbers of Palestinians yields about five million Arabs and five million Jews living west of the Jordan River. About 15 percent of West Bank territory claimed by the Palestinians lies on Israel's side of its 425-mile security fence. Some 270,000 Jews live on the West Bank settlements, and another 180,000 live in East Jerusalem. Some 60 percent of Israel's water crosses the West Bank on its way into Israel, and if Israel withdraws would fall under Arab suzerainty.

It strains credulity to believe that a single all-purpose settlement can be reached. What little prospect there is lies in breaking down the problem into smaller units. Rather than think in terms of a single Palestinian state, which entails creating a land bridge linking Gaza and the West

Bank, one idea that has surfaced is a two-state Palestinian solution, with Gaza linked closely to Egypt, and the West Bank population linked, as it was for decades, to Jordan. The populations of Gaza and the West Bank differ: 84 percent of residents in Gaza are "refugees"—a designation that for the Palestinians alone, the UN defines to include descendants of those displaced. Some 50 percent still live in camps, with 35 percent unemployed; on the West Bank only 26 percent are "refugees" and 18 percent are unemployed. Standing alone or in federation with Jordan, perhaps the West Bank is viable. Why tie its fate to that of Gaza?

Thus, creating secure areas within the West Bank and pushing out terror and corruption offer perhaps the best chance for some progress. Top-down governance has been an abject failure in the Palestinian territories, leading first to Arafat's dictatorship and then to an elected terrorist government. Building small secure areas enables progress metrics to be applied: more progress, more territory, but no territory without progress first. Given the hyper-bellicized state of Palestinian society, with weak, venal and terrorist leaders, peace is an unlikely prospect.

But given international political pressure pushing the Arab-Israeli dispute to the forefront of Mideast affairs, something different than the current diplomatic bootstrap policy—asking Israel to cede territory to the Palestinians to end a terror campaign whose ending is the necessary precondition for peace—should be tried. Such a strategy might work were the struggle seen by the Palestinians as truly territorial, rather than as the existential one they continue to pursue—seeking to destroy the State of Israel. Natan Sharansky believes that separating the Palestinian people from their rulers would quickly yield positive results. For this to happen the terror apparatus—Hamas, Fatah, and Hezbollah—will have to be dismantled.

The wrong move is to back Fatah, unless it ends terror, a prospect that appears chimerical. This echoes what has been done before, to ill effect. One senior Fatah operative told a reporter that U.S. training given to Fatah's elite Force 17 unit helped the Palestinian assault launched against Israel in September 2000 (after Yasser Arafat spurned a peace offer at Camp David). When Hamas seized control of Gaza in 2005 it captured Fatah documents with U.S. intelligence secrets—documents and spy technology. The U.S. government says nothing fundamental was compromised, but whatever Hamas learned will be shared with every radical Islamist group around the globe.

Although President Bush has tried to hold Palestinians accountable for terror, and to make democracy a goal, the Mideast "peace process" remains the paradigm for the region, despite its utter failure in the Palestinian territories. Its twin trumpeted successes, the Egyptian and Jordanian Accords, are explicable as much by Israel's military superiority as by treaties signed.[62]

Asia and Elsewhere: Will the Periphery Be Sucked Into the Mideast Vortex?

Afghanistan. Al-Qaeda's home base in Afghanistan was America's first post-9/11 target, but the organization is truly global. By 2007 arrests of al-Qaeda suspects had been made in 102 countries. Osama bin Laden prepared for battle by retiring to his home labyrinth of mountain caves in the Afghan highlands, awaiting a protracted replay of the Soviet debacle. But America fared better than earlier invaders. Bin Laden found himself on the receiving end of an American blitzkrieg, with thermobaric weapons (which literally ignite the air around a target and suck out the oxygen) torching cave redoubts while U.S. special ops riders on horseback with laptops and laser pointers directed Afghan irregulars and American aviators. Soviet Russia's ten-year Vietnam became America's few-months turkey-shoot. Three years later, in October 2004, Afghans marched to the polls in impressive numbers, defying death threats, and democratically elected a moderate regime.

---

62. As this book went to press, a 49-nation conference on Arab-Israeli issues was hosted by the U.S. at Annapolis, Maryland. The risk to Israel—and the U.S.—is that Israel makes irrevocable, tangible concessions in return for revocable, intangible promises. In 1993 Israel traded "land for lies" at Oslo; in 2000 Israel traded land for suicide bombers in vacating Lebanon; in 2005 Israel traded "land for rockets" in vacating Gaza. What might be next?

Then the Taliban struck back. Hamid Karzai's government controls the cities, but warlords control the countryside. Despite defeat of the Taliban and an election, many Afghans cling to traditional ways. Working to undermine the U.S. position in Afghanistan are several factors. Pakistan's 12,000 *madrassas* mint new terrorists continuously. This is especially alarming in a country with 80 percent illiteracy. Afghanistan's opium poppy crop jumped 50 percent in 2005 to a record 6,000 tons, and supplies 95 percent of Europe's opium demand. In 2006 it soared again, to 8,200 tons, valued at $3 billion, but growth became more concentrated as central and north provinces were cleaned. Columnist Anne Applebaum suggests we allow poppy farming and direct the produce to lawful medical uses, rather than attempt to eradicate the crop. Another columnist reports that the drug war has become the Taliban's most effective recruiter. USAID states that poppy cultivation is *seventy times* more lucrative than farming wheat. Investing $3 billion to buy up the crop and pay farmers each year not to grow it involves an annual investment equal to an additional *one-tenth of one percent* of America's annual budget.

We can rely on low-profile activities, including paying generous bribes to warlords, to secure more peaceful conditions. The big challenge is to find a long-term economic solution that undercuts incentives to produce drugs. If we decide we will not buy up the opium crop, we can permit its export for lawful medical uses. As General David Petraeus has put it: "Money is a weapon."

On the bright side, we have invested $8.6 billion for a two-year doubling of the Afghan army, from 32,000 to 70,000. Increased Army pay has cut 2005's desertion rate of 25 percent to ten percent in 2006. American troop strength there was boosted from 18,000 to 24,000 in 2006. In February 2007 President Bush proclaimed his commitment to provide substantial continuing aid, including an additional $3 billion in non-military aid: increasing national police by end-2008 from 61,000 to 82,000; adding 1,000 miles to the 4,000 miles of roads so far built; offering credit, seeds and fertilizer in order for poppy farmers to switch to other crops (thus denying drug revenues to the Taliban); training judges and prosecutors and establishing judicial facilities.

Key metrics already show substantial improvement in Afghanistan since liberation from the Taliban. By 2007 the Afghan economy had doubled, and attracted $800 million in foreign investment. Children attending school increased from 900,000 (all males) to five million (1.8 million girls). The U.S. has built 681 health clinics, thus enabling 80 percent of Afghans to receive health care. Women are advancing in government, too; there are 91 women serving in the Afghan Parliament, and the nation's first female provincial governor was appointed by President Karzai. Afghans living in cities may well be safer than they would be living in certain U.S. cities. In Khost, a city roughly the size of Detroit (one million), 58 people were killed in 2006 by IEDs. In Detroit, 373 people were murdered in 2006.

The enemy's strategy is encapsulated in quotes. The Taliban say, "The Americans may have all the wristwatches, but we have all the time." And Taliban leader Mullah Omar said in 2002:

> I am considering two promises. One is the promise of God, the other of Bush. The promise of God is that my land is vast. If you start a journey on God's path, you can reside anywhere and will be protected. The promise of Bush is that there is no place on Earth where you can hide that I cannot find you. We will see which promise is fulfilled.

We need not accept Mullah Omar's assessment. Polls show that only seven percent of Afghans support the Taliban, versus 75 percent having a positive view of America. With 77 percent of Afghans supporting democracy and 63 percent thinking the country is moving in the right direction (though down from 83 percent a year earlier), there is much to celebrate. But reconstruction efforts get negative marks from 58 percent.

It would be a shame to squander that goodwill by grossly under-investing in a winnable conflict, when a piddling fraction of what we spend in Iraq, an amount little more than a rounding error in our gargantuan federal budget, could significantly improve our chances of prevailing.

Pakistan. Especially dangerous is the situation in Pakistan, a nuclear-armed Islamic state with a significant Islamist radical presence. President Musharraf is a reluctant and part-time ally who made a pact with Islamists not to aggressively push the search for al-Qaeda in Waziristan, the region of Pakistan that abuts Afghanistan, where the writ of law has never fully run. Under the Waziristan Accord, signed September 5, 2006, al-Qaeda and Taliban fighters received a safe haven. Since then attacks in Afghanistan and Pakistan have increased several-fold. An estimated 40,000 Taliban fighters operate in Waziristan and neighboring regions, despite $11 billion in U.S. aid sent Pakistan since 2001. In the event, the Waziristan Accord collapsed in July 2007, another failed attempt to appease terrorists. In September 2007 the Taliban and al-Qaeda declared war on Pakistan's government.

Given that Pakistan is armed with nuclear weapons (by one estimate, 55 to 115 warheads), it is obviously unthinkable to push for an election that hands the country over to Islamist militants, but fortunately Islamists represent perhaps only 11 percent of the electorate. The administration thus astutely seized the opportunity to press for Benazir Bhutto, twice Prime Minister until ousted in 1999 and forced to flee the country to avoid prosecution on corruption charges, to return to Pakistan and run for the ceremonial post of President. By not putting all our eggs in one basket (Musharraf) the U.S. is well positioned for constructive change. Any unease Bhutto might have entertained in taking on the Islamists surely was dispelled by their near-miss assassination attempt that greeted her October 2007 return to Pakistan. Bhutto may not be as pro-Western as she claims, but she is not Islamist.

The administration also deserves credit for brokering a first-ever cross-border *loya jirga* (tribal council) between Afghan and Pakistani tribes, with Musharraf and Afghan President Karzai attending. The successful August 2007 meeting lasted four days, and brought together over 600 tribal leaders.

President Musharraf says that of 160 million Pakistani Muslims, a full one percent—1.6 million—are violent extremists. Musharraf is thus reluctant to move directly against Islamofascists, even turning a blind eye to honor-killings of Pakistani women. The country as a whole is anti-American, but terror attacks by al-Qaeda and Taliban have killed Pakistanis, and consequently support for suicide bombing and Islamist terror in general has dropped sharply. As with Iraq and elsewhere, when Islamist terror strikes home, the locals change their minds. Another factor in anti-American attitudes, cited by Benazir Bhutto, is the stop-go pattern of U.S. aid to Pakistan: up in the 1960s, when Pakistan aided U.S. Cold War efforts, including U-2 overflights of Russia and the 1971 opening to China; down in the 1970s, after the India-Pakistan War (in which East Pakistan split off from the Western half and became Bangladesh); up in the 1980s when Pakistan was an indispensable staging base for channeling aid to Afghans fighting the Soviet invaders; down in the 1990s when the Soviets had left Afghanistan, and Pakistan ran afoul of U.S. anti-proliferation policy; and up since 9/11, with $11 billion in aid sent there by the U.S. A crucial period was during the 1970s and 1980s, as Pakistan developed into a strongly Islamic state. In 1971 there were 900 *madrassas* in all Pakistan; by 1988 there were 8,000 official religious schools, plus 25,000 unregistered ones.

The sensitivity of hunting down al-Qaeda leaders in Pakistan, without Pakistani permission, caused the U.S. to stand down in 2005 after "high confidence" intelligence suggested that al-Qaeda number two Ayman al-Zawahiri was to attend a meeting of al-Qaeda leaders in tribal areas. The Pentagon feared that sending hundreds of troops into Pakistan could jeopardize relations with Pakistan and ignite anti-American, pro-Islamist sentiment. In 2006 an airstrike aimed at taking out Zawahiri hit a place where he was supposed to be, but the intelligence proved faulty.

Intelligence is *never* airtight. Witness the March 2003 Dora Farms strike aiming at Saddam at the start of the Iraq War, that destroyed the wrong site. That risk was worth taking, as the goodwill of the Iraqi government we were preparing to overthrow was not an issue. One suggestion is to turn such operations over to the CIA, which has had some success in recent years with special operations, notably in Afghanistan in 2001. Small covert operations are more likely to stay below the radar screen, and thus are politically preferable. Assassinations are a more discriminate way to target leaders while minimizing collateral casualties, essential to keep local goodwill.

In November 2007, President Musharraf declared a state of emergency, packed the Supreme Court with friendly judges, and postponed the January 2008 election. Thousands of protestors took to the streets, as thousands of regime opponents were arrested—ominously, they were pro-democracy opponents, and not Islamist supporters. Ms. Bhutto was briefly placed under house arrest. Strong American pressure induced Musharraf to restore the scheduled election date and to free Ms Bhutto. Pakistan will remain a fluid, volatile environment for some time, with many possible outcomes, from hostile Islamist dictatorship to a pro-U.S. democracy (and many other results in between). The administration wisely declined to cut off the $150 million monthly stipend it has given Pakistan since 9/11, as that would very likely backfire. Patient diplomacy behind the scenes may yield positive results, ideally, a democratic ally that fights Islamists and not its democratic opponents.

Elsewhere. Terror havens in places like Sudan, Somalia and the Philippines cannot be ignored. Low-profile operations there can be conducted with minimal manpower, firepower and media scrutiny, leveraging the power of local allies (most notably, Australia and Japan). In 2007 the leader of Abu Sayyaf, the main Islamist terror group in the Philippines, was captured, and the estimated 2,000 fighters at his disposal have been reduced to a few hundred. Also in 2007 the leader of Jemaah al-Islamiyeh ("Islamic Group") was captured in Indonesia. Indonesia's Islamic tradition is a moderate one, based upon Sufism, an eclectic, mystic branch of Islam that is highly tolerant of other faiths; radical Islam began to gain a foothold in the 1970s, but Indonesia made the transition to democracy in 1998 and is now the world's third largest democracy, as well as the most populous Muslim nation (200 million Muslims out of

235 million total) and the fourth-ranked in country population. Success there is a vital element in countering Islamist terror in Asia.

The success of Ethiopian forces, working in tandem with American special operations in the last days of 2006, drove the Islamic Courts Union, an al-Qaeda affiliate, out of Mogadishu (Somalia's capital). Preventing a retaliatory insurgency and establishing a stable government are the task list of the victors. Terrorist affiliates of al-Qaeda are increasingly active in Morocco and Tunisia, moderate Islamic states whose loss would give militant Islam significant victories at the western tip of the great crescent of Islamic communities that stretches from Southeast Asia through the Mideast into Africa.

Another potential Asia terror threat is that posed by the Uighurs, Islamic people living under Chinese rule in a region (Xinjiang) that covers one-sixth of China's vast area and holds major oil and mineral deposits.

In South America, the chief threat is Venezuelan dictator Hugo Chavez, whose vast oil wealth makes his collaboration with al-Qaeda, coupled with his evident desire to emulate Fidel Castro, a menace to the region. Chavez is stirring unrest in several Central and South American countries, including Nicaragua, Ecuador, Bolivia and Argentina. But Venezuelan voters have dimmed Chavez's star by rejecting his bid to amend the constitution, so he could run indefinitely.

Mismatching Resources and Strategy

The common denominator in battlefield shifts is probable acceptance of middling—in place of ideal—outcomes. In Iraq, our reach exceeded our grasp—partly due to failure to invest adequate resources, and partly due to failure to conduct operations with sufficient—but highly discriminate—ruthlessness. *We must above all seek outcomes that do not amount to total defeat.* The consequences of a perceived total defeat would be devastating. An energized radical Islamic community thus inspired would mount more deadly attacks against a West they see as in retreat.

Would the Mideast be more stable today, and the U.S. making greater progress against al-Qaeda, had George Bush, Tony Blair and John Howard (Australia's Prime Minster) left Saddam in power? Critics say yes. Saddam, they assert, could have been contained. But once the UN's Hans Blix had finished inspection and found nothing, Saddam would have slipped the sanctions regime entirely. He could have reconstituted his WMD programs, restarted production of anthrax within a few weeks, and restarted other WMD programs in short order. Saddam would have been able to continue to kill Iraqis (having killed hundreds of thousands during his reign, not to speak of launching several wars), and to send $25,000 payments to families of Palestinian suicide bombers. Freed from sanctions, with no plausible prospect of their resumption, Saddam would have been at liberty to expand his support for terrorism.

The Democracy Project Now

Thus the overall Mideast picture nearly five years after Saddam's fall is a shaky Iraqi government whose legislature is infested with terrorist parties and corruption; a Lebanese elected government held hostage by one of the world's worst terrorist groups, Iran-backed Hezbollah (which is also aided by Syria); and an explicitly terrorist Palestinian elected government in Gaza. In all, not a pretty picture for President Bush's 2002 pro-democracy initiative. Yet there is much good news in places where America's role was minimal, with Ukraine's 2004 Orange Revolution and Georgia's 2003 Rose Revolution. Georgian GDP was $3 billion in 2002, is $8 billion in 2007 and is expected to double again in three years. It is led by ardently pro-U.S. Mikheil Saakashvili, who has committed 2,000 Georgian troops to fight in Iraq. But both are shaky.

In Iraq and elsewhere, terrorist parties were not made to disarm as a condition of participation in the legitimating process of electoral politics—*bullets or ballots, but not both, should be our rule.* Most dispiriting of all, the Arab world may prove—at least, for some time still to come—the dismal exception to the universalist proposition advanced by Jefferson in the Declaration of Independence. While Arabs are not intrinsically less capable than others of embracing democracy, many Arab societies may be too fractured to take the medicine of self-rule for the foreseeable future.

The President's Mideast democracy vision had plausible grounding. Democracy had spread among many countries historically undemocratic: in Latin America, Asia, Eastern Europe, Russia, and even a few spots in Africa. About one-third of the Islamic world's 1.3 billion people live in societies featuring some form of democracy, including Indonesia. These include a minority in India larger than all Muslim country populations save for that in Indonesia; and Turkey. Immediately after the 9/11 attacks, more than one million Iranians turned out to protest Iran's Islamofascist misrule.

So the assumption was made that Muslim countries should be next in line. And 9/11 had shown that the order of tyrannies in the Mideast produced not "stability," but transnational terror funded by petrodollars. Democracy promoters believed that even if Islamofascists triumphed in fair elections they would face a public that would insist on routine governance. Voters would expect that, with the revolution over it would be time to take out the trash and build roads. The "trash collection" theory, thanks to Hamas, is now in history's trash can. State Department types resisted Bush's goal. One former official had this exchange with a State Department bureaucrat, discussing State's defiance of Bush's pro-democracy policy: "It's our policy." "What do you mean?" "Read the President's speech." "Policy is not what the President says in speeches. Policy is what emerges from interagency meetings." Sadly, often the bureaucrat is right.

Arab societies are still founded on clan loyalty. As author Francis Fukuyama writes, tribal societies are "low-trust societies," whereas liberal democracy and capitalism require "high-trust" societies, in which loyalty is not tribal but rather attaches to constitutional and legal norms of conduct. There are only two forms, writes Fukuyama, of trust: *cultural* trust that reflects shared *values*, traditions and history; or an *impersonal* trust reflecting shared *interests*. Why would the Iraqi Sunni accept a constitutional guarantee from Shia and Kurds that the Sunni had so cruelly oppressed for decades? Or trust a United States that delivered them into the hands of their victims? The urbane Iraqi exiles who pleaded in the West for help in liberating their native country from Saddam were startlingly unrepresentative of their countrymen. Yet there are some contrary signs: Polls indicate that between 2004 and 2006 Iraqi support for an Islamic state fell from 30 to 22 percent, while those supporting separation of Church and State rose to 41 from 27 percent. The revolt of the Anbar sheiks against al-Qaeda, and the success of the surge, has boosted Sunni-Shia cooperation.

Was Iraq an exercise in nation-building? It is often said that conservative advocates of forcing regime change ignored their prior position during the Somalia debacle (1993) and the Kosovo War (1999), that "nation-building" is a task fundamentally beyond the competence of the United States. But Iraq seemed different, because it did not appear to be an obviously failed state, but rather a real country under the tyrant's rule. Iraqi exiles had convinced pro-democracy outsiders that beneath Saddam's jackboot was a real nation waiting to emerge once order was established and infrastructure rebuilt.[63] Democracy had been transplanted successfully outside the Mideast without formal exercises in nation-building.

It may be that the predicate for liberal democracy in the Mideast is precisely what the late Israeli Prime Minister Golda Meir (1969–1974) said about the predicate for Arab-Israeli peace: It will come if and when the Arabs decide that they love their children more than they hate the Jews. Consider the Palestinian mother who campaigned for Hamas in early 2006 by noting that three of her six sons had blown themselves up to kill Israelis, and that she hoped her remaining progeny would follow suit. Or consider the late 2006 suicide bombing by a 64-year old Palestinian grandmother who left 41 descendants. The Arabs largely ignore

---

63. The author recalls a conversation shortly before the 2003 war with an Iraqi-American friend who said that his relatives in Baghdad couldn't wait for the Americans to liberate them. There were, it now seems, not enough Iraqis who felt that way.

such atrocities. Thus they are nowhere near the standard laid down by Golda Meir. We may be more than one generation away, yet.

President Bush, for his part, defends his Mideast democracy promotion, citing progress in Jordan, Qatar, Morocco and the Gulf sheikdoms. Kuwait now allows women to vote. A fair election of a non-terrorist government took place in Yemen in 2006, the poorest Arab country and one long a haven for terrorists. In Libya there is a strongman, but he apparently no longer backs terrorism. In other key Mideast nations—Egypt, Jordan—radical Islamic factions, far better organized than the moderates, are given the best chance of winning if genuine elections are held.

Egypt is a particular black mark, having received $45 billion in U.S. aid since 1979. Egypt holds over 100,000 political prisoners. Having conducted a fairly honest election in 2005 Egyptian President Hosni Mubarak pushed through constitutional changes in 2007 that enshrined emergency powers he had hitherto exercised without legal authority. Thus he has created what has been called "a Constitution for a Pharaoh." Worse, he has consistently repressed moderates while placating radicals, the converse of what our democracy program needs.

The picture is mixed in Saudi Arabia. On the positive side, the Saudis are creating a 35,000-man security force to protect their oil infrastructure, and have rolled up a number of terror cells. Additional good news is that several court cases have been allowed to proceed against the Saudi religious police, and in an oddity, the Kingdom has permitted Muslim couples to shop for roses for Valentine's Day, despite it being a *kaffir* ("unbeliever") holiday. Yet the Saudis still send money to support radical mosques and *madrassas* around the world, and when called on it in print, have used "libel tourism" to sue authors under England's strict libel laws, giving them a chance to win in England cases that they would lose under American libel laws, which are far more protective of the press.

But a little perspective is in order. Switzerland gave women the right to vote in 1971, and Portugal waited until 1976. We should promote *liberal* democracy *later*, not *illiberal* democracy *sooner*. Early setbacks suggest that we take a slow track; demand of parties that they choose bullets or ballots, not both, and covertly fund favored parties. We must look for countries where the radicals are not organized, or if organized are not much better organized than moderates; and where we can protect and support moderates, preferably clandestinely, that they may avoid the taint of being labeled a client of ours. Is it *unfair* to clandestinely support moderates? The enemy will underwrite the radicals, whether or not we help our side. Extremists are, in the event, organized better than moderates in fragile societies, by virtue of their superior focused energy, compared to the diffuse interests of moderate factions. We need to compensate moderates for this disadvantage.

Lebanese commentator Fouad Ajami puts his finger on the central, irreversible Mideast reality created by America's toppling of Saddam: "We can't shy away from the very history we unleashed. We had demonstrated to the Arabs that the rulers are not deities; we had given birth to the principle of political accountability."

Natan Sharansky explains his rationale for promoting the spread of liberal democracy. He quotes the Soviet scientist and dissident Andrei Sakharov, who said: "A country that does not respect the rights of its own people will not respect the rights of its neighbors."

Sharansky explains that neither elections nor constitutions (the Soviet Union had one) make for a true democracy. Only with a free press, rule of law, independent courts and political parties can true democracy take root. He concludes: "Freedom's skeptics must understand that the democracy that hates you is less dangerous than the dictator that loves you.... Today, the dictator's enemy may be your enemy. But tomorrow, his enemy may be you."

In the end, failure is simply not an option. The potential consequences are simply too ghastly: genocidal strife between Sunnis and Shia, nuclear detonations—possibly including Israeli weapons on Iranian soil, Pakistan and Afghanistan sucked into the vortex of disintegration, sky-high oil prices that severely disrupt the world economy, and Islamic terrorists energized worldwide. And there is also a profound moral obligation. A war that a U.S.-led coalition started has led to 2.25 million Iraqi refugees, one third of whom crossed into Jordan, an Arab state we are allied with, but which is fragile (the rest are in Syria, an ally of Iran). This amounts to eight percent of Iraq's population. True, it is the barbarous violence of the insurgent terrorists and sectarian militias that have forced them to flee, but in failing to establish security after the fall of Baghdad the U.S. cannot escape sharing the blame. Good intentions have paved the road to Hell for the very people we intended to rescue from the grip of a brutal dictator.

Former National Security Adviser and Secretary of State Henry Kissinger counseled:

The radical jihadist challenge knows no frontiers; American decisions... will affect the confidence and morale of potential targets, potential allies and radical jihadists around the globe. Above all, they will define the U.S. capacity to contribute to a safer and better world.

Some critics regard President's Bush's position as hopelessly idealistic. But as the author-essayist Norman Podhoretz has pointed out, it is no more, and arguably even is less, ambitious than the famous words spoken at other Inaugurals.

Consider the famous call of John F. Kennedy in his Inaugural, considered one of the greatest such addresses in American history:

Let every nation know, whether it wishes us well or ill, that we shall pay any price, bear any burden, meet any hardship, support any friend, oppose any foe, to assure the survival and success of liberty.

JFK, too, warned that we were locked in "a long, twilight struggle" (against Communism). And he, too, understood that such work is a long-term project:

All this will not be finished in the first one hundred days. Nor will it be finished in the first one thousand days, nor in the life of this administration, nor even perhaps in our lifetime on this planet. But let us begin.

We have begun the twenty-first century's "long, twilight struggle."

CHAPTER VI
RESOURCE CHALLENGES
CHEAP NOW, COSTLY LATER

> The greatest threat to the world order in this century will be the next Hitler or Lenin, a charismatic leader who combines utter ruthlessness with a brilliant strategic sense, cunning, and boundless ambition—and who gains control over just a few weapons of mass destruction.
> FRED CHARLES IKLÉ, *ANNIHILATION FROM WITHIN* (2006)

After five years at war America is using but a fraction of its available material and monetary resources to address a challenge to its very existence. Fear of adverse economic impact of burgeoning federal budget deficits has us fighting with far fewer resources than were devoted to America's major twentieth-century wars. Ballistic missile defense moves slowly, as dangers gather over the horizon. Hardening and otherwise protecting critical infrastructures competes with congressional "earmarks"—pork projects for member districts and states. And our government is just as vulnerable to sudden incapacitation, should a WMD strike kill most top leaders, as it was on 9/11.

Certain special challenges merit immediate attention, either because the long lead time requires immediate commencement, or because the change can be made rapidly anyway. Steps to address these challenges can be divided into two types of resource allocation: money and material to fund essential defense programs and infrastructure, and managing affairs after a catastrophic strike.

Matching Material Resources to Defense Needs

Financial Resources. The only wars accountants ever win are against the IRS—and they lose more than they win. We cannot expect to win a world war with a green-eyeshade mentality. Massive deficits are routine in wartime. Spend what you must, and figure out how to foot the bill afterward. Taxation levels are best set to maximize economic growth. Policy and resources available should be brought in line, but resources are greater than revenues.

Are you horrified by a $9 trillion total debt and a $250 billion federal budget deficit? No discussion of these makes sense without reference to productivity and assets. We generate over $13 trillion in GDP annually; our total assets exceed $165 trillion, of which roughly one-third is tangible and two-thirds intangible. (The asset total does not even include the value of over 700 million acres of federally-owned land.) Thus our annual deficit in 2007 is just over one percent of GDP, compared to the peak of 6 percent it reached in 1983. Our debt is about two-thirds of annual GDP, about 18 percent of tangible assets and about 6 percent of total assets. The United States spent 7.1 percent of its federal budget on national security in 1949, rising in 1955 to 11.4 percent (between the Korean and Vietnam conflicts). We spent 9.8 percent in 1963, but are spending only 3.8 percent today (one-third the 1955 level). Even to reach the 1949 level would take an increase *equal to America's entire 2001 national security budget.* In terms of Gross Domestic Product, the U.S. spent 35 percent of GDP in World War II, 15 percent in Korea, 10 percent in Vietnam, 6 percent in the Gulf War and 4.4 percent in 2005. The military represented less than one percent of the U.S. labor force from 2003 to 2005, compared to 2.5 percent in the 1970s. In 2004, 6 percent of domestic capital investment and 2 percent of domestic industrial production came from defense and space equipment providers. Military R&D accounted for 16 percent in 2003, a jump of only 2 percent from 2000's pre-9/11 share of 14 percent. It was a whopping 53 percent of the total in 1988.

All these comparisons mean that we can *easily* afford to spend more to win this war—for troops, new weapons systems, new homeland security systems, etc. Suppose we add $1 trillion, or even $2 trillion, over the next decade. During that time we will generate, even if GDP is static, over $130 trillion. Let GDP grow at 3 percent annually over the next decade (it grew 3.5 percent in 2005), and cumulative U.S. GDP for the next decade will be $150 trillion. We are a vastly wealthy country, and can afford pretty much anything. Yes, we have lots of debt, but would you rather be a street beggar who owes $100 or a billionaire who owes $100 million? *The one thing we cannot afford is to lose a war of survival— better a live bankrupt than a dead tycoon.* Consider a WMD strike causing mass casualties, possibly equivalent to 100 9/11s, perhaps even 1,000. Besides catastrophic loss of life, it would be a multi-*trillion* dollar event.

There is now consensus that our military is dangerously over-stretched. The surge that in 2007 created the first prospect of success in Iraq can last only 15 months, unless combat tours are extended. Thus, inadequate resource commitment may undermine an otherwise success-ful strategy. That a battle with the stakes of that in Iraq could be lost for such a reason is testimony to a massive *bipartisan* failure to provide ad-equately for the common defense. One expert sees our ground forces as being underfunded by nearly half—$112 billion in 2007 versus around $200 billion needed, with a 50 percent increase in troop strength from today's 510,000 needed.

General Robert Scales, a retired commander of the Army War Col-lege, provides more detail. It takes three brigades (3,000 soldiers each) to keep one combat-ready: one is in the field, one is recuperating and one is being refitted for combat. All Army brigades save one in Korea have seen combat since 2001: 22 have done two tours, nine have done three tours and two have done four tours. We have about *half* the number of brigades we need.

Vietnam and Gulf War hero General Barry McCaffrey recently de-scribed the danger to our Army: "The Army is beginning to show signs of great strain…. Recruiting standards are being lowered. Our equip-ment is shot. By [2008] we will be forced to downsize our deployment to Iraq or the Army will unravel." The military says it will take two years to restore material resources to prewar levels. We send our soldiers into battle without full body armor and in under-protected Humvees, causing Lt. General Peter Chiarelli, one of America's most successful military leaders in Iraq to say: "Our current problems raise the legitimate question of whether the U.S., or any democracy, can successfully prosecute an extended war without a true national commitment."

Regarding deficits, there are two other arguments to be addressed. First is the legitimate concern about why our deficit is being run up. Deficits are economically constructive when run to finance vital capital needs, such as building public infrastructure. But they are economically destructive when run to finance uneconomic subsidies, often the case today.[64] It should also be noted that deficits do less to boost the economy during times of growth than they do when the economy is in recession.

But the impact of deficits on interest rates is dwarfed by massive asset value shifts in the global economy. This is why over the past quarter-century during which deficits have been run, there is no correlation between deficits and interest rates. They frequently move in opposite directions, because of the work of larger forces. Further, deficit increases due to funding a war of survival are a good societal investment, regardless of the economic impact. We could, of course, substantially ameliorate the problem were the administration and Congress to act to reduce non-essential spending. But this will rarely happen because to every constituency the rewards it receives are "essential," and the benefits of deficit-financed rewards are seen now, while the bill is presented later.

This brings up one final argument often made against incurring added debt: the burden we thus place on future generations. *If future generations share in the benefits, it is reasonable to ask them to foot part of the*

---

64. While deficits can increase inflationary pressure, other factors also affect inflation, and often swamp whatever impact budget deficits may have. Fears that larger federal budget deficits would cause higher inflation have often not been borne out historically: in the 1980s the federal budget deficit widened—its 1983 number of 6 percent of GDP remains the high-water mark (as noted in the text)—while inflation fell sharply between 1981 and 1985, and remained low for more than a decade thereafter. There is thus no good reason to believe that expenditures of a few hundred billion extra war dollars will inflict significant economic harm on America, via higher inflation. Even if they did so, if the better war capability thus purchased averts even one mega-catastrophe, the higher inflation will have been worth its weight in monetized gold.

bill. My generation helped pay the costs of financing World War II, and lived freer and vastly more prosperously as a result. It was an excellent investment. The same will be true for future generations if we defeat those plotting acts of apocalyptic terror. Future generations will live much better lives as a result.

How we finance the deficit is only a secondary question where survival is concerned. (If you do not think this war one of survival, it is a co-primary question.) There are four ways to finance increased spending in a given sector: cut spending elsewhere, change tax rates (up or down), borrow and pay interest and inflate the currency (the government prints money to "monetize the debt"). The best choice is to cut spending elsewhere. Tax rates can be altered—the 2003 Bush tax cut yielded a revenue bonanza for the Treasury and cut the deficit by more than half. Passing costs on to future generations, as noted above, is defensible if benefits are shared. The worst choice is to accelerate inflation—debauching the currency—by printing money, with consequent economic misery to follow. In the event, the federal budget deficit, $413 billion in 2004 (3.6 percent of GDP) is estimated to be $158 billion in 2007 (1.2 percent of GDP). *When defeat can mean a ghastly dictatorship, and perhaps a thousand years of darkness, be a spendthrift.*

Missile Defense. A key area for defense is the ability to destroy incoming missiles, but arms control diplomacy often gets in the way. Despite a 1999 successful test at White Sands, New Mexico, in which a ground-based laser destroyed a Katushya rocket in flight, the weapon, a Northrup system dubbed the Sky Guard tactical laser, was never deployed because of diplomatic objections lodged by Russia and China. A second factor was that the laser was believed to be cost-ineffective, relative to cheap rockets. Tell the latter to residents of northern Israel, who endured thousands of Katushyas fired by Hezbollah. What are the economics of one-third of Israel spending a month in bomb shelters? Israel paid in the coin of innocent human life for its decision not to deploy lasers.

Lasers have a longer-term dimension, too. Space-based systems could destroy missiles worldwide, seconds after launch. But arms control advocates would deprive us of the best defense against missile launches, in pursuit of idealized international amity. *When dealing with rogue, revolutionary or terror states, it is best to bet on defense, not on diplomacy.* Self-restraint on deployment of missile defense technology has a long pedigree, even outlasting the 1972 ABM Treaty's 2002 expiration. Radar-based systems, which are now being deployed by the U.S. among others, are limited by the Earth's curvature, which limits warning time for interception.[65] Missile defense expert Angelo Codevilla argues that far more effective would be space-based lasers, a dozen of which, orbiting at a 500-mile altitude, could protect America from launches anywhere on the planet. Critics point to the 1967 Outer Space Treaty, which bans orbiting WMD systems and the use of "celestial bodies" for non-peaceful purposes.[66] Space laser missile defense is reasonably regarded a peaceful use and thus should not be interpreted to violate the Outer Space Treaty.

The Bush administration believes, apparently, that deploying missile-defense lasers would be too upsetting to Russia and China, who object because their own arsenals would thus be neutralized. Russia also objects to the planned deployment of a BMD radar site in the Czech Republic and ten missiles in Poland, to protect against a possible missile launch from Iran. Russian President Vladimir Putin proposed that the site be located in Azerbaijan. If joint U.S.-Russian authority is needed to launch such missiles, this would enable Russia to decide to let missiles land on two Eastern European countries it hates. In the few minutes in which a launch decision must be made, any Russian stalling would be tantamount to allowing missiles to land. Worse, Russia has been a prime mover of Iran's nuclear program. It is what insurers call "moral

---

65. The latest missile defense radar, known as the sea-based X-band radar, vastly increases range of detection to thousands of miles, and also can distinguish between live warheads and dummy decoys (by virtue of improved image resolution).

66. Article IV of the Outer Space Treaty does not explicitly ban all BMD systems. Only BMD systems armed with WMD or based on "celestial bodies" are banned by the treaty.

hazard"—relieving someone of the consequences of reckless behavior, which thus encourages more reckless behavior by the beneficiary—to exempt Russia from the consequences of its decision to aid Iran's program. Such proposals are and should always be unacceptable.

Another potentially promising BMD opportunity is the Airborne Laser (ABL), a triad of BMD lasers mounted on a Boeing 747. The ABL would enable destruction of ballistic missiles in their launch phase, when they are rising slowly and over the territory of the launcher country. The program may make ballistic missile attacks obsolete. A prototype may be available in 2009, and if successfully tested could be used in an emergency. Other laser systems may be used to counter SAM (surface-to-air missile) launches.

Israel has the world's most advanced operational BMD system, the Arrow. Designed to shoot down theater missiles, Arrow intercepts warheads up to roughly 50 miles away, at altitudes of five to ten miles. It uses an explosive warhead with a kill range of 45 to 55 yards. It is deployed in batteries of 24 to 48 missiles. There are three Arrow bases, covering all of Israel. Arrow has performed well in tests. But given Israel's concentration of population in a few urban centers, a few nuclear warheads can effectively extinguish the Jewish state. Thus, Israel may decide to strike Iran pre-emptively if the U.S. does not, and Israeli intelligence concludes that Iran is about to cross the nuclear threshold. Iran, however, has stated that it has 600 medium-range Shahab-3 missiles aimed at Israel. *Suppose Iran fires 600 missiles, with six of them nuclear-armed: How will Israel figure out in a few minutes of flight time which ones—the lethal one percent—are nuclear-tipped?* (Even if Iran has only 300 missiles, finding 6 nukes is a daunting task.)[67]

A related area is anti-satellite weapons (ASAT) that can blind communications and surveillance satellites, upon whose operations the American military absolutely depends. China's January 2007 successful test of an ASAT, matched only by a 1971 Soviet test and a 1985 Ameri-

---

67. The U.S. X-band system is not integrated with Israel's Arrow system, and thus its decoy detection is not available to the Israelis.

can one, signals its intent to have that capability in event of a conflict with the United States. In 2006, a Chinese laser blinded a U.S. satellite.

Author-soldier Ralph Peters warns that the inability to defend orbiting satellites leaves America with "a Maginot line in the sky." Our modern military is utterly dependent upon communications between satellites and myriad air, sea and ground systems, without which our real-time battlefield intelligence and our pin-point targeting accuracy would simply disappear. Both Russia and China know this well and surely would, in event of a conflict with the U.S., make our military and communications satellites among their highest-value targets.

Another critical defense need is to forestall an Electromagnetic Pulse (EMP) strike. As noted in the prologue, a 2004 report to Congress by a senior panel warned that a nuclear-armed missile launched from a barge offshore could inflict massive damage on the nation's electronic infrastructure; such a threat could well emerge before 2020. The U.S. has already successfully tested an intercept of a missile launched from a barge. One quick BMD option is to modify the Navy's existing fleet of some 60 AEGIS cruisers to shoot down single-missile EMP launches offshore.

Because retrofitting equipment is expensive, hardening the next generation of equipment is more promising. *Ironically, modern countries are more vulnerable than others, because electronic semiconductors are more vulnerable than older, vacuum tube technology, still found mostly in less advanced infrastructures (such as Iran's).* Because of inter-dependencies among key infrastructures (meaning that major failure of one infrastructure induces major failure in one or more others)—electric power, communications, energy, banking and financial, water, and emergency care—an EMP strike could disable the U.S. economy for months, possibly even years.

The 2004 report provides a detailed blueprint for protecting key elements of diverse infrastructures. Notable is that wireless communications are especially vulnerable to EMP disruption; wireline networks are far less so, because optical fiber networks that form the nation's long-distance and inter-office communications fabric are immune to EMP effect.[68] But as noted earlier, though direct damage from an EMP strike will not bring down optical networks, a massive loss of electric power that lasts long enough to exceed the back-up power capability of network providers will enable an EMP hit to accomplish indirectly what it cannot accomplish in the first instant.

The EMP panel's recommendations are commendable, but do not go far enough. The next generation of PCs must be manufactured with hardened components. Over the next decade every current PC should be replaced by hardened PCs. Congress, ever fond of imposing unfunded regulatory mandates on business, should do so here, by requiring PC manufacturers to manufacture hardened PCs as soon as possible. Whatever the cost of hardening is, compare it to the multi-trillion dollar impact of losing the nation's electrical and communications grids for months, perhaps even a year. These, and computers networked into them, practically run modern economies.

EMP attacks are a terrorist's dream: immense economic damage inflicted at minuscule cost, with little in the way of effective retaliation that might deter the strike in the first place. EMP vulnerability must be addressed forthwith. (This fact is hardly a secret. Terrorist states who might contemplate developing such a weapon know its potential. Americans may as well know.)

The Homeland: America's Extended and Vulnerable Infrastructures

Homeland security covers a vast set of vulnerabilities, involving not only loss of life but considerable societal disruption. A bio-terror attack that unleashed a flu pandemic could force closing schools for three months, and require that even healthy adults stay home for seven to ten

---

68. They operate in higher transmission frequency bands unaffected by EMP, so long as they do not have electronic amplifiers, which are being supplanted by optical amplifiers. Amplifiers boost signal power and are used in long-distance transmission. All-optical networks are immune to EMP effect. But any electronic equipment connected to all-optical networks—telephones, computers, etc.—is just as vulnerable as equipment connected to older networks.

days. The FY2006 federal budget allocated ten times as much money ($16.5 billion) to protect military bases and facilities (two-thirds are located in the homeland) as the $1.65 billion spent for homeland security covering America's major cities. In the five years since 9/11, Los Angeles, the largest port on the Pacific Coast, got a total of $25 million—only $5 million per year—to protect an absolutely vital port.

Of particular note are America's two most critical infrastructures, energy and communications (financial and other infrastructures are largely based upon these two), and our seaports, which our highly trade-dependent economy needs for continued growth and prosperity.

Communications. Modern communications networks have four fundamental characteristics. They are global, accessible, programmable and fragile. Global networks have "cascade" vulnerability. Failures in one point can rapidly spread to the remainder of the network. Accessible networks are accessible not only to legitimate users, but also to hostile users (hackers, terrorists). Programmable networks can have their operation altered by hackers who cause networks to crash, shut out legitimate users, or tie up computing resources, thus denying them to others. Communications networks are increasingly fragile. Software complexity makes problems hard to repair. (Anyone who has experience using a personal computer and trying to fix a software glitch—by now, most Americans—will understand this last point very well.)

Prime examples of this vulnerability are the major network failures of the early 1990s, when far-flung telephone networks crashed due to software glitches that cascaded throughout their switching fabrics. A single faulty line of software code in an upgrade caused more than 50 percent of AT&T's long distance network to crash on Martin Luther King Day in 1990, one of the year's busiest calling days. It took AT&T two weeks to find the error, hidden in millions of lines of software code. In 1991, faulty software upgrades caused several major local telephone network crashes, affecting phone service in multiple states. A software hacker who gained access to system software could trigger a shutdown. While defenses against such attacks have been the focus of industry efforts for more than a decade, software is hard to make tamper-proof or foolproof.

Increasingly, wireless networks can provide flexibility after a disaster or terror attack. They offer four benefits: *portability*—location-independence; *mobility*—motion-independence; *separability*—device-independence; and *ubiquity*—pervasive network access points. Portability means that the user can use his PC or cell phone or other access device the same way anywhere—in Los Angeles as in New York, or Paris, or Tokyo, or Sydney. Mobility means that communicating while in motion (on foot, car, ship, plane) is achievable. Separability means that one can operate a device without being physically tied to it—e.g., a hands-free speakerphone or cellphone. Ubiquity means that wherever the user goes there are network access points to connect to. Wireless capacity has yet to expand enough to cover large-scale customer demand in the wake of a disaster, however. On 9/11 appeals were made for people to refrain from calling relatives and friends in New York City and Washington, so as to keep networks open for emergency communications. Cracks appear in odd places. A program for distributing to nearly 400 state and local bomb squads "Cobra kits" (costing $12,000 each) to enable detection of explosives and WMD materials foundered because the localities decided that they couldn't afford to pay the phone bills for wireless transmission associated with use of the kits.

For absolutely critical communications network nodes there are general strategic principles that can be applied to prevent disaster. Networks with critical single points of failure should be provided with backup. Four types of separation are desirable. First is to physically separate critical hardware for highest value targets. This is already done for access to essential military operations. Second is to separate software, so that easily available software is not used for critical applications, because hackers target such software. Third is to separate levels of command, so that no single person can make a decision with catastrophic consequences. Thus nuclear missiles cannot be launched by one person, and nuclear warheads cannot be solely armed. Fourth is to employ at least two, and ideally, three levels of authentication to clear personnel involved in critical operations. There are three types of authentication: who you are—fingerprints, etc.; what you have—*e.g.*, a smart card; and what you know—*e.g.*, encrypted passwords.

In the not-too-distant future digital technology will permit creating phony Presidential speeches, with results that will look and sound authentic to the lay viewer-listener. The doctored photographs that Reuters aired during the 2006 Israeli-Hezbollah war were amateurish. Future efforts will be more skillful. *Authenticating source material and those communicating it, plus authorization of those purporting to act with authority is critical.* Biometric identification and multiple layers of security will be required. But the task is daunting: lies can survive forever on countless servers in cyberspace. "Digital watermark" authentication may not suffice to prevent abuse. (A digital watermark is a software-embedded, indelible visual identification tag invisible to the viewer.) Millions of people who see a video that ostensibly shows an American President calling for holy war against Muslims are not likely to have learned about invisible digital watermark authentication in school, or to know through hands-on computer experience how to find an authoritative indicator of authenticity.

Problems of authentication already plague global communications. One example: jihadist websites post "reports" purporting to recount events, including in March 2007, 966 claims about battlefield casualties posted by 11 self-identified jihadist groups, targeting impressionable Muslim minds globally. There are conflicting priorities here: We want dissidents living under dictatorship to remain anonymous; but we want terrorists worldwide to be traceable. China, which worries far more about domestic dissidents than terrorist attacks, has launched a major crackdown on bloggers, with 18,000 sites shut down. To accomplish this task, China employs an estimated 30,000 snoops looking for unauthorized Internet use.

Thus there is an inherent tension between authentication of a remote user, authorization for that user to engage in a transaction and acceptance of

such legitimacy, on the one hand, and the desire many remote users have for
network anonymity, on the other. Terrorists will seek to use anonymity to
gain spurious authentication and authorization, in hope of winning network acceptance of their transactions, without surrendering their cloak
of anonymity.

Internet websites are increasingly used to support jihad around the
globe. Hezbollah has aired a computer game about killing Israelis called
"Special Force 2," that is based upon the 2006 Lebanon-Israel war. Players become holy warriors out to kill Israelis. On the brighter side, bloggers in the Arab world, where Internet access reaches about ten percent
of the population, are increasingly rising up to challenge their dictatorial
governments.

Perhaps most dangerous of all, the Internet also exponentially em-
powers charismatics. Instead of preaching to a few hundred souls inside
a mosque, a cyber-imam using the virtual mosque on the Internet can at-
tract countless millions. Cyberspace enables widespread ideological in-
doctrination—call it anti-social distance learning. It creates virtual space
in which all jihadists can exchange messages. It serves as a clearinghouse
for information on techniques of terrorism, from planning to operations
to escape. A recent study comparing how U.S. government agencies use
the Web, versus how Islamic terrorists do, found that the latter use the
Internet far more effectively, especially as to use of video and multimedia
technologies. It is a supreme irony that the Internet, crown jewel of the
twenty-first century information age, may prove to be as much a force for
spreading ignorance as for spreading worthwhile knowledge.

In an August 2007 report the New York Police Department, which
has America's—perhaps the world's—best counter-terror capability
among police forces, warned that second and third generation Muslims
inside the U.S. were being radicalized by Islamist Internet videos and
chat rooms devoted to jihad. NYPD regards this as the most serious
growing threat, as these groups are not affiliated with al-Qaeda, but get
inspiration and education from foreign groups like al-Qaeda.

The Internet is vulnerable to "cyberwar." In May 2007 a landmark event in cyberwar occurred: the first documented cyber-attack by one country against another country. The attack from Russia targeted Estonian government, financial, communications and news sites. Although Estonia is a member of NATO, the NATO Treaty doesn't define cyber-attacks as a "military action" requiring a NATO response. Cyber-jihadist websites now number more than 5,000.

To counter cyber-attacks, there will be increased use of "digital rights management"—a legal concept that entitles those with intellectual property rights to restrict unauthorized use of their hardware or software. Technical devices such as anti-copy technologies, embedded in television and PC hardware within the next few years, will facilitate authentication of specific machines and authorization of legitimate users. Such devices will use public key cryptography.[69] Over time a "trusted computing base" can be grown that will make fraud far more difficult, though never impossible. In September 2007 the Air Force activated a "provisional" Cyber Command, which will develop offensive and defensive capabilities to be used in cyberspace.[70]

The Department of Homeland Security's SAFECOM Initiative has made considerable progress in equipment interoperability, a key problem in managing communications infrastructure disaster recovery. Two-thirds of agencies nationwide reported some level of interoperability at the end of 2006. SAFECOM's RapidCom 1 Initiative has established command interoperability at the ten highest urban threat areas, with assured connectivity within one hour of a "major" event. Full interoperability is a long way off.

Ports. Seaports are another essential infrastructure element for fighting terrorists. Ninety percent of imports and export pass through them.

---

69. Public key cryptography involves matching a combination of published and unpublished keys. The keys are complex digital identifiers that authenticate who is an authorized user for a given transaction. They provide very high levels of security.

70. In its 2007 annual report to Congress the U.S.-China Economic and Security Review Commission warned that China continually probes U.S. government networks, and that the largest leakage of advanced U.S. technology is due to China's massive espionage effort.

Commendably, the Bush administration has implemented several programs to address shipping and port vulnerability. But by the end of 2006, the Department of Homeland Security Container Security Initiative (CSI) covered only six percent of the 26,000 containers that daily enter America's 361 ports; Hong Kong, according to a former senior official, inspects 100 percent. Worse, most foreign inspectors clearing cargo overseas decline U.S. requests for specific inspection 80 percent of the time. CSI did not cover the 20 percent of U.S. cargo that is carried on commercial airliners, which get only spot-check inspection. A complementary program, the Customs Trade Partnership Program, offers reduced inspections to qualified companies, but only 11 percent of companies in the program had been vetted as of late 2006. In December 2006 DHS launched its Secure Freight Initiative, aimed at enhancing capability to detect nuclear and radiological materials. Key foreign ports are to inaugurate the program.[71] Since 2003 the Department of Energy has been implementing its Megaports Initiative, with similar goals, working in tandem with DHS programs.[72]

Congress passed the SAFE Port Act of 2006, to further govern port procedures and to require that by the end of 2007 the 22 busiest U.S. ports have modern screening equipment to detect nuclear and radiological material. New scanner technology has performed so well that the government will likely recommend deployment at 400 ports, supplanting existing systems that generate hundreds of false alarms daily at a large port. Major port vulnerability stems also from large LNG (liquefied natural gas) tankers that unload cargo near major population centers. The potential for a terror attack killing many thousands exists, unless LNG cargo is unloaded further offshore. LNG is too cold to ex-

71. Six ports are the first ones to participate: Port Qassim, Pakistan; Puerto Cortes, Honduras; Southampton, United Kingdom; Port Salaah, Oman; Port of Singapore; and Gamman Terminal at the port of Pusan, South Korea.

72. At the end of 2006 six countries were fully operational participants in the Megaports program: Greece, the Bahamas, Sri Lanka, Spain, Singapore and the Netherlands. Twelve other countries are part of the program, but with only partial implementation: Belgium, China, Dubai, Honduras, Israel, Oman, the Philippines, Thailand, Egypt, Jamaica, the Dominican Republic and Taiwan.

plode, but it burns at 1,000 degrees Fahrenheit. Once ignited it cannot be doused. A large LNG tanker on fire will incinerate everything within four-tenths of a mile. Port security is a welcome case of bipartisan recognition of a grave vulnerability, and agreement between the branches on ways to address them.

Energy. There have been repeated calls for energy independence since the Arab oil embargo was imposed in 1973. By one tally, the goal was included in 24 of 34 Presidential State of the Union addresses since then. Nonetheless, American dependence upon imported oil has risen from 34.8 to 60.3 percent since 1973. Steps we can take include reducing consumption of petroleum by adopting the French solution of using nuclear power to provide electricity, allowing the price to rise to reduce gasoline consumption or subsidizing alternative energy producers to explore non-oil options without fear of sudden undercutting by price drops. Conservation alone rarely helps, because increased energy efficiency historically has simply led to more consumption, rather than less usage. Hybrid fuels eventually may make a modest contribution, with one possibly promising source being electricity.

But as energy expert Peter Huber writes, for the foreseeable future two sources of fuel, carbon (oil and gas) and uranium (nuclear), will dominate the energy field. America spends $500 billion annually on them, and the market capitalization behind the supply of such fuels is several trillion dollars, numbers that dwarf the piddling sums governments appropriate to support alternative fuel research and development. Ethanol currently accounts for but two percent, with an estimated potential of ten percent, of total U.S. gasoline consumption. Proposals to create a price floor high enough to encourage investment in alternative fuels may become feasible, with the public now inured to stratospheric oil prices. Various energy tax proposals may have merit, in that they discourage consumption.

Huber and co-author Mark Mills offer a key insight about energy needs, that explains why conservation efforts are offset and why waste of energy is the least of our worries:

What most of us think about energy *supply* is wrong. Energy supplies are unlimited; it is *energetic order* that's scarce, and the order in energy that's expensive.... Energy begets more energy; tomorrow's supply is determined by today's consumption....

What most of us think about energy *demand* is even more wrong. Our main use of energy isn't lighting, locomotion or cooling; what we use energy for, mainly, is to extract, refine, process and purify energy itself. And the more efficient we become at refining energy in this way, the more we want to use the final product.

Proof of these propositions comes from several sources. First, compare wide swings in the price of oil to far smaller swings in the price of coal and uranium. Most of the cost of oil-based products is in the oil itself, whereas most of the cost for the latter two are in the infrastructure of transportation and energy refining that supports their production. Second, most energy is wasted to produce useful output. Only about one to five percent of raw energy emerges at the other end, in refined, purified form, to perform useful work. The microchips and lasers that increasingly run modern economies waste most of the energy put into them, but generate highly valuable economic output. Third, energy efficiency increases are cancelled out by increased usage. Thus, since 1950 U.S. GDP per unit of energy used has more than doubled, but energy consumption has tripled. The authors note a "productivity paradox" that complements this "efficiency paradox." "The more power it puts to increasingly clever use, the more productive a workforce becomes, the more payrolls expand, and the more new jobs emerge." Thus information technology, itself highly energy-intensive but highly ordered, spurs job growth and economic productivity.

America's energy infrastructure is robust enough to withstand ordinary supply shocks—embargoes or major price jumps. But as major power outages show, its electric grid is vulnerable to disruption, whether accidental, as in the past, or intentional, as may prove to be the case in the future. One concern about relying more on nuclear plants is possible terrorist strikes, such as with a hijacked airliner. Technology exists to program air traffic control software to automatically re-route airliners headed for prohibited areas.

America will remain an energy mega-consumer, unless its citizens are prepared to return to the pre-industrial age—essentially, the time of its Centennial. Protecting energy nodes thus becomes central to America's continued prosperity.

One quick fix is that for an estimated $20 million to $30 million per oil refinery, at a cost of an additional one cent per gallon of gasoline, if amortized over three years, refineries could jettison highly toxic hydrofluoric acid for less toxic sulfuric acid. The former could, given a successful attack on a refinery, generate a lethal cloud and kill many thousands, while the latter would not do so.

A major impediment to America accepting change in energy policy is that the public harbors many misconceptions about energy matters. It overestimates our dependence on Mideast oil, the potential of alternative energy sources (solar, wind power, ethanol), the extent of environmental pollution and consequent damage, and safety risks associated with use of nuclear power. Thus the public accepts an environmentalist stranglehold that prevents exploiting available energy resources to their fullest. And it tolerates serial waste of billions of federal tax dollars on boondoggles: myriad alternative energy projects mounted in several administrations to little effect to date.

An exploration of myriad energy issues lies well beyond the scope of this book. One point above all is worth making: The single most important change in America's energy policy would be a shift towards nuclear power. Its energy potential is vast, and its safety risks minuscule. *In the entire history of the U.S. commercial nuclear power industry no one has ever perished due to radiation from a nuclear accident.* Driving an automobile, by one calculation, carries one million times the risk of death as dying from a nuclear power accident. New technologies offer promise of even safer operation of nuclear plants, including fuels that make diversion to weapons use far more difficult.

But what about the 1986 Chernobyl disaster in Ukraine that so horrified the world? Unlike with the 1979 Three Mile Island accident in Pennsylvania, a significant release of radiation occurred. At Chernobyl the reactor had no containment vessel, the massive covering designed to withstand a direct hit from a jetliner, that contains radiation in event of a spill at all U.S. plants. The Soviets largely ignored safety in building their nuclear plants, including on ships and submarines. The sterling safety record of the American program stands in stark contrast to the appalling documented toll of sailors on Soviet vessels, exposed to unshielded or minimally shielded radiation.

But there is one truly vital fact about Chernobyl, one little known: According to a UN report, the number of fatalities due to the accident has been far lower than originally feared. Through mid-2005, the toll for 19 years of exposure to radiation that within ten days had spread over Europe has been *fewer than 50 deaths*, most being workers involved in the initial clean-up at the site. Thyroid cancer directly caused nine child deaths: 4,000 children in the region developed the cancer, with a survival rate of 99 percent. There was no "spike" in fertility problems and birth defects. Scientists originally anticipated 4,000 radiation fatalities among the 600,000 people living in the region. Worse, continued intense monitoring has caused mental health problems among otherwise healthy members of the population, because pervasive monitoring induced the healthy to fear that they were sick. Currently, 5 to 7 percent of government spending in Ukraine targets largely non-existent health problems. (To put this number in perspective, this would mean, given a $2.8 trillion-dollar U.S. federal budget, an annual expenditure of $140 to $196 billion.) Beyond a 20-mile circle around the site, radiation levels are at a level deemed acceptable by scientists. Most people there receive more radiation dosage from natural sources. New technology allows "inherently safe" reactors that "fail safe" without meltdown, and ameliorate waste disposal problems. It is time to lay to rest once and for all a nuclear energy policy driven by irrational fears.

Emergency Human Resources: Authority, Continuity and Public Education

Federal disaster law currently vests primary authority with the state governors. Federal martial law has been declared several times in America's history, first by General Andrew Jackson in 1814 after winning the Battle of New Orleans. The last declarations came from military governors during the post-Civil War Reconstruction. Since then local martial law has been declared by military leaders when soldiers were used to suppress labor riots or race riots, from the late nineteenth century to the early twentieth. Yet in 1962 President Kennedy reportedly told emergency planners that "nationwide martial law is not an acceptable planning assumption" even given a nuclear attack. In an emergency, divided authority can delay critically-needed disaster response. Thus, in the aftermath of Hurricane Katrina, a full four days after the levees broke and New Orleans was flooded, the Governor refused a Presidential request to federalize the National Guard, with the result being further delay of desperately needed assistance that the State could not competently provide by itself.

The fact that Kennedy never faced the situation in reality makes his objection seem reflexive and theoretical. The chaos following a nuclear detonation on American soil, amplified a thousand-fold by today's pervasive, high-octane media, could well generate mass hysteria were order not quickly established. The President should be given formal statutory authority to declare martial law for 30 days, free of review by Congress or the courts, in the wake of a mega-disaster, whether natural or man-made. The President should have 30 days with sole executive discretion to act in emergencies that threaten life and essential national assets. There should then be the option of serial renewal for 90-day periods, upon executive request, but these should be subject to congressional authorization and judicial review.

It is possible in theory to give Congress a limited time to review the initial executive decision, failing which the President may act. But this is impractical in reality for two reasons: (1) Congress is not set up to act quickly; (2) if a divided Congress fails to approve, a President who then acts could find his authority politically impaired after a divisive debate during emergency times, when nationwide unity is most urgent. *Flip the famed football maxim, "speed kills." In a crisis with potential catastrophic impact, undue delay kills.*[73] Might a President abuse such broad power? It is possible, but intuitively at least as likely is a President paralyzed by the magnitude of a catastrophic event. The catatonic performance of Louisiana officials, who failed to implement either the state or city evacuation plan for New Orleans when facing Katrina, illustrates this possibility.

The strongest executive is most needed when the worst disasters strike. The public in times of severe crisis inevitably looks to the President for leadership. As power should equal responsibility, Presidential authority should be pre-eminent at times of greatest national crisis. Rest on the philosopher whose writings were the main source for Thomas Jefferson's Declaration of Independence. The President would, in effect, exercise what seventeenth-century English philosopher John Locke called "executive prerogative":

> For the Legislators not being able to foresee, and provide, by Laws, for all, that may be useful to the Community, the Executor of the Laws, having the power in his hands, has by the common law of Nature, a right to make use of it, for the good of the Society, in many Cases, where the municipal Law has given no direction, till the Legislative can conveniently be Assembled to provide for it…. 'tis fit that the laws themselves shall in some Cases give way to the Executive power, or rather to this Fundamental Law of Nature and Government, *viz.*, that That as much as may be, *all* the Members of the Society are to be *preserved.*[74]

Jefferson added a stern qualifier: "The line of discrimination between cases may be difficult, but the good officer is bound to draw it at his own peril, and throw himself on the justice of his country and the

---

73. In Federalist 70, Alexander Hamilton argued "for energy in the executive" that encompasses "unity, duration, adequate provision for its support; and competent powers." A unified executive can act with "decision, activity, secrecy and dispatch."

74. (Emphasis in original.) Chapter XIV, sec. 159 of John Locke's *Second Treatise of Government* sets forth "inherent executive Prerogative to protect society and public safety."

rectitude of his motives." This is an intellectually sound qualifier, but in a poisonous political atmosphere with opposition and media in full assault mode, mercy seems to be in short supply in the nation's capital.

But can federal martial law be squared with the Constitution's reservation of police power to the states? If Katrina is used as a test case, the answer is "yes." First, recovering a major port that is the gateway for traffic coming down the Mississippi from many states is hardly a local matter. The south Louisiana Port Complex is the country's largest and the world's fifth largest port, with 15 percent of U.S. energy supplies (40 percent of U.S. natural gas), a significant share of U.S. agricultural products and maritime products for 36 states passing in transit. The Louisiana coast provides one-third of all domestic seafood.

Second, the Framers lived in a world where the infant federal government had near-zero resources—an era when travel between Washington, D.C., and New York City took a week on horseback. Naturally the police power had to lie with the states. And so it should still, for *local* matters. But when issues of substantial national or global impact are at stake, or when Uncle Sam is picking up most of the tab, federal supremacy is essential. Put simply, far less in our lives is truly local than was the case in 1787.

The federal government plays a far larger role in American life today. In the 1920s the federal government consumed four percent of GDP, versus 18.6 percent today. It was not until 1936 that federal spending topped the combined spending of state and local governments, having exploded to nine percent of GDP, a doubling in a decade.

Third, as the President has 60 days of sole authority to commit American forces under the 1973 War Powers Resolution, a period of 30 days regarding extreme domestic emergencies seems reasonable.

The proposed executive prerogative is *discretionary*: A President who finds local authorities highly competent (as with NYC and 9/11) and able to manage a situation can decline to exercise extraordinary emergency power. This last point bears emphasis: An ambiguous division of federal, state and local power can be made to work if the leaders in question enjoy mutual trust, as after 9/11. But when leaders don't share a trusting collaborative relationship, as after Hurricane Katrina, divided authority is a prescription for paralysis.[75]

Equally important is the need to enact "continuity of government" measures that in extraordinary circumstances provide for effective governmental authority that also is publicly recognized as lawful and legitimate. The main problems are four-fold: mass vacancies, incapacitated leaders, credible elections and Presidential succession. United Flight 93, we now know, was headed on 9/11 for the Capitol building, not the White House, because the former is much easier to see from a plane.

Vacancies in the House of Representatives are filled per Article I, Section 2, Clause 4 of the U.S. Constitution, which provides: "When vacancies happen in the Representation from any State, the Executive Authority thereof shall issue Writs of Election to fill such Vacancies." Senatorial vacancies are filled per the Seventeenth Amendment, Clause 2 of which provides that vacancies are filled by special election, with interim senatorial appointments as the state legislatures may provide; the states have delegated such power to their governors.

Because governors can make interim appointments, and most, if not all, will likely survive most WMD attacks, there is less of a serious problem in the Senate. But the problem is acute in the House, because there is no interim appointment power as to replacing House members. In recent years the typical time to fill a House vacancy has been 126 days (four months), with a range from two and one-half to nine months. Article I, Section 5 provides for each House of Congress that a majority constitutes a quorum (currently 218 in the House, 51 in the Senate), but smaller numbers may call for adjournment (such as might be the case after a terrorist strike). A precedent dating to the Civil War re-defines a quorum as a majority of members "chosen, sworn and living." Incapacitation intrudes here; If 220 members of the House are alive but incapac-

---

75. Hamilton's injunction against dividing executive authority anticipated the Katrina trainwreck by 217 years: Divided authorities "lessen the respectability, weaken the authority, and distract the plans and operations of those whom they divide."

itated—by a chemical or nerve agent, for example—a majority of the House could constitute a quorum, but couldn't act. Replacement would have to await the next general election, possibly close to two years. Senate replacement would similarly be delayed, up to six years in some cases. A related problem is if a terror attack forces one or more jurisdictions to cancel an election, as happened on 9/11 in New York City. Statutory provision of timetables can help. Holding an election within 90 days for a national election might entail everyone voting again, to preserve the contemporaneous judgment of the electorate.

The Continuity of Government Commission, convened after 9/11, recommends that state governors be empowered to fill vacancies in the House and Senate, in event of mass incapacitation, until elections can be held. A Constitutional amendment is needed to amend the Constitution's provisions to cover such exigencies; among the unresolved issues is who determines what constitutes a mass incapacitation and how is such determination is made. Rapid adoption and ratification occasionally happens, when the public recognizes an urgent need for amendment, and thus should be achievable here, if proposed with broad bipartisan support.

On May 9, 2007, President Bush issued a national security directive designating the White House as primary supervisor of continuity issues, and the Department of Homeland Security as primary Cabinet department for same. The directive defines eight "essential functions" whose continuity must be assured. They encompass the three branches of government, and address the ability to defend the country, recover from a disaster, revive the economy and protect "national health, safety and welfare."

Presidential and Vice Presidential disability is dealt with per the twenty-fifth amendment, ratified in 1967 (prompted by the confusion after the 1963 assassination of President Kennedy). Section One provides that in event the president dies, the Vice-President succeeds; this re-codifies practice dating to the origin of the republic. Section Two provides that given a Vice-Presidential vacancy, the President nominates a candidate, to be confirmed by majority vote of both houses. This happened twice during the Watergate years. In 1973 Vice-President Spiro Agnew resigned, to be replaced by Michigan Congressman Gerald Ford. When in August 1974 President Nixon resigned, Ford became President, and New York Governor Nelson Rockefeller was later confirmed as Ford's number two. Section Three provides that the President can transmit a message to the leaders of both houses that he cannot perform his duties, and thus the Vice-President becomes acting President until the President signals his fitness to return. This was first invoked when President Ronald Reagan underwent surgery. Section Four provides a complex procedure by which a majority of the Cabinet officers or such other body as Congress may provide can declare the president incapacitated. Upon the request of the President to be allowed to return he can do so, unless a majority of the Cabinet or other body established by Congress vetoes his return.

Congress currently provides by statute the line of succession in event both President and Vice-President are disabled, a line that begins with the Speaker of the House, then the President *pro tempore* of the Senate, then Cabinet officials, beginning with State, Defense, Treasury and the Attorney-General.[76] This law, originally passed in 1947 and amended as new Cabinet posts have been added, is of dubious constitutionality, in that it arguably conflicts with the Constitution's Presidential Succession Clause, which requires that an "officer" succeed to the Presidency in event of a double vacancy. Some scholars interpret "officer" to refer solely to the executive branch. Another infirmity is that given a 50–50 Senate (which was the case from January to May of 2001), if the Senate's presiding officer becomes President, Senatorial control might change, were the replacement Senator to come from a different party. (No one can serve in both the legislature and the executive: The Incompatibility Clause of

---

76. Presidential Succession Act, 3 U.S.C. sec. 19 (1947, as amended). The President *pro tempore* ("temporary") presides over the Senate when the Vice-President is not presiding. The first succession law had the President *pro tempore* first and then the Speaker. In 1886 the law was changed to provide for Cabinet succession only. But in 1947 President Truman persuaded Congress to pass the present law.

the U.S. Constitution provides: "[N]o Person, holding any Office under the United States, shall be a Member of either House during his continuance in Office.")

The continuity of government recommendations noted above should be adopted. As for succession, American Enterprise Institute scholar John Fortier argues that the 1947 law should be repealed, and a pure executive line of succession adopted (as was the case from 1886 to 1947). This preserves the choice of administration and congressional control voters made in the immediately preceding Presidential election. Above all, action is needed to provide for continuity and succession by enshrining in law a process that commands respect across a broad political spectrum of leaders and voters.

Another emergency issue is the need to educate the public more thoroughly about specific dangers posed by various types of attacks, so they know which attacks are truly lethal and which are far less so, and can take action accordingly. One major fear is that of a "dirty-bomb." The lethality of a radiological weapon is critically dependent upon which specific toxic substance is used in the bomb. If a bomb is laced with plutonium it could contaminate an urban area for decades. But if it is laced with Potassium-40, found in our bodies, the resulting contaminant might raise one's risk of getting cancer by a fractional percentage over several decades. This would be nettlesome but hardly worthy of provoking mass hysteria. We can, alas, depend upon mass media to hype risk and thus amplify panic, as with Chernobyl.

This is where ex-Presidents and current celebrities can help. All willing former Presidents should tape a series of public service ads—appearing together so as to catch the viewer's attention. The ads would explain what precautions to follow after an attack, and how to find out the estimated magnitude of the hazard. Newspaper and magazine ads can complement the TV ads. Celebrities (those with credibility for sobriety and intelligence) can also do ads like this, as they command lots of viewer attention. An educated public is far less likely to panic. At present, 28 percent of the public has disaster kits, 36 percent have made evacuation plans, and 48 percent have first aid or CPR training.

Spend Less Now or More Later

America must take steps now to reduce to the lowest feasible risk level the chance of suffering a society-destabilizing catastrophe. A United States without the support services of its electrical and communications infrastructure for any extended period would be crippled. A mass panic after a "dirty bomb" attack could kill thousands needlessly. We have the resources, and in no meaningful economic way are we constrained by the federal budget deficit, which is but modest compared to overall public debt and, more importantly, compared to the immense store of tangible and intangible financial asset wealth of America.

We must as well take steps to mitigate, as much as possible, the impact of catastrophe by giving the President adequate emergency authority, providing prudently for continuity of government after a catastrophic strike, and educating the public about certain threats so as to minimize unnecessary loss of life.

After a major WMD event, there will be martial law, albeit perhaps not formally declared. In a democratic republic, it is best that such powers, while inevitably deriving their scope and scale from the triggering event, should be bounded as to duration. Doing so precludes conflicts over legitimacy of executive authority. Complementary to this, continuity measures protect legislative legitimacy and executive succession. Together, they ensure legitimacy of governance when it is most needed.

Our resource challenges test not our immense pocketbook, but our flagging political will and our economic misconceptions. We can afford what we need. Sharing the cost with descendants is fine so long as they benefit, as of course they would, hugely. Frugality on homeland defense today courts catastrophe tomorrow. *One WMD catastrophe will make our frugality seem the most expensive policy choice we have ever made.*

CHAPTER VII
THE SHORT WAR
WMD AND BETTING THE COMPANY

"Appeasement," where it is not a device to gain time, is the result of an inability to come to grips with a policy of unlimited objectives.
But it is the essence of a revolutionary power that it possesses the courage of its convictions, that it is willing, indeed eager, to push its principles to their ultimate conclusion. Whatever else a revolutionary power may achieve, therefore, it tends to erode, if not the legitimacy of the international order, at least the restraint with which such an order operates.... And because in revolutionary situations the contending systems are less concerned with the adjustment of differences than with the subversion of loyalties, diplomacy is replaced either by war or by an armaments race.
HENRY KISSINGER, *A WORLD RESTORED* (1957)

Diplomacy without force is like music without instruments.
FREDERICK THE GREAT

The Short War is, as noted earlier, a war of prevention: preventing a WMD catastrophe whose destructive effects—massive loss of life, long-lasting severe economic damage and a shredded social fabric—could overwhelm the West's ability to cope. Victory in the Short War is a predicate for success in the Long War. While biological pathogens may ultimately prove the gravest threat, for the near term the threat of nuclear detonations appears to be the most pressing problem. Foremost among potential nuclear menaces would be an Islamist Pakistan, already nuclear-armed, but at this writing the Islamists do not appear positioned to take power. Rather, it is Iran's nuclear program, in service of its leaders' revolutionary aspiration and messianic creed, that appears to pose the most urgent threat in the near future.

The critical question that now confronts the West regarding Iran is, which side is "betting the company"? This is a huge risk no one should want to take, if it can be avoided. Are the bigger gamblers those who seek to destroy Iran's nuclear program before it succeeds, or those who prefer to rely on traditional notions of deterrence after Iran goes nuclear? *The critical policy imperative for Western powers as regards any adversary state in search of WMD is to never limit themselves to the three "apocalyptic options" of surrender, suicide or genocide (whether pre-emptive or retaliatory).*

It should be noted that the 9/11 Commission Report mentions Iran's connection to al-Qaeda and terrorism. The June 1996 Khobar Towers bombing that killed 19 U.S. servicemen and injured scores was carried out largely, perhaps exclusively, by the Saudi branch of Hezbollah. But the relationship between Iran and al Qaeda dates back to 1991, when Hezbollah began training al-Qaeda operatives. The 9/11 report states: "The relationship between al-Qaeda and Iran demonstrated that Sunni-Shia divisions did not necessarily pose an insurmountable barrier to co-operation in terrorist operations." Yet the panel concluded that it could not establish a direct connection with the 9/11 plot, stating that while there is "strong evidence" that Iran facilitated the transit of al-Qaeda operatives out of Afghanistan prior to 9/11, which may have included some 9/11 hijackers (many of whom did not know their ultimate mission), "we cannot rule out the possibility of a remarkable coincidence" (*i.e.*, that more than one terrorist operation was underway) that would explain the contacts without directly implicating Iran in the 9/11 plot. The panel recommended that the government further investigate the matter.

Whether diplomatic negotiation can halt Iran's nuclear program boils down to a single question: Is Iran a *status quo* or a *revolutionary* power? The former seeks adjustment in the terms of the existing international order, the latter seeks its destruction and replacement by a new order. Nazi Germany was a revolutionary power, as was the Soviet Union for much of the Cold War. Then came Mikhail Gorbachev, a man Margaret Thatcher famously said she could "do business with." With his *glasnost* (openness) and *perestroika* (restructuring) policies adopted in 1987, the Soviet Union abandoned its revolutionary aspirations, which had been based on a totalitarian ideology of world revolution. Then came the miracle year of 1989. Soviet spokesman Gennady Gerasimov told American television audiences that the Brezhnev Doctrine—once a country goes socialist it stays socialist—had been supplanted by the "Frank Sinatra Doctrine"—"My Way" for the countries of Eastern Europe. The new Russian way was letting Eastern European satellites go. By this action the Soviet Union signaled that it had become a *status quo* power, one no longer seeking to overturn the existing world order. By the end of 1991 the break-up of the Soviet Empire was complete.

Diplomacy, multilateral coalitions and sanctions, as options short of military action, are hard put to constrain a revolutionary power. Yet these tools are commonly considered by many Americans to suffice for conducting foreign policy in accord with alliances and the United Nations. But America sometimes forgets who its real friends are and is tempted to try to placate its enemies.

Recalibrating Diplomacy: Dance with Friends, not Wolves

We can place nations in five broad categories.

1. **Friends: Stand By Them.** These will stay with us even when we are losing (think Britain, Australia, Israel, Japan).

2. **Fence-Sitters: Deal at Arms Length.** Neutrals (think Switzerland) or fair-weather friends (think of our Mideast Arab "allies") will stay with us so long as we look like winners.

3. **Rivals: Use Carrots and Sticks.** These aim to surpass us in influence, but not necessarily to destroy us (think China).

4. **Rogues: Use More Sticks Than Carrots.** These engage in criminal or terrorist activities in pursuit of a lone-wolf agenda, and will destroy us if, in their view, that is the only way to achieve their goals (think North Korea, Syria). Regime change is preferable.

5. **Revolutionaries: Seek Regime Change.** These seek to *forcibly* overturn the international order (think Iran), and thus intend specifically to destroy us, because a strong America is their major obstacle. For

such adversaries our only secure remedy is to seek regime change—theirs, before they can change ours. Regime change is imperative.

Categories 4 and 5 are, of course, *enemies*. With revolutionaries, an important distinction arises between those who seek by force or the threat of force to overthrow the existing world order, so they can impose a dictatorial world order, versus democratic nations that seek to liberate captive peoples. The United States is a revolutionary power, in that it upholds the right to "life, liberty and the pursuit of happiness" as the birthright of every person on Earth. As Michael Ledeen has argued, America has for two centuries been the world's most revolutionary power, but America has sought to spread liberty and prosperity. It is the spread of *tyranny* by revolution that America rightly opposes.

Placing nations in these categories is not intended as a suggestion that we should expect nations to follow other than their own perceived best interests in dealing with us. Thus India, whose relations with America have never been better, also has entered into negotiations with Russia and China, two rivals of America, to seek ways to counter American power and create a more "multi-polar" world. Together these three countries represent 40 percent of the world's population, 20 percent of the world economy and more than 50 percent of the world's nuclear warheads, and thus can exert considerable influence in concert. We should expect that fence-sitters will switch sides from time to time, or simultaneously play both sides, as Pakistan has done since 9/11.

How, in fact, do we treat enemies? Often too well. We offer carrots to rogues like North Korea, support largely toothless UN resolutions and go back to the bargaining table.[77] Until 2007 revolutionary Iran got a partial pass despite doing much to undermine our position in Iraq, where the President calls victory absolutely essential; Iran supplies insurgents with sophisticated IEDs (Improvised Explosive Devices) and

---

77. In his magisterial memoir, *Surrender is Not an Option* (2007), former State Department official and U.S. Ambassador to the UN John Bolton shows in detail how the U.S. State Department bureaucracy pushes accommodationist policies even in deliberate contravention of Presidential policies.

EFPs (Explosively Formed Projectiles), plus it foments sectarian violence through its stooge militias. We have engaged, from time to time, in a diplomatic dance with Syria, a rogue state that has aided the Iraq insurgency and, as well, aided Hezbollah in its war with Israel. Syria also has its own WMD program.

The once "Grand Alliance" of America and Europe is no longer so grand. On the plus side, Europe has cooperated with the U.S. in many law enforcement counter-terror ventures. And Europe has a major force commitment in Afghanistan. But the minus side may be greater. In 2002 a French book claiming that the U.S. orchestrated the 9/11 attacks to justify invading Afghanistan spent six weeks on the bestseller list, and broke the French record for first-month book sales. Europe unleashed one mass fusillade against American detention practices and a second in opposition to the idea of preventive counter-terror strikes. European solicitude for detainees who would kill European families in an instant is a curious way to fight Islamofascist terror. So is piling on in the Abu Ghraib dispute. Europe went public in an apparent effort to placate Muslim residents. Europeans have also been hypocritical, simultaneously accusing the U.S. of abusing Guantanamo detainees, while refusing to accept detainees whom the U.S. sought to return to their home country for detention there. Compounding European hypocrisy is that in 1978 the European Court of Human Rights held permissible the combined use of detention practices similar to those the U.S. used at Guantanamo: wall-standing, hooding, playing loud music, sleep deprivation and even food and drink deprivation via a reduced diet. The reality is that at Guantanamo, detainees are fed 2,700 calories per day. (A lightly active 20-year-old, 6-foot, 200 lbs. male requires 2,717 daily calories to maintain his weight.)

Worse, Europe does not seriously challenge the terrorists to live up to comparable standards of treatment. This should be done not because the terrorists would do so, but to show the difference between the two sides. This also holds for Hezbollah and Hamas, whose atrocities Europe largely ignores, as compared to Israel, whose errors Europe trumpets. A

2007 poll shows that 72 percent of European Union leaders believe that Tehran's nuclear program is purely defensive in nature, while 70 percent of the European public, to their credit, believes otherwise. With many European elites fearing the U.S. more than Iran, it is clear that the days of close, even sentimental friendship with much of Western Europe are over. America has truer friends in Eastern Europe and elsewhere.[78]

But, one asks, should not friends offer honest criticism when they think you are wrong? Absolutely—such advice is essential. But in doing so, real friends should follow a rule of discretion: Severe criticism should be offered behind closed doors, and thus nothing said in public should be calculated to injure or in any way undermine one's ally. The chorus of screams over detainees at Guantanamo violates this rule. Outrageous— mostly totally untrue—accusations were hurled at us, thus inflicting great damage on America's image.

No effort was made to put accusations in perspective. America was publicly pilloried. From friends, this is simply unacceptable. American expatriate author Claire Berlinski divines a "first principle" of European attitudes toward America, one which suggests the problem is endemic and oblivious to reasoned counter-persuasion:

> European anti-Americanism is a cultist system of faith, rather than a set of rational beliefs, and as such is impervious to revision upon confrontation with facts, logic, evidence, gestures of good will, public relations campaigns, or attempts on the part of the American secretary of state to be a better, more sensitive listener.

Europe's anti-Americanism goes hand in hand with European willingness to pass the buck to America. Just after the Cold War joined history's ash-heap, the Secretary-General of NATO, Germany's Manfred Woerner, told President George H. W. Bush: "The United States should not expect others to deliver much. They are waiting for the Americans."

The differences between America and Europe are, international lawyers David Rivkin and Lee Casey point out, deep, and may repre-

---

78. On November 7, 2007, French President Nicholas Sarkozy addressed a joint session of Congress. His speech expressed sincere and deep friendship towards America. But there is little reason to believe that France's foreign policy elite shares this view.

sent an unbridgeable chasm. Europe's faith in legal process against terrorism stems from its inquisitorial system, superior to our adversary system, which affords far fewer rights to defendants and gives the state broader investigative powers than does America's common law system. The inquisitorial system features extended preventive detention, secret proceedings, judges instead of jurors, the requirement that defendants testify, and open-ended prosecutorial power. The Bush administration's military tribunals do not go nearly so far in limiting common law rights.

But as to war-fighting, Europe's refusal to recognize the unlawful combatant concept, which stems from its ratification of the 1977 Genera Protocol I, makes it far less effective in war-fighting than the U.S., which declined to ratify Protocol I. As Rivkin and Casey explain, Protocol I makes it nearly impossible to target terrorists embedded within civilian populations without arguably committing a war crime, while giving terrorists the benefit of Geneva rights despite their deliberate targeting of civilians. No compromise is likely to fully reconcile these sharply opposing, strongly-held views.

Yet we, too, have at times failed to take steps to preserve alliance relations. A notable debacle, for which both parties bear some responsibility, is between the U.S. and Turkey, a key country whose geography spans Europe and Asia, and an ally that gave the U.S. considerable support during the Cold War and the Gulf War. Turkey failed to allow the U.S. to send its strongest ground unit, the Patriot Division, into Iraq in March 2003, thus prolonging the war. But the U.S. only belatedly tried to control the Kurdish separatist terrorists crossing into Turkey from Kurdistan, creating the prospect that Turkey will invade Kurdistan and come into direct conflict with its NATO co-member, the U.S.

In sum, we should treat our true friends best, treat fence-sitters less well, treat rivals at arms-length (albeit cordially, with a proper diplomatic formality), make rogues fear us, and undermine revolutionary regimes. We are resolutely ambivalent about Saudi Arabia, whose financing of Islamic extremism created much of the monster we now are trying to defeat. We plan to sell $20 billion worth of top-of-the-line weaponry to the Saudis, despite their perfidy in the 1980s and 1990s. Ironically, we sold AWACS and F-15s to the Saudis in 1981 to cement a "special relationship" with them. Still, the Saudis spread fanatical hatred of the West, even in mosques in the U.S. Saudis are prominent among jihadist fighters infiltrating into Iraq to wreck America's Iraq project. True, they did help in the Gulf War, but that was in their survival interest. Absent American intervention Saudi Arabia would have become a vassal of Saddam's. Time will tell if this latest arms sale will bear fruit in constructive cooperation. *Curbing Saudi financing of fanaticism worldwide, by whatever combination of carrots and sticks is required, must become a preeminent American foreign policy goal.*

Coalitions and Consensus: The Perils of Reflexive Multilateralism

Begin with the absurd pretensions of some Secretaries-General who aspire to be, as former U.S. Ambassador to the UN John Bolton put it, the "Planet President." The S-G's role is defined per Article 97 of the UN Charter as "the chief administrative officer of the Organization."[79] The adjective "administrative" shows that the S-G is not even an *executive* officer. He is a *bureaucrat*. Yet two S-Gs immediately prior to the present one have used their access to global media in an attempt to morph their powers into those of a planetary executive. Kofi Annan branded the U.S.-led Coalition's 2003 invasion of Iraq illegal, despite a March 27, 2003, vote at a UN session in Geneva—the only vote on legality taken at the UN—that rejected a motion declaring the invasion illegal. In fact, the S-G has *zero* authority to independently deliver an official opinion on *any* issue of legality under the UN Charter. Article 99 of the UN Charter provides: "The Secretary-General may bring to the attention of

---

79. Former UN Secretary-General Kofi Annan openly proclaimed himself a "secular Pope." Article 97 of the UN Charter refutes this, as does Aman's dismal performance, which gave no intimation of Papal infallibility.

the Security Council any matter which in his opinion may threaten the maintenance of international peace and security."

Then factor in that the UN can hardly work as originally intended when the top eight donor members shoulder 72.5 percent of the cost while the bottom 48 pay a whopping 0.001 percent, an average of $19,000 each. The 128 lowest-paying members (two-thirds of the UN's 192 total members) combined pay less than *one percent* of the UN's budget. When members vote themselves money from other nations the result is another example of "moral hazard"—decoupling risk from responsibility.[80]

The UN has never adopted a formal declaration defining terrorism. Also many countries regard any act of legitimate self-defense taken by America or Israel as inherently suspect. In the event, the manifest failure of UN "peacekeepers" on the Israeli-Lebanon border in 2006 informs us anew that we cannot expect much from such multilateral ventures.

Dramatic proof of UN fecklessness was provided after the December 26, 2004, tsunami in Southeast Asia that killed over 200,000 people. Rapid rescue work by a coalition of the willing reached Indonesia (by far the hardest hit) long before the UN could trouble itself to pitch in. Australia, New Zealand, Singapore and Japan joined the U.S. to do most of the heavy lifting, along with the locals, for the first few weeks. The UN, for its part, sent officials to hold press conferences and meetings, while denouncing the relief efforts as "uncoordinated." One UN official called America "stingy" as American aircraft carriers led the relief effort. The UN only counts government funding through certain programs in tabulating aid; sending an aircraft carrier with on-board hospitals, medical supplies, water purification plants, power generators and skilled crews fails to qualify, nor do the efforts of private charities. More than half of U.S. aid is sent via private channels. Meanwhile, a full *one-third* of UN aid went to cover administrative overhead.

---

80. Ambassador Bolton believes that only if financial contributions are voluntary and transparent, can the UN work better. The operations that work best, such as the International High Commissioner for Refugees, the World Food program, and UNICEF, are funded this way.

Worse still is UN amoral neutrality in the face of genocide. After Bosnia, Kofi Annan said that the UN had "an institutional ideology of impartiality even when confronted with attempted genocide." UN investigations of nuclear facilities (performed by the International Atomic Energy Agency—IAEA) are sharply limited. The IAEA inspects only facilities *declared* by member states; it cannot verify secret weapons or facilities, and the inspection is subject to approval of personnel and conditions by the country whose facilities are to be inspected.

International institutions can work, but only in specialized circumstances where commonality of interest is sufficiently broad. Thus, the World Health Organization (WHO) can function reasonably well, because virtually all nations, except for a few outliers that aid bio-terror efforts to weaponize pathogens, share common goals in combating disease. The International Telecommunication Union offers an example of generally constructive cooperation in the economic sphere.[81] Placing the WHO and ITU inside the UN's vast, Soviet-style bureaucracy makes them subject to UN political currents. There is reason to believe that they could do better if freed from the bureaucratic embrace of their current parent.

But the areas in which goals are least likely to be common are those which raise questions like use of force and nuclear proliferation. Thus, the chief UN inspector in charge of monitoring Iran's nuclear program has stated that he does not see anything wrong with Iran acquiring nuclear weapons capability.

Most illustrative of all is the massive oil-for-food scandal, largest in the history of the planet, which siphoned off desperately needed aid intended for the Iraqi people. Journalist Claudia Rosett, whose articles did more than any others to expose the oil-for-food mess, writes that of $65

---

81. The first international organization, the International Telegraph Union, was formed in 1865, for the purpose of regulating international telegraphy. It survives as the International Telecommunication Union, and is subsumed under the UN organizational structure. An excellent discussion of the subject is found in pp. 115-123 of Robert J. Oslund's essay, "The Geopolitics and Institutions of Satellite Communications," in *Communications Satellites: Global Change Agents*, (Joseph N. Pelton, Robert J. Oslund & Peter Marshall Ed., 2004).

billion in oil-sales and $46 billion in relief purchases, $11 billion was siphoned off by Saddam, cronies inside Iraq and abroad and even UN officials, and on top of that the UN Secretariat collected $1.4 billion in commissions. While this was going on, the U.S. was being blamed for the sanctions, allegedly causing the deaths of hundreds of thousands of Iraqi children. Except that the sanctions never barred food or medical supplies. That "inconvenient truth" was simply ignored by American critics.

Another danger to America's effective exercise of power is the UN's Law of the Sea Treaty (LOST), which President Reagan declined to submit to the Senate, but President Bush, backed by military advice and former senior Reagan officials, has decided to support. It defines international boundary lines of demarcation at sea, rights of access to navigable waters, seabed mining rights, etc. Even if the administration and its supporters are right as to the substantive provisions of the treaty, disputes over access are required to be submitted to international arbitration. Such panels will be drawn from judges of all nations, and likely will feature a majority who are hostile to the U.S. and cannot be counted upon to rule honestly. We have experience with such abuse. In 1984 the World Court held that the Court had jurisdiction over U.S. mining of Nicaragua's harbors, despite the U.S. having conditioned its ratification of the UN treaty on the U.S. consenting to accept court jurisdiction in a given case, and despite Nicaragua never having actually accepted the Court's jurisdiction.

Another excellent demonstration of how the UN caters to terror states is its refusal to condemn Iran's March 2007 seizure in international waters of British sailors. During her two-weeks of captivity one female hostage was forced to wear a head-scarf in public. This flagrantly violates Article 34 of the Third Geneva Convention, to which Iran is a signatory, which states that "[p]risoners of war shall enjoy complete latitude in the exercise of their religious duties." Hudson Institute scholar John O'Sullivan points out that had Britain illegally seized Iranian sailors and mistreated them, there would have been an instant global uproar, with pressure on Britain to immediately release the Iranians. But the world community was largely silent regarding Iran's outrage, with the UN failing even to deplore Iran's unlawful conduct.

Negotiations: The Perils of Process

Oft quoted is Winston Churchill's aphorism: "To jaw-jaw is always better than to war-war." But Churchill's remark was made during his final stint as Prime Minister, at a White House luncheon on June 26, 1954, when *nuclear war* between the United States and the Soviet Union could easily have entailed mutual suicide. Mr. Churchill took the opposite position between 1936 and 1939, when Adolf Hitler was annexing land in Europe. War then would have toppled Hitler and saved more than 50 million lives. "Jaw-jaw" proved exceedingly unhelpful on December 7, 1941, as U.S. diplomats sparred with their Japanese counterparts in Washington while Japanese bombers sank U.S. ships.

Negotiations can work against adversaries only to the extent that power lies behind promises made and inspection can verify compliance. During the Cold War the former Soviet Union massively violated strategic arms agreements, yet never was meaningfully called to account for doing so.

In his Inaugural address, John F. Kennedy proclaimed, "Let us never negotiate out of fear. But let us never fear to negotiate." It often seems that in the West the second clause is taken more seriously than is the first. Negotiations too often can represent the triumph of process over substance and a way to avoid hard decisions. Six practical principles as to diplomacy and negotiations seem evident:

1. Negotiating from weakness—out of fear—is likely a losing effort, ceding advantage to adamant opponents.

2. Our adversaries can cheat and repudiate with impunity, but we can't (media, public pressure for "good faith"—giving them "another chance," etc.).

3. We Westerners tend to view all differences as splittable, but often our opponents do not.

4. The desire to preserve a good "atmosphere" usually freezes non-diplomatic options (sanctions, human rights pressure, military options).

5. Adversaries can "move the goal posts" by making new demands once their demands have been met (as happened with North Vietnam).

6. We fail to grasp that negotiations with adversaries based upon falsely presumed common interests are never "can't lose" propositions.

Rogue and revolutionary states are expert at offering mini-carrots just when less patient parties are ready to walk away. Such concessions are honored in the breach, but serve their purpose of keeping the negotiations open and freezing other options, especially the use of force. *A simple rule of thumb would help: When negotiations between civilized countries and rogue or revolutionary states break down, 99.9 percent of the time the fault lies with the barbarians.* States that habitually deal in bad faith should presumptively be blamed. Thus, blaming American administrations because talks with the likes of North Korea or Iran get nowhere is a form of diplomatic masochism. The most one can realistically hope for when negotiating with a rogue or revolutionary power is to force a tactical retreat; strategic defeat cannot be won solely by negotiation.

The West must get over the self-deluding attitude that all differences are resolvable. The concept of irreconcilable differences is ruled out even when the adversary manifestly shows revolutionary intent, as with Iran. In terms of probable outcome, the side that needs negotiations more will most likely prove the loser in any deal struck. It will feel pressure to make a deal for the sake of making one. The only times that one can reasonably anticipate success in negotiation with enemies is when we have the upper hand, and our enemies know that we do. This was the case when Ronald Reagan and Margaret Thatcher negotiated with Mikhail Gorbachev in the late 1980s. Gorbachev had famously been told by Marshal Ogarkov, his defense chief, that the Soviet Union simply was unable to keep up with American technological superiority. He thus knew his position was weak and getting weaker, and negotiated accordingly.

There is nothing like that situation with Iran in 2007, which sees itself as in a superior position *vis-à-vis* the U.S. So long as this remains the case, there can be no reasonable expectation that the mullahs will give us help in Iraq. Our defeat, and an ignominious exit from Iraq, is what will most enhance Iran's power in the region. The mullahs cannot be expected to bargain victory away to suit us.

Lest we fall for the fallacy of mirror-imaging on Iran, think in terms of how polite behavior and brutish behavior are viewed, depending upon social setting. In a nice restaurant, the first is admired and the second is unacceptable; in a prison yard, the first marks one as a target, while the second earns street-level respect, essential in the jungle of prison.

The point was made eloquently, as regards the Soviet Union, in 1982, by the late Senator Daniel Patrick Moynihan. He warned that we court great danger when we invite the contempt of totalitarians. The prescience of Moynihan's warning was made clear on 9/11. Dealing with the world's worst regimes by progressively sweetening offers in the face of non-compliance courts precisely such contempt.

Sanctions: Time and Targeting

Sanctions offer a way to squeeze an adversary into agreement without resorting to military force. But sanctions must clear five hurdles to work well:

1. Control by a sole supplier or a group of suppliers who equally agree on the sanctions regime.

2. The ability to direct pain at the regime and its leaders, by withholding goods or services deemed essential to the regime's ability to stay in power and carry out its policies.

3. A regime weak enough to be unable to circumvent sanctions or endure under them.

4. Honest and effective administration of the sanctions program.

5. Enough time for sanctions to achieve their intended purpose.

The Reagan administration wrote the sanctions playbook. Ronald Reagan lifted the grain embargo imposed by Jimmy Carter on the Soviet Union, in response to its December 1979 invasion of Afghanistan, because alternate suppliers—Canada, Argentina and Australia—were supplying the grain anyway. The losers had been American farmers, not the Soviet leaders. But in 1982 Reagan imposed a high-technology embargo—including products only the U.S. made—that targeted the Soviet regime by denying essential technology to its military. This helped bring the Soviet Union down, because without high technology, its economic and military stagnation was inevitable. The Bush Sr./Clinton oil-for-food sanctions against Saddam failed all five tests given above.

A test of the efficacy of sanctions policy is ongoing with North Korea. In February 2007 the U.S. and its negotiating partners struck a tentative deal with North Korea, trading economic aid (mostly fuel oil) for ending its nuclear program and presenting a list of its entire program within 60 days. Targeted for lifting were highly effective sanctions denying the North access to international credit markets, perhaps the strongest card the West has in its diplomatic deck. Later in 2007 a "breakthrough" was announced. The North would surrender its nukes and end its program, in return for which the West would recognize its legitimacy and America would take the North off its terror watch list. But the North merely promised again what it had promised to do—and failed to do—in the February agreement. Clandestine hoarding of nuclear bombs can be accomplished, and the North may well have facilities buried deep underground, unknown to the inspectors. After the Iraq WMD debacle, how much confidence can one have in America's ability (or anyone else's ability) to conduct WMD verification? President Bush, who approved a draft agreement in October 2007, is a believer.

Of all this, former U.S. Ambassador to the UN, John Bolton, who when serving in the Bush State Department crafted the innovative, highly successful Proliferation Security Initiative (which interdicts un-lawful shipments of nuclear material) said: "If you hold out long enough and wear down the State Department negotiators, eventually you will get rewarded." The administration's old "CVID" policy—complete, veri-fiable, irreversible disarmament—is history. While the North appears to be closing its aging Yongbyon reactor, absent intrusive inspection we cannot verify dismantling of the North's program. We released $25 mil-lion in frozen funds in return for commitments we cannot verify.

We know that the North has provided nuclear material to Syria, where a suspicious facility was destroyed by an Israeli night air raid on September 6, 2007. In its aftermath, the silence of Arab states in the Mideast attests to their growing fear of Iran's drive for hegemony in the region. The raid, which bypassed Syria's advanced air defenses, also is a warning to Iran that its own Russian defenses may fail, too.

On the plus side is the establishment of the Kaesong Industrial Zone, where South Korean companies are getting a foothold, and may in time set in motion the kind of forces that spurred economic reform in China. Also, Kim Jong-Il has been less of a risk-taker than his late fa-ther, Kim Il-Sung who, among other acts, launched the Korean War in 1950. Former Secretary of State Henry Kissinger has written that our chances for success in negotiating with the North lie in keeping sanc-tions pressure on, and in refusing to let the North's grievances dominate the negotiation.

Iran's Revolutionary Aspirations

Iran is playing a diplomatic double game on the world stage. For-mer President Mohammed Khatami tells Americans that Iran desires peace. Yet Khatami has never delivered any genuinely significant regime moderation, though it was hoped for by many in the West. And Iran's current President, Mahmoud Ahmadinejad, already faces indictment abroad.[82] Noting that America won World War II, Ahmadinejad vows

---

82. In 2006, a warrant was issued by an Argentine judge seeking extradition of Ahmadinejad, to face trial in Argentina for his role in the 1992 bombing that killed 29 and wounded 242

that America will lose World War III. "Iran," he says, "will win the coming war and America will be beaten."

Consider this triad of chilling quotes, two from Iranian leaders, and one from Iran's top agent in the terrorist group Iran founded, Hezbollah. Iranian President Mahmoud Ahmadinejad said in 2006 that Iran must "wipe Israel off the map." An earlier Iranian President, one often called pragmatic, Hashemi al-Rafsanjani, said in 2001 that it would be worth it to kill five million Jews in Israel, even if an Israeli retaliatory strike killed 15 million in Iran—a small "sacrifice" for the world's Muslims to make. And Hezbollah chief Sheik Nasrallah said in 2006: "If Jews all gather in Israel, it will save us the trouble of going after them worldwide."

Who then to believe? As former Senator Bob Dole said, during the 1986–1987 Iran-Contra scandal (Reagan's messy, semi-accidental arms-for-hostages affair), an Iranian "moderate" is a radical who has run out of ammunition. Bear in mind that all aspiring candidates are vetted by the 86-member Assembly of Experts, so that no one the mullahs disfavor can run for office. The sounder view of apparent divisions within the regime is that Iran plays "good cop/bad cop" with the West.

Especially disturbing is the messianic character of the ideology of Iran's mullahs. Their brand of messianic faith is more lethal than that of Communism. The Marxist-Leninist messiah was a secular, earthly one, whose performance could be judged by real-world standards. The child Messiah who Iran's mullahs prepare to welcome is a religious authority who will bring about an Islamic version of what we in the West call an apocalyptic end of times. In the case of Iran, the practical, real-world vehicle for bringing on the apocalypse may well be via nuclear weapons. The likely targets are Israel and America. Leaders seized of messianic certitude are not reliably amenable to the rational calculus that is the *sine qua non* of a successful policy of deterrence.

---

people in Buenos Aires. The move is symbolic, as Iran's President will never show up. Only if there is regime change in Iran, and Ahmadinejad is captured alive, might the Argentine judicial warrant be executed.

By fair weight of evidence available to us—actions and statements—
Iran is a *revolutionary* power whose desire to overturn the existing world
order makes negotiations a poor wager. Iran's mullahs will be stopped, if
at all, either by regime change from within or regime change from without.

Deterrence and Revolutionary Regimes

What about deterrence as an option? Begin with a working definition: A policy of deterrence aims to implant in the mind of an adversary
the credible fear that certain consequences, unacceptable to the adversary, will foreseeably occur, in the event the adversary takes certain action, despite having been warned not to do so. Put more prosaically, if
you launch one or more nuclear bombs in our direction, one (or more)
will be sent to your home address. A policy of deterrence presumes three
things: (1) a *rational adversary* who will calculate costs versus benefits
and carefully assess relative estimated risk; (2) a threat of retaliation that
is *considered credible by the adversary*; and (3) an *identifiable home address
for the attacker*, against which retaliation can be directed in the event deterrence fails.

Now, herewith is a brief historical retrospective, because what is
"known" about deterrence during the Cold War is mostly popular fiction. Unfortunately, a false history underpins the arguments of those
who advocate a reprise of Cold War deterrence, this time against a nuclear-armed Iran. We are continually told that the doctrine of deterrence
that worked in the Cold War was called Mutual Assured Destruction
(MAD). Only in the *public declaratory* sense was that true—MAD was
said to be our doctrine and that of the Soviets.

MAD meant that each side would deliberately hold its civilian
population hostage to the other side's nuclear forces (missiles, bombers,
submarines). Equally, each side would refrain from deploying missiles
whose "lethality" (*i.e.*, combination of accuracy and warhead yield) gave

them "counter-force" capability—the ability to destroy the other side's nuclear forces.[83]

But neither declaratory proposition was actually true in practice. First, the Soviet Union ran a massive urban civil defense program (derided in the West as "Duck and take cover!"). This was an effort to protect civilians, who were supposedly hostage to our forces in the event of nuclear war. Even if ineffective, the very effort showed *intent* on the part of the Soviets to reject holding all of their population hostage, as MAD entailed. Further, Soviet missile accuracies improved sufficiently so as to give their strategic forces a plausible ability to kill "hard targets" (U.S. missiles in silos). Soviet MAD doctrine might better have been called "Mainly America's Destruction."

From the U.S. standpoint, every administration during the Cold War sought intermediate options between "all or nothing." Thus, even the famously dovish Carter administration adopted a doctrine of targeting command and control assets in event of war—the very assets that would direct nuclear strikes. This doctrine was plainly inconsistent with a strict application of MAD, which entails an all-out strike. For this reason the 1972 ABM Treaty banned only missile defenses to protect the *population*. Limited deployment to protect missile sites was permitted. As noted earlier, President Bush exercised America's right to withdraw from the ABM Treaty. (In 2006 the first post-treaty-withdrawal operational missile defense site was deployed on Kodiak Island, Alaska.)

Explaining these niceties in the hurly-burly of public debate was, as pretty much everyone in the field understood, next to impossible. The Reagan administration once tried to convince skeptics that the Soviet Union's military doctrine held that—in theory, at least—it was possible to fight and win a nuclear war. After being pilloried in the press, the administration shelved attempts to persuade the public of this, despite evidence supporting its view. Meanwhile, the Soviets kept building, whether we were building or not. As President Carter's Defense Secre-

---

83. In the parlance of nuclear theologians, strikes against population are "counter-value."

tary, Harold Brown, once famously said of the "arms race": "When we build, they build; when we cut, they build." Yet the talisman of an all-out arms race took hold of the public imagination.

This history illustrates a prime difficulty of trying to discuss nuclear deterrence: the mind understandably reels at thinking in too much detail about horrific scenarios. Thus in 1959 the nuclear strategist Herman Kahn said: "In spite of our reliance on the idea that deterrence will work, we usually do not analyze carefully the basic concepts behind such a policy. This somewhat lackadaisical interest in bedrock concepts is probably related to a subconscious fear that our foundations cannot stand close examination."

Thus, even during the Cold War, deterrence was never as simple as, "You kill us, we kill you." It worked well enough, however, because the Soviets were rational and cautious most of the time. They usually played nuclear brinkmanship with care.[84] Much credit can be given, in retrospect, to the uncertainty inherent in human affairs. Finely calibrated theories of war-fighting, deterrence and more esoteric aspects of nuclear theology could not eliminate the bedrock unpredictability of human affairs, and knowledge of the risk of fatal miscalculation by either side.

This point, of course, was understood fully by every serious participant in theological and policy debates. No one assumed that nuclear scenarios could be predicted in advance. And no one should make such an assumption today. Yet however unpalatable it was, "thinking about the unthinkable," in an effort to reduce the possibility of catastrophe, was an obligation keenly felt by those who made a living trying to grapple with these issues. This equally holds true *vis-à-vis* Iran.

Another factor regarding Iran: If it joins the nuclear club, it will have a small arsenal. As Central Asia expert S. Enders Wimbush explains:

---

84. The most notable exception was the Cuban Missile Crisis of October 1962. The U.S. quarantined (not a full blockade; for example, medical and food supplies were permitted) sea lane access to Cuba, and Russia pulled back. Russian leader Nikita Khrushchev paid for his recklessness two years later, when he was removed by a coup. A second nuclear face-off came during the Yom Kippur War in 1973, when in response to Soviet moves and threats President Nixon declared a nuclear alert; the matter was resolved when the war ended.

Arsenals will be small, which sounds reassuring, but in fact it heightens the dangers and risk. New players with just a few weapons, including Iran, will be especially dangerous. Cold War deterrence was based on the belief that an initial strike by an attacker could not destroy all an opponent's nuclear weapons, leaving the adversary with the capacity to strike back in a devastating retaliatory blow. Because it is likely to appear easier to destroy them in a single blow, small arsenals will increase the incentive to strike first in a crisis. Small, emerging nuclear forces could also raise the risk of preventive war, as leaders are tempted to attack before enemy arsenals grow bigger and more secure.

There are reasons to believe that reliance on deterrence with a nuclear Iran is a far dicier proposition than it was with the Soviet Union. The traditional reliance on leaders being conscious of the substantial endemic uncertainty in human affairs may well be, in the Iranian case, pushed aside by its leaders reaching through revelation a transcendent certainty that Judgment Day is here.

Strategic Options

Iran's Economy. Sanctions, given time, might well work. Iran's petroleum industry is potentially vulnerable. Its 137 billion barrel proven reserves (an estimate of what can be extracted at current prices) as of 2007 is deceptive. Sixty percent of its production comes from fields over 50 years old. At the end of 2006 Iran's daily output of nearly four million barrels was five percent below its OPEC production quota. It is well below its six million barrels per day figure for 1974, at the start of the OPEC bonanza, but above its 1.2 million daily figure during the 1980–1988 Iran-Iraq War. In many old fields production could fall eight percent annually over the next decade, meaning that its oil exports could ultimately fall to zero. Its problem is made worse because the regime's refusal to invest in a four- to six-year timeline to bring new fields into production, plus the six percent annual leakage rate, squeezes the supply, while the regime's subsidy of gasoline prices (35 cents per gallon), has sent Iranian consumer demand soaring to a world-leading six percent annual growth rate. Oil exports, $47 billion in 2006, were half the government's revenue. Iran's gasoline consumption has tripled since 1980, and it actually imports 170,000 barrels a day for gasoline, out of 1.5 million daily consumption of barrels of oil. But some investment in energy may be included in the $18 billion in loan guarantees Iran received from Europe in 2005.

Iran's energy vulnerability already imposes severe economic strain on the regime. It spends 38 percent of its national budget (nearly 15 percent of GDP) on subsidizing gas pump prices. Put in terms of America's $2.8 trillion budget or its $13.8 trillion GDP, were we to do the same we would be spending $1.06 trillion or $2.07 trillion, respectively. Further amplifying the regime's economic hardship is that an estimated 30 percent of gas stations were destroyed in the 2007 riots, inflation is running 17 percent, and there is a 14 percent unemployment rate among college graduates. Iran's President, Mahmoud Ahmadinejad, threw more sand in the gears of Iran's economy when he imposed a 12 percent interest rate ceiling on bank lending, forcing rate reductions and thus reducing capital available to fund investment. Its economy has experienced much labor unrest, and the regime has outlawed unions, jailing and torturing union leaders. One poll taken in June 2007 showed 88 percent of Iranians favoring improving their economy, 80 percent for allowing full nuclear inspection, 79 percent for democracy in Iran, 70 percent for normalization with the U.S., and even a majority for recognizing Israel.

Iran's international trade volume was $110 billion in 2006. Iranian dependence upon Europe is substantial, as 40 percent of its imports come from the EU (out of the 50 percent in total coming from the West), and 25 percent of its exports go to the EU. France alone has nearly $40 billion invested in Iran. Generous credit is common. Germany has underwritten 65 percent of recent exports to Iran. U.S. trade with Iran is negligible, some $150 million to $200 million since 2000 (we trade that much with China every eight hours). Another source of Iranian vulnerability, given the U.S. freeze on Iranian financial assets, is that 30 percent of Iran's $60 billion in bank reserves is dollar-denominated. Iran is beset by inflation, with the *rial* in 2007 at less than *one-hundredth* of its value in 1978, the year before the mullahs took over.

Since 2000 Iran has inked over $150 billion in major international contracts, but pressure on Iran is mounting. Two UN Security Council resolutions imposing sanctions (1737, barring nuclear material trade, and 1747, barring trade in arms and also imposing visa restrictions) were passed early in 2007.

In the United States, a dozen states are considering legislation mandating that stockholders divest Iranian assets, as was done globally with South Africa over apartheid. The U.S. and Israel have been promoting "terror-free investing" as a strategic tool—in effect a benign application of public and private investments. Beginning late in 2006, the governments of England, France and Germany have pulled back from underwriting Iranian contracts. Iran continues, however, to get aid from the World Bank, to which the U.S. contributes $950 million per year.

A special factor in Iran's political and economic equation is the elite Revolutionary Guard Corps, the "Pasdaran," which is an arm of the regime's Spiritual Leader, the supreme authority in the country. In addition to providing elite military forces, including those clandestinely operating inside Iraq against the Americans, the IRGC sends its alumni commanders into Iran's senior political councils. Of 21 Cabinet members, 14 are IRGC alumni, as are 80 of 290 members of the Iranian Parliament. In addition, they govern 20 of 30 provinces. The IRGC also funds Iran's nuclear program ($10 billion to date) and its terror group sponsorship—most notably, Hezbollah. The IRGC has about $6 billion in contracts, equal to three percent of Iran's $204 billion GDP. It has targeted strategic industries for investment—oil and gas, military, telecommunications, and construction. One analyst suggests that unless sanctions target IRGC investments, by hurting non-IRGC investors, the result could be to strengthen the relative position of the IRGC.

Above all, Iran's position at the Straits of Hormuz, the choke-point through which 20 percent of the world's oil passes (and 25 percent of America's supply) gives it considerable blackmail leverage with major oil-consuming countries. But there are two potentially promising avenues of limiting Iranian leverage, as noted by non-proliferation expert Henry Sokolski. First, an international accord affirming the right of unhindered passage for all commerce through the Straits would make it politically costly for Iran to block tanker traffic. Second, by upgrading the trans-Saudi-Arabian oil pipeline, to handle 11 million barrels of oil daily, and by bringing back into service the Iraqi-Saudi pipeline, supplies could bypass the Iran-controlled choke-point; such a project is estimated to cost only $600 million, a pittance compared to the economic damage an oil blockade would inflict on the world economy.

Iran's Nuclear Program. Since 9/11 Iran has made considerable progress toward crossing the nuclear threshold, while flummoxing European and U.S. diplomatic efforts. It has been caught cheating and lying about its cheating, and with sketches of nuclear weapon design. Iran lied for 18 years, from 1984 to 2002. A 2006 U.S. House of Representatives staff report concluded that Iran "probably" has not yet produced a nuclear weapon, "likely" has an offensive chemical weapons R&D capability, "probably" has an offensive biological weapons program, "bears significant responsibility for the recent violence in Israel and Lebanon," has "no rational reason" to clandestinely pursue peaceful nuclear energy, has "extensive" involvement in destabilizing Iraq (transferring IED technology and covertly backing militant and insurgent groups), and "could at any time significantly ramp up its sponsorship of violent attacks against U.S. forces in Iraq and elsewhere in the Middle East." Iran is also developing the Shahab-4 ballistic missile, whose estimated 4,000 kilometer (2,400-mile) range would put all of Italy, most of Germany, all of Eastern Europe, all of India, and the southern reaches of Norway and Sweden within range. While in November 2007 U.S. intelligence reversed its 2005 estimate that Iran is pursuing nuclear weapons, Iran's uranium enrichment and missile programs continue. Both Israeli and British intelligence disagree with the U.S. intelligence reversal. Past U.S. intelligence failures are legion and give no cause for credence in their latest product.

In choosing diplomacy, the West chose to ignore signs auguring possible regime change from within Iran, if aided by outside help. We could have promoted democracy by supporting the opposition. When after 9/11 one million Iranians demonstrated in Tehran against the mullahs, Western leaders mostly ignored them, too, preferring to engage in diplomacy.

There is a long, dismal history of diplomatic negotiations with the Iranians. In 1981, on the eve of President Reagan's inauguration, the Carter administration obtained release of the 52 American hostages (U.S. Embassy personnel in Tehran) who had been held 444 days, in return unfreezing Iranian financial assets, settling claims against the regime, and pledging non-interference in Iran's internal affairs.[85] In its second term the Reagan administration traded arms to Iran in a futile effort to obtain the release of hostages held by Iranian surrogates in Lebanon. The first Bush administration sought, in vain, engagement with Iran, during a period when Iran continued to lead the planet in sponsoring terrorist acts. The Clinton administration's continual courting of Iran led it to ignore illegal shipments of arms and nuclear materials into Iran by Russia, ignore Iran's sponsorship of the 1996 Khobar Towers terror bombing, and look the other way as Iran shipped arms to the Bosnian Muslims rather than send U.S. arms. While operating inside Bosnia, Iran recruited and trained terrorists, including three involved with the 9/11 attacks. The second Bush administration, despite "Axis of Evil" rhetoric, cut a deal with Iran after the initial phase of the Afghanistan campaign, despite solid evidence that Iranian-backed terrorists had attacked U.S. troops there.

There is pro-U.S. sentiment among Iran's youth, who have no memory of life under the Shah (who, in the event, was far less repressive than the mullahs have been, though far more criticized for abuses due to his alliance with the U.S.). In 2006, an Iranian female college student en-

---

85. The 1981 hostage release was effected using the Algerian government as intermediary, as after the November 4, 1979, seizure of the hostages the U.S. severed diplomatic relations with the new Iranian regime.

gagingly told a *Washington Post* reporter: "Please know this: We are not Saudi Arabia. We are not Iraq. We are not Yemen. Please tell them we are not the same as these places!" (Too many Americans, alas, tend to learn about foreign places and peoples only when America gets in a war with them.) Reports indicate that Iranian students are pressing the regime for more academic and personal freedom. What Iran expert Michael Ledeen calls "the War of the Persian Succession" has opened splits in the Iranian leadership, with a leading dissident ayatollah, close to the Ayatollah Khomeini but later jailed by his successors, calling for an end to repression.

Far from encouraging dissidents, American policy has been passive. What was set up by Congress as Radio Free Iran, to broadcast the kind of public affairs programming that was a staple of Radio Free Europe during the Cold War, is now a station broadcasting Western music. Hudson Institute Central Asia specialist S. Enders Wimbush proposes that a true Radio Free Iran should broadcast into Iran programs that undermine the regime's legitimacy, show its disunity and focus on Iran's cultural and economic decline.

Iran's leaders openly express their confidence that they are on the rise and the U.S. is slipping toward defeat in Iraq. Former President Rafsanjani, still one of Iran's most powerful figures, said in July 2007 that he did not think America a superpower, "when it can easily be trapped in a small country like Iraq." In August, Supreme Leader Ali Khamenei said: "America and its followers are stuck in a whirlpool and they sink deeper as time passes. A dangerous future is predicted for them." In September President Ahmadinejad flatly called Iran's nuclear program "non-negotiable." The topper also comes from Ahmadinejad, expressing his supreme confidence in his own ability to calculate that America will not attack Iran. He said on September 3:

> They do not dare wage war against us and I base this on a double proof. I am an engineer and I am a master in calculation and tabulation. I draw up tables. For hours, I write out different hypotheses. I

reject. I reason. I reason with planning and I make a conclusion. They cannot make problems for Iran.[86]

Such statements recall Senator Moynihan's assertion noted above, as to the dangers of inviting the contempt of totalitarians. Worse, if Israel's estimate that Iran will go nuclear in 2009 is accurate, sanctions may not have time to work. The status of the Bushehr I reactor is currently unclear, with some reports indicating a delay in its operational cutover. The number of uranium enrichment centrifuges Iran has is in dispute. The International Atomic Energy Agency now concedes that Iran has 3,000 centrifuges running, and that it does not know whether Iran's nuclear enrichment is directed towards commercial or military use. Iran's ultimate goal for its Natanz facility is 54,000 centrifuges.

Bushehr I will, upon its becoming fully operational, be able to use its 3,000 centrifuges to enrich its uranium commercial fuel to weapons-grade within *five weeks*. With 330 kilograms of weapons-grade plutonium waste, the Iranians could produce 55 Hiroshima-size atomic bombs per year. This situation differs from the WMD assessment re Iraq, in that Iran's nuclear program is known to be a weapons program. As noted earlier, they have no serious commercial need for nuclear power now, have been caught cheating and also possessing weapons design sketches. Above all, *a nation with a purely commercial program has no incentive whatsoever to cheat*, because peaceful nuclear power is perfectly legal. Iran also has the opportunity to seek nuclear material from abroad, in Russia or former Russian republics, or obtain aid from Pakistan or North Korea. One vital counter to this is the Nuclear Threat Initiative, which has secured 7,000 nuclear warheads since the mid-1990s, and also secured over 100 pounds of nuclear material in Serbia (as part of a program to secure nuclear material located outside Russia).

Therefore either America or Israel may have to act to end the Iranian nuclear quest. Ideally this would be accomplished by aiding regime change from within, and that must be our first priority. If military action

---

86. Ahmadinejad's statement came three days before Israeli's surprise strike against Syria, which did not enhance his credibility as master calculator.

proves necessary, Islamofascists worldwide will explode (amplified by protests from predictable quarters in the West). Thus in event of taking military action we should try to *decapitate the regime*, rather than settle for bombing a few buried facilities. If such a strike proves impossible, we should disable as much of Iran's military assets as possible. Otherwise we will have but wounded and thus infuriated the regime, and may expect retaliation, including strikes within America, where Iran's terrorist creation, Hezbollah, has embedded assets. In the event, *the political costs of a small and large strike are essentially the same. It therefore makes sense to prefer regime change.*[87]

Even if deterrence stops a nuclear first-strike, a nuclear Iran could subvert our efforts in the Mideast, safe from attack behind its nuclear shield. Thus, Iran must not be allowed to go nuclear. We may not have ironclad "beyond the shadow of a doubt" proof, but that comes only with a detonation announcing that a new nuclear state has joined the club. Recall that with North Korea, we considered its nuclear membership uncertain until its October 2006 test. Despite the North having publicly said that it had a nuclear capability back in 2002, we wondered if perhaps it was bluffing.

Some measure of uncertainty is endemic in human affairs. If we intend to take action to preclude Iran's acquisition of a nuclear capability, we must accept less than 100 percent certitude as a standard. But whatever it takes, we must stop Iran's march toward nuclear membership.

---

87. The President does not need approval from Congress for such a strike. Besides that seeking such would compromise necessary secrecy, the power of Congress to "declare" war leaves the power to "make" war with the President as Commander-in-Chief. James Madison's notes on the 1787 Convention explain that declaration refers to starting a war, whereas making war refers to response to attack. Iran has been attacking the U.S. since the mullahs took power in 1979, beginning by seizing American hostages. It used terrorism to kill Americans abroad, killed 241 Marines in Lebanon in 1983, and has been responsible for an estimated more than half of U.S. 2007 combat deaths in Iraq. Thus we are at war already, with no need for a declaration. Escalation decisions are made by the President as Commander-in-Chief. Congress retains the power of the purse to curtail Presidential war policies, and can exercise its consultation prerogatives under the 1973 War Powers Resolution, albeit the latter is of debatable constitutionality.

Failing to do so would fatally undermine America's power and influence in the Mideast.

Such action is not, strictly speaking, pre-emption. A pre-emptive strike is premised upon ascertaining imminent hostile action. Rather we would be taking *preventive action*. Prevention aims to preclude even the *possibility* of a program or a hostile act. Preventive action does not rest on actual evidence that the feared action is imminent. Pre-emption presumes that intelligence will provide concrete evidence of imminent attack, or, as in Iran's case, evidence of imminent completion of its nuclear program. *When one deals with small nuclear tests using small amounts of diverted nuclear material—or, for that matter—transfer of same to hostile groups—imminence lies below the threshold of real-world ability to detect in advance.*[88]

Given that America and/or Israel must prevent a mullah-ruled Iran from crossing the nuclear threshold lest catastrophe come to pass, it is *essential* that every possible support be given to forces in the Mideast coalescing against Iran and Syria. The effort must be made, with or without Europe's blessing. It surely must be made without much help from the UN, which regards it as unacceptable to distinguish between nations as

---

88. Establishing that an attack is imminent is harder than many people realize. Despite having intercepted a Japanese diplomatic code signal before Pearl Harbor was bombed, the U.S. did not act, partly because Japanese diplomats were still in Washington, ostensibly negotiating. In 1967 Israel struck at Egypt's air force, because after weeks of hysterical Arab propaganda about driving the Jews into the sea, Egypt's expulsion of a UN peacekeeping force from the Sinai, and imposition of an illegal blockade, Israel feared absorbing a first blow would be too damaging. Israel struck, and after the war it became understood that Egypt was bluffing. But as related in Michael B. Oren's masterful *Six Days of War: June 1967 and the Making of the Modern Middle East* (2002), it could not take that chance. New evidence compiled by Israeli journalists Isabella Ginor and Gideon Remez in *Foxbats Over Dimona* (2007) strongly suggests that the Soviets deliberately fed false intelligence to Egypt to foment the war, during which they planned to destroy the Israeli nuclear reactor at Dimona; Israel's rapid victory scuppered the Soviet plans. Michael R. Gordon and Gen. Bernard E. Trainor recount in their authoritative book, *The Generals' War* (1995), that in August 1990 the U.S. decided that Saddam's massing of land forces on Kuwait's border was a military exercise, and not the invasion it turned out to be. Intelligence is always ambiguous, with mixed signals. Separating wheat from chaff (in intelligence parlance, "signals" from "background noise") is an art, not a science, and a highly fallible one. The acknowledged classic work on this, which I note with familial pride, is the late Roberta Wohlstetter's *Pearl Harbor: Warning and Decision* (1962).

to their nuclear programs. It may also be noted that Israel successfully stopped one nuclear program—Iraq's, in 1981. This is one more nuclear program than the UN has stopped.

President Bush stated his position twice, shortly after 9/11. In his September 20, 2001, address to Congress he declared that nations were either with us or with the terrorists. And in his 2002 State of the Union address he named Iraq, Iran and North Korea (the "Axis of Evil") as states in search of WMD. But despite the President's soaring rhetoric, North Korea has joined the club, and we continue to try to press Iran to end its program, but with limited sanctions, considering Iran's repeated violations of prior commitments.

One likely consequence of our perceived failure to stop Iran is already evident. In late 2006, six Mideast nations announced plans to collaborate in developing nuclear technology.[89] Their decision echoes that of French President Charles DeGaulle, who in the 1960s deployed France's independent nuclear deterrent, because, as he famously put it, he didn't believe America would see New York destroyed if it incinerated Moscow after a Soviet nuclear strike on Paris. Unless checked soon, the weather forecast for the Mideast, it seems, could well be not sandstorms but mushroom clouds.

Diplomacy alone will not succeed with Iran for several reasons. Iran thinks it is winning, and revolutionaries on a roll do not make concessions—at least, not those they will honor. European powers, despite public declarations against Iran's program, are not likely to press hard enough to have a chance to make a difference. The UN is essentially irrelevant, especially given that three permanent members of the Security Council (Russia, China and France) have helped Iran's nuclear program at one time or another.

Much of our present predicament might well have been avoided had stern sanctions been imposed when Iran was first caught cheating. Instead the Europeans dithered, meeting each Iranian rebuff and each

---

89. The six nations: Algeria, Egypt, Kuwait, Morocco, Saudi Arabia, Tunisia.

instance of Iranian duplicity with offers of new negotiations. When Iranian dissident Shirin Ebadi received the Nobel Peace Prize in 2004, the West passed up an opportunity to use her case to highlight human rights abuses and thus diminish the regime's prestige and increase pressure for reform. Rewarding bad behavior yielded, predictably, more bad behavior by the Iranians. Demonstrators in the Iranian city of Shiraz reportedly mocked President Bush, chanting: "Bush, you told us to rise up, and so we have. Why don't you act?"

There is enough evidence already to justify preventing Iran from achieving its goal. True, the CIA believes that Iran's nuclear window is 2010–2015. But who believes the CIA on the status of WMD programs, based upon their perfect record of failure to predict prior nuclear tests? Intelligence reform is a long-term process. We cannot decide what to do with Iran's nuclear program based upon CIA estimates.

Sanctions can take a long time to bite. A virtual monopoly of force resides with the government, and only if military elements inside Iran switch loyalty does revolution have a realistic chance.

Orientalist Bernard Lewis sees in Iran a confident regime that believes the West will back down, that genuinely wants revolutionary change and may well use nuclear weapons in pursuit of its goals. On the brighter side, Lewis sees favorable trends in Sunni Arab states that fear Iran's rise to Mideast dominance. Also, the Arab world is opening up a bit, at long last; Jordanians can (and many do) watch *Israeli* television, which gives them a different picture of life in Israel than they get in the mosque. Over time, this may help change attitudes. But such a change will not likely happen, if at all, before the Iran issue is decided.

On the diplomatic front, it must be made quietly clear to Russia and China, lest they be tempted to rapidly transfer a nuclear weapon to Iran, that consequences of a most serious (unspecified) nature will be the result. China must also be told that as it holds the effective power to control North Korea's behavior (by threatening to withhold the energy supplies the North needs to stay in existence, of which China supplies

80 to 90 percent), that it will be held responsible, too, if North Korea exports nuclear weapons to any state or terrorist group.[90]

The longer we postpone a final decision, the greater the risk that Iran will spring a surprise as did North Korea in 2002, announcing it has gone nuclear. In the interim we should do everything possible to help those within Iran who seek regime change. But we have waited far too long to sit comfortably awaiting a change that is hard to effect quickly. On the evidence we have, we wait at our peril. To do so is the "bet the company" wager. Why so?

Iran could activate terror groups like Hezbollah and launch attacks around the globe. It could subvert regional governments. It could block the Straits of Hormuz. *Iran could accomplish these things more easily if secure behind a nuclear shield, and thus virtually immune from military retaliation upon its homeland.*

Further, consider what else could happen if Iran goes nuclear. Iran could transfer nuclear material to terrorists, or launch a missile attack on Israel. Israel could launch its own preclusive strike against Iran. And, in the event, "Great Satan," America, will surely be blamed if "Little Satan" Israel acts. If we are to be blamed anyway, shouldn't we carry the mission out, and do a more thorough job? Also possible is that Israel may conclude that its conventional munitions cannot penetrate buried, reinforced concrete, and that it will have to rely on one-kiloton nuclear warheads to destroy key Iranian facilities. Such a strike, if executed preemptively, would be the first nuclear strike since 1945. The impact of mushroom clouds on the world Islamic communities surely would be immense, and could well bring on the all-out interfaith war the West fears most.

In the context of Iraq, the "bet the company" wager turned out to be not WMD, but removing Saddam and trying to promote stable Iraqi

---

90. The U.S. missed a golden opportunity to pressure China to cut off energy supplies, and thus rapidly bring down Kim John-Il's regime. China derives nearly 70 percent of its GDP from world trade. The U.S. held a veto over China's entry into the World Trade Organization. We chose not to use this powerful lever.

representative government. But we acted on what was known then—and not disputed by any major country's intelligence community.

Perhaps the ultimate trap for leaders is to wait for certitude before acting. To influence events it is necessary to act in advance. For a leader who acts later risks becoming prisoner of events as they unfold. And burdens of proof can be treacherous. Whenever debate over policy centers upon establishing a conclusive factual predicate, the side with the burden of proof can rarely act effectively in advance, because the requisite certainty will be lacking.

We should hugely prefer non-military solutions, but neither time nor the world political environment appears hospitable to their success. Should non-military measures fail, forcing regime change will become an urgent necessity. Halfway measures won't eliminate the threat posed by Iran's revolutionary leaders.

CHAPTER VIII
LESSONS LEARNED SINCE SEPTEMBER 11, 2001

Fool me once, shame on you; fool me twice, shame on me.

CHINESE PROVERB

Now that we have looked at various aspects of the wars we are engaged in, it might be useful as well to consider lessons learned, recognizing that even though history does not repeat itself identically, we can avoid making mistakes more than once (though fallible we all are, so we will surely make new ones instead). Here are fifteen lessons, drawn from the first six years of the Long and Short Wars.

1. Marshal far more resources than you think you need to fight.

Right after 9/11 was the time to ask for the moon, so to speak. Boosting defense spending 50 percent was simply not enough; doubling was probably the minimum benchmark. Our troops are doing three and four stretches in Iraq, and National Guardsmen serve there, because we failed to recruit enough soldiers. Few believe today that we could fight a major war in another theater outside the Mideast, while engaged deeply in Iraq. This is a state of affairs that must not be allowed to continue. Nor should we have to choose between preparing for counter-terror operations and possible future conventional conflicts that may arise. By preparing for both we do better in the current war and are more likely to deter possible future wars. It will of course be said that "We can't afford it." Should war ensue due to our lack of preparation, we will realize that what we most cannot afford is lack of preparation.

2. Define complex war challenges precisely for formal planning purposes, but define them simply for practical public purposes.

Right now our prime enemy is militant strains of Islam. But even to-day we face non-Islamist threats, too—mainly North Korea. And eventually the most dangerous enemy we face may be bio-terror Unabombers, whose motivation to strike may not even be ideological. Thus, General Abizaid's "Long War" focuses our attention on the multi-generational length of the civizational struggle over values before us; the "Short War" encapsulates the urgency of preventing a WMD catastrophe.

3. Challenge the media on accuracy and on airing of hostile propaganda, and on control of Presidential access to broadcast air time.

Terrorists cannot defeat us on the battlefield. Mass media is their greatest weapon, by which they demoralize Western publics. We should adopt truth-in-sourcing rules to prevent mass media from serving as propaganda facilitators for terrorists. And private media gatekeepers holding broadcast licenses from the government should not be allowed to keep a President from reserving air time; the public will tame Presidential excess, and the opposition party should have equal time. We need not formally declare war to do any of this, as most wars we have fought have been undeclared ones.

First Amendment purists will object. But countless restrictions of speech—time, place and manner, for instance—already exist. Disclosure of sourcing does not prevent airing or publication of stories, but merely identifies their source—which need not be by name. A free press heedless of its manipulation by terrorists may report itself into extinction.

4. Fight battles on your terms, not the enemy's.

In Iraq we allowed the insurgency to flower with help from Syria and Iran. We should have slammed Syria at the first sign of interference, and done the same with Iran. *What strategists call "horizontal escalation" is a prime tool in this war, allowing us to shift the battle from defense to offense, and migrate the main action to more favorable battle theaters.* In this instance this means taking the battle to the Iranian regime itself, and to Syria as well, when the proper opportunity arises. Prior to the surge in

Iraq, we were fighting on al-Qaeda's terms. Now, fighting on our own terms, we have al-Qaeda on the run.

5. Promote liberal democratic societal change incrementally.

We lack the colonial experience to manage well large-scale societal transition in alien cultures. Learning on the fly in Iraq has been a costly experience that has damaged U.S. prestige worldwide. Having demonstrated that nation- and democracy-building are skills America has not mastered, prudence dictates re-booting democracy promotion after a thorough review. Should we decide to effect regime change in Iran, while a liberal democracy is preferable, we should be willing to settle for a non-terrorist leadership, even if undemocratic. Iran might well prove far more fertile ground for democracy than other parts of the Mideast. But if an opportunity arises to aid the replacement of the current revolutionary regime with a non-revolutionary one that is less than democratic we should take it, in that the best is the enemy of the good. The mess in Iraq suggests that a non-democratic solution would hardly have been the worst choice. Regime change must focus first on establishing non-terrorist governments, then on democracy over the longer term. Stability requires neutralizing the extremists, to clear the field for moderates. Thus, asking moderates and extremists to join and form a coalition government, as is the case in Lebanon and Iraq, is a recipe for trouble.

6. De-emphasize multi-ethnic integration of tribal societies.

We reflexively shrink from accepting separatism. The former Yugoslavia taught us nothing, or else in Iraq we would not have felt committed to keep intact Britain's artificial cobbling together of three ethnic provinces to create Iraq. Western publics are of modernist temper, and thus are almost bound to underestimate the potency of tribal passions in alien cultures. We should bear in mind that racial tensions persist even in Western societies, and thus we should hardly be surprised when ethnic tensions persist in other cultures. A recent real-life lesson was provided by the former Communist satellite countries of Eastern Europe: Where heterogeneous populations existed, partition followed—sometimes peaceful (Czech Republic and Slovakia via their "velvet divorce"), other times violent (several conflicts in the former Yugoslavia). In 2007 Belgium gave signs that a Fleming–Walloon ethnic split may come to pass. Iraq may yet hang together, but we cannot force an outcome.

7. Confront and defeat multi-culturalist tendencies.

Right after 9/11 Muslim activists in Western societies began characterizing any unflattering but truthful remark about radical Islam or its votaries as "Islamophobia" or "hate speech." In Europe there are laws that back up these outrageous positions. Attempts to implement rational airport security screening were met by cries of "ethnic profiling." Such tactics can be very harmful. We must prevent P.C. constriction of our options in discussing these issues. We must not allow militants to "define the territory of insult."

8. Keep the UN as far out of matters as politically possible; bypass the UN with coalitions of the willing when it obstructs.

On the fair evidence of it, the United Nations is at best a nuisance, often a menace, save for very rare "alignment of planets" cases. The nations with the most to lose from obstructionism, delay and deceit at the UN are the Western nations, who are a minority of members, outnumbered by nations who use their votes to block actions that might protect the West. The democracies can ameliorate this problem by refusing to continue to financially support UN operations that produce such results. The current system, in which the major Western countries carry nearly 90 percent of UN costs, but have far less than half the votes, creates moral hazard: Smaller nations are able to act irresponsibly, at no cost to themselves. Irresponsible behavior can be curbed if those who indulge in it are made to carry all costs associated with such acts.

9. Reject "suicide pact" constructions of domestic and international law.

A functioning legal system is essential for any advanced society. It can be a menace, however, during wartime, especially during wars of survival. Lawyers and judges can lose a war, but cannot win one. The less we allow the legal system to tie us up in knots the better our chances of prevailing. Baseline adherence to certain norms is essential to maintain public support in Western societies, but adopting Geneva rules for detainees is unnecessary and risks loss of information crucial to preventing catastrophic WMD strikes.

Laws are, legalists argue, most necessary above all in times of war, when liberty is most threatened. But the greatest threats to liberty will come after, should it happen, a nuclear detonation occurs on Western soil, or a super-lethal pathogen kills millions. Anyone who thinks martial law will not be imposed to curb widespread panic, regardless of civil liberties, lives in what Lady Thatcher calls "cloud cuckoo-land."

Justice Jackson's admonition that unless judgments are "infused with a little practical wisdom" law will become "a suicide pact" is one many of today's judges and lawyers not infrequently ignore. Benjamin Franklin's maxim on essential liberty and temporary safety must be read with its converse proposition: We should be willing in wartime to surrender non-essential liberty in pursuit of essential safety.

But above all is the importance of limiting the role of judicial mandarins appointed for life. *In a society premised upon representative government, the most fundamental decisions must be made by officials who answer directly to the people.* Decisions that might significantly affect a society's chances of prevailing in a struggle for civilizational life are those that above all must be commended to those politically accountable. Neither rule of law, nor constitution nor treaty can justify courts taking such decisions into their own hands.

10. Avoid "suicide pact values" and moral relativism traps.

If, as Justice Jackson said, the Bill of Rights is not a suicide pact, neither are "our values." We must observe certain minimum unilateral protocols, to be sure. No one suggests that we, as an interrogation tactic, replicate Saddam's rape rooms, or sic Dobermans on prisoners. But dunking 9/11's mastermind in the drink for a couple of minutes hardly amounted to anything like what Saddam did, or what al-Qaeda and Hezbollah do. It likely saved thousands of innocent lives. And while we must avoid gross levels of collateral damage to innocent civilians, an effort like Israel's in Lebanon must be permissible. Thus it is imperative to preempt Iran's nuclear option, lest there be a nuclear exchange in which Western retaliation murders millions of innocent Iranians who have no say in what their government does. Such a retaliatory strike is the quickest way we could lose the "moral high ground" *vis-à-vis* our adversaries. In fighting counter-insurgencies, we must—as our military does—take reasonable steps to minimize civilian casualties, in accordance with our battlefield values, while employing realistic rules of engagement that permit effectively engaging the enemy.

Those who use civilians as shields must be denied the "moral high ground," a term that should be defined relative to what adversaries do, rather than be set against an Olympian standard (as has been done) for America to match. As in all cases where we will be held to high standards, we must insist that our adversaries be held to an equally lofty standard by the world community. Our critics seem to see the war as an exercise in public confessional exhibitionism, parading America's shortcomings across the world stage. This is a prescription for defeat. It would have cost us World War II.

We must balance benefits of taking actions we normally refrain from, against the risk of alienating Western publics. A cardinal principle should be recognizing that our choice in these kinds of conflicts often is the lesser of evils, with no victorious course that is likely to make us completely comfortable.

11. Negotiate only with adversaries who seek or can be made to accept genuine compromise, and avoid the trap of endless negotiations freezing alternative measures.

Diplomatic negotiation differs fundamentally from business negotiation: The acceptance of common values and rules of conduct that eases bargaining in business does not prepare a negotiator for dealing with revolutionaries. Trying to negotiate with revolutionary powers is useful only to buy time to implement better strategies, or to demonstrate the futility of negotiations to a skeptical public. Negotiations work well *vis-à-vis* adversaries only when there is sufficient leverage to yield results. Thus we cannot unilaterally negotiate a successful deal with North Korea or

Iran, as we lack sufficient plausible leverage to do so—neither believes that we will actually take decisive action if negotiations fail.

12. Sanctions work as a policy tool only under special conditions.

No powerful nation will quickly be brought to its knees by sanctions. Even a relatively weak country like North Korea can defy them, given willingness to endure hideous hardship. Only a concerted group of nations committed to a broad sanctions regime might give Iran's leaders pause. So long as a regime is revolutionary, sanctions are a stopgap at best.

13. Force must be decisive, precise and preventive if necessary.

Five lessons from this war may be gleaned about the use of force: (1) prepare for worst cases; (2) follow Machiavelli's "kill the king" rule— no halfway measures; (3) target charismatic leaders as a top priority; (4) prevent terrorist acquisition of nuclear weapons at all costs, by force if necessary; (5) Target precisely to minimize collateral damage. Targeting leaders and pre-empting WMD are essential to preserving our security. Precise targeting protects our values.

14. The Internet's potential for manipulating communications, and spreading lies and distortions, will grow over time, thus forcing stringent authentication and authorization issues to the forefront.

The time to think seriously about this is now, *before* the coming cyberspace deluge of virtually undetectable image/identity fraud. Terrorists turned industrial technology against us on 9/11; information technology is ripe for the taking. Problems of authentication, anonymity, authorization and acceptance must be examined, so that strategies will be in place as technology enables more sophisticated use by our adversaries of the Internet's global reach and instantaneous impact. Today's computer security is grossly inadequate, almost begging to be compromised by foes. We must monitor how fanaticism spreads over the Internet and vastly improve our own ability to use global networking to promote positive alternatives to fanaticism.

15. Broadly exploit the full panoply of advanced technologies to improve battlefield effectiveness and homeland security.

Advanced technologies can reduce the chance of successful catastrophic strikes on the homeland and can also improve battlefield intelligence. Advanced aerospace technologies such as lasers, optics and microwaves can enable more precise and more rapid targeting of high-value targets, render enemy ballistic missiles obsolete and disable enemy communications.

Conclusion

We reached for the stars, but failed to marshal adequate resources to get there. We ignored our operational limits. We imprisoned ourselves in absolutist interpretations of values, thus making them ill-suited to enable us to effectively fight a war of survival. And we failed to grasp how ingrained radical tendencies are in Arab and many Muslim lands, in which the three worst ideas in human history run deep: Nazism, Communism and Islamofascism. We face now intermediate second- or third-best outcomes in engagements already underway, and yet must prepare for bold action—sooner rather than later—to ward off emerging, grave dangers.

Acceptance of defeat in the Short War would leave a diminished West facing a revolutionary, nuclear-armed Iran. The result would be an ascendant global, revolutionary Islamofascist foreign policy shaped by an Iran free to step up its subversion in the Middle East and export terror elsewhere, secure from military retaliation. Should Iran's mullahs act on their apocalyptic impulse and unleash nuclear weapons, the result could be Israel's extinction, or the death of one or more major Western cities, or the crippling of Western economies by disabling critical infrastructures for long periods of time.

Betting that Iran will not act on fanatical, genocidal impulses amounts to "betting the company." If we make that wager—as well we may—we had better be right.

Failure to win the Short War could well render ultimate victory in the Long War hollow. The tragic truth may then be that we could well have prevented the kind of WMD catastrophe that will permanently scar free societies, but that we failed to do so. We owe it to ourselves and future generations to do everything possible, investing all necessary human and material resources to prevail.

SELECTED BIBLIOGRAPHY

Agresto, John. *Mugged By Reality*. 2007.

Armstrong, Karen. *Islam*. 2000.

Ashcroft, John. *Never Again*. 2006.

Barr, James. *Setting the World on Fire*. 2006.

Bawer, Bruce. *While Europe Slept: How Radical Islam Is Destroying the West From Within*. 2006.

Berlinski, Claire. *Menace in Europe*. 2006.

Bolton, John. *Surrender is Not an Option*. 2007.

Bowman, James. *Honor: A History*. 2006.

Coll, Steve. *Ghost Wars*. 2004.

Emerson, Steven. *Jihad in America*. 2002.

Flynn, Stephen. *The Edge of Disaster*. 2007.

Friedman, Thomas. *From Beirut to Jerusalem*. 1989.

Fromkin, David. *A Peace to End All Peace*. 1989.

Fukuyama, Francis. *The End of History and the Last Man*. 1992.

Gaffney, Frank J. *War Footing*. 2006.

Gold, Dore. *The Fight for Jerusalem*. 2007.

Gold, Dore. *Tower of Babble*. 2004.

Goldsmith, Jack. *The Terror Presidency*. 2007.

Guttman, Stephanie. *The Other War: Israelis, Palestinians and the Struggle for Media Supremacy*. 2005.

Kaplan, Robert D. *Imperial Grunts*. 2005.

Karsh, Ephraim and Inari Karsh. *Empires in the Sand*. 1999.

Kedourie, Elie. *The Chatham House Version*. 1984.

Kirkpatrick, Jeane. *Making War to Keep Peace.* 2006.

Kupperman, Robert and Jeff Kamen. *Final Warning.* 1989.

Lane-Poole, Stanley. *The Barbary Corsairs.* 1894.

Ledeen, Michael A. *The Iranian Time Bomb.* 2007.

Ledeen, Michael A. *Machiavelli on Modern Leadership.* 2000.

Lord, Carnes. *Losing Hearts and Minds: Public Diplomacy in the Age of Terror.* 2006.

Moynihan, Daniel Patrick. *Secrecy.* 1998.

Peters, Joan. *From Time Immemorial: The Origins of the Arab-Jewish Conflict Over Palestine.* 1984.

Peters, Ralph. *Fighting for the Future: Will America Triumph?* 2001.

Phillips, Melanie. *Londonistan.* 2006.

Podhoretz, Norman. *World War IV.* 2007.

Posner, Richard. *Countering Terrorism.* 2007.

Posner, Richard. *Not a Suicide Pact.* 2006.

Pryce-Jones, David. *Betrayal: France, the Arabs, and the Jews.* 2006.

Scheuer, Michael. *Imperial Hubris.* 2005.

Sharansky, Natan. *The Case for Democracy.* 2004.

Steyn, Mark. *America Alone.* 2006.

Strum, Philippa. *When the Nazis Came to Skokie.* 1999.

Tuchman, Barbara, *Bible and Sword.* 1956.

West, Bing, *No True Glory.* 2005.

Wright, Lawrence. *The Looming Tower.* 2006.

Yoo, John. *War by Other Means.* 2006.

Zacks, Richard. *The Pirate Coast.* 2005.

Printed in the United States
107464LV00002B/71/P